COMMON CORE ENGLISH WORKBOOK

GRADE 1

prep@ze   www.prepaze.com

Author: Ace Academic Publishing

Ace Academic Publishing is a leading supplemental educational workbook publisher for grades K-12. At Ace Academic Publishing, we realize the importance of imparting analytical and critical thinking skills during the early ages of childhood and hence our books include materials that require multiple levels of analysis and encourage the students to think outside the box.

The materials for our books are written by award winning teachers with several years of teaching experience. All our books are aligned with the state standards and are widely used by many schools throughout the country.

Prepaze is a sister company of Ace Academic Publishing. Intrigued by the unending possibilities of the internet and its role in education, Prepaze was created to spread the knowledge and learning across all corners of the world through an online platform. We equip ourselves with state-of-the-art technologies so that knowledge reaches the students through the quickest and the most effective channels.

For inquiries and bulk orders, contact Ace Academic Publishing at the following address:

Ace Academic Publishing
3736 Fallon Road #403
Dublin CA 94568

www.aceacademicpublishing.com

This book contains copyright protected material. The purchase of this material entitles the buyer to use this material for personal and classroom use only. Reproducing the content for commercial use is strictly prohibited. Contact us to learn about options to use it for an entire school district or other commercial use.

ISBN: 978-1-949383-15-7

© Ace Academic Publishing, 2021

INTRODUCTION

About the Book

The content of this book includes multiple chapters and units covering all the required common core standards for the grade level. Similar to a standardized exam, you can find questions of all types - multiple choice, fill in the blanks, true or false, match the correct answer and explain your answers. The carefully chosen reading comprehension passages will help students gain key comprehension skills, such as themes, understanding figurative languages, character traits, and contextual vocabulary. The questions also cover writing standards that are not covered by most of the other commonly available workbooks. The exercises help students learn proper language conventions and effectively use resources to research topics for writing essays. The detailed answer explanations help the students make sense of the problems and gain confidence in solving similar problems.

For the Parents

This workbook includes practice questions and tests that cover all the required Common Core Standards for the grade level. The book comprises of multiple tests for each topic so that your child can retake another test on the same topic. The workbook also includes questions for the writing standards and teaches your child to write essays and free responses. The workbook is divided into chapters and units so that you can choose the topics that you want your child to practice. The detailed answer explanations will teach your child the right methods to solve all types of questions, including the free-response questions. After completing the tests on all the chapters, your child can take any common core standardized exam with confidence and can excel in it.

For additional online practice, sign up for a free account at www.aceacademicprep.com.

For the Teachers

All questions and tests included in the workbook are based on the core state standards and include a clear label of the standard name. By following the chapter by chapter units, you can assign your students tests on a particular topic. The workbook will help your students overcome any deficiencies in their understanding of critical concepts and will also help you identify the specific topics that may require more practice. The grade-appropriate, yet challenging questions will help your students learn to strategically use the appropriate tools and persevere through common core standardized exams.

For additional online practice, sign up for a free account at www.aceacademicprep.com.

www.prepaze.com   Copyrighted Material

Other books from Ace Academic Publishing

Ace Academic Publishing
ACHIEVING EXCELLENCE TOGETHER

TABLE OF CONTENTS — GRADE 1

1. READING: LITERATURE

- **1.1. Key Ideas and Details** 8
  Story Details • Central Theme • Character Development
- **1.2. Craft and Structure** 17
  Understanding vocabulary • Story structure • Narrator's point of view
- **1.3. Integration of Knowledge and Ideas** 22
  Story moods and illustrations • Compare/contrast story elements
- **1.4. The range of Reading and Level of Text Complexity** 29
  Read prose and poetry of appropriate complexity
- **1.5. Chapter Review** 35

2. READING: INFORMATIONAL TEXT

- **2.1. Key Ideas and Details** 50
  Text details • Main idea • Sequence
- **2.2. Craft and Structure** 55
  Understanding vocabulary • Locate information • Author's point of view
- **2.3. Integration of Knowledge and Ideas** 62
  Visual illustrations • Text connections • Compare/contrast key details
- **2.4. Chapter Review** 68

3. READING: FOUNDATIONAL SKILLS

- **3.1. Print Concepts** 80
  Organization and basic features of print
- **3.2. Phonological Awareness** 86
  Syllables and Sounds
- **3.3. Chapter Review** 94

4. WRITING

- **4.1. Text Types and Purposes** 102
  Opinion pieces • Informative/explanatory writing • Narrative writing
- **4.2. Chapter Review** 109

5. LANGUAGE

- **5.1. Conventions of Standard English** 118
  Forms of Nouns • Past, Present and Future tense • Adjectives and Pronouns • Other Grammar Topics

GRADE 1
TABLE OF CONTENTS

5.2. Vocabulary Acquisition and Use **122**
Multiple-meaning Words and Phrases • Distinguish Words Differing in Manner and Intensity

5.3. Chapter Review **127**

END OF YEAR ASSESSMENT 134

ANSWER KEY 159

1. READING: LITERATURE

1.1. KEY IDEAS AND DETAILS   8
- Story Details
- Central Theme
- Character Development

1.2. CRAFT AND STRUCTURE   17
- Understanding vocabulary
- Story structure
- Narrator's point of view

1.3. INTEGRATION OF KNOWLEDGE AND IDEAS   22
- Story moods and illustrations
- Compare/contrast story elements

1.4. THE RANGE OF READING AND LEVEL OF TEXT COMPLEXITY   29
- Read prose and poetry of appropriate complexity

1.5. CHAPTER REVIEW   35

1. READING: LITERATURE

1.1. Key Ideas and Details

Common Core State Standards: CCSS.ELA-LITERACY.RL.1.1, CCSS.ELA-LITERACY.RL.1.2, CCSS.ELA-LITERACY.RL.1.3

Skills:
- Ask and answer questions about key details in a text
- Retell stories, including key details, and demonstrate an understanding of their central message or lesson
- Describe characters, settings, and major events in a story, using key details

> **Directions:** *Read the passage and answer the questions below.*

THE HARE AND THE TORTOISE

A Hare was making fun of the Tortoise one day for being so slow.

"Do you ever get anywhere?" he asked with a mocking laugh.

"Yes," replied the Tortoise, "and I get there sooner than you think. I'll run you a race and prove it."

The Hare was much amused at the idea of running a race with the Tortoise, but for the fun of the thing, he agreed. So the Fox, who had consented to act as judge, marked the distance and started the runners off.

The Hare was soon far out of sight, and to make the Tortoise feel very deeply how ridiculous it was for him to try a race with a Hare, he lay down beside the course to take a nap until the Tortoise should catch up.

The Tortoise meanwhile kept going slowly but steadily, and, after a time, passed the place where the Hare was sleeping. But the Hare slept on very peacefully; and when at last he did wake up, the Tortoise was near the goal. The Hare now ran his swiftest, but he could not overtake the Tortoise in time.

1. READING: LITERATURE

FREE RESPONSE

1. **Your teacher tells you to read this passage and then ask a friend two questions about the text. What would you ask your friend?** (RL.1.1)

   _____
   _____
   _____
   _____

2. **Why did the Hare choose to take a nap?** (RL.1.1)

   _____
   _____
   _____
   _____

3. **What lesson is this passage teaching us?** (RL.1.2)

   _____
   _____
   _____
   _____

1.1. KEY IDEAS AND DETAILS

1. READING: LITERATURE

MULTIPLE CHOICE

4. **The line "Do you ever get anywhere?" is evidence of what?** (RL.1.1)
   A. Tortoise asking Hare a question.
   B. Hare making fun of Tortoise for being slow.
   C. Hare being kind to Tortoise by offering to help.
   D. Hare making fun of Tortoise for being fat.

FILL IN THE BLANK

5. _____ served as judge for the race. (RL.1.1)

6. **Tortoise's progress was slow but** _____. (RL.1.2)

7. **It seemed as though** _____ **was going to win the race.** (RL.1.1)

TRUE OR FALSE

8. **The Tortoise thought that he was going to lose the race.** (RL.1.1)
   A. True
   B. False

1.1. KEY IDEAS AND DETAILS

> **Directions:** Read the passage and answer the questions below.

THE SHEPHERD BOY AND THE WOLF

A Shepherd Boy tended his master's Sheep near a dark forest not far from the village. Soon he found life in the pasture very dull. All he could do to amuse himself was to talk to his dog or play on his shepherd's pipe.

One day, as he sat watching the Sheep and the quiet forest, and thinking what he would do, should he see a Wolf, he thought of a plan to amuse himself.

...continued next page

1. READING: LITERATURE

His Master had told him to call for help should a Wolf attack the flock, and the Villagers would drive it away. So now, though he had not seen anything that even looked like a Wolf, he ran toward the village shouting at the top of his voice, "Wolf! Wolf!"

As he expected, the Villagers who heard the cry dropped their work and ran in great excitement to the pasture. But when they got there they found the Boy doubled up with laughter at the trick he had played on them.

A few days later the Shepherd Boy again shouted, "Wolf! Wolf!" Again the Villagers ran to help him, only to be laughed at again.

Then one evening as the sun was setting behind the forest and the shadows were creeping out over the pasture, a Wolf really did spring from the underbrush and fall upon the Sheep.

In terror, the Boy ran toward the village shouting "Wolf! Wolf!" But though the Villagers heard the cry, they did not run to help him as they had before. "He cannot fool us again," they said.

The Wolf killed a great many of the Boy's Sheep and then slipped away into the forest.

FREE RESPONSE

9. **What is the lesson of this passage?** (RL.1.2)

_____

_____

_____

10. **Describe the main character of this passage.** (RL.1.3)

_____

_____

_____

1.1. KEY IDEAS AND DETAILS

1. READING: LITERATURE

FILL IN THE BLANK

11. **Where is this story set?** (RL.1.3)

The story is set in a _____.

TRUE OR FALSE

12. **The townspeople ignored the Shepherd Boy to teach him a lesson.** (RL.1.2)

   A. True   **B.** False

> **Directions:** Read the passage and answer the questions below.

THE SELFISH CROCODILE

Deep in the mysterious forest, in the muddy river, lived a large Crocodile. He was thought to be a very selfish Crocodile. He didn't want any other animals and fish to drink or bathe in the river. He thought it was HIS river. As a result, it was usually a very quiet place.

Every day, he shouted to the animals of the magical forest, "Stay away from my river! It's MY river!! If you come into my river, I'll eat you all!" So there were no fish, no tadpoles, no frogs, no crabs, no crayfish in the river. All were afraid of the selfish Crocodile.

Even the forest animals kept away from the river as well. Whenever they were thirsty, they went a long distance to drink in the other rivers and streams. It was so unfair.

NAME: .... DATE: 13

1. READING: LITERATURE

=== FREE RESPONSE ===

13. Describe the area where the Crocodile lives. (RL.1.2)

_____

_____

_____

_____

14. Why do you think the Crocodile does not want the other animals and fish to drink or bathe in the river? (RL.1.2)

_____

_____

_____

_____

1.1. KEY IDEAS AND DETAILS

=== MULTIPLE CHOICE ===

15. Why did the forest animals go a long distance to find water and drink? (RL.1.2)
   A. They didn't like the forest.
   B. They had enough water already.
   C. They were afraid of the Crocodile.
   D. They wanted to see other rivers.

1. READING: LITERATURE

> **Directions:** *Read the passage and answer the questions below.*

The Dog and its Shadow

A hound dog found a bone and held it tightly in his mouth. He growled and scowled at anyone who attempted to take it away. Off into the woods he went to bury his prize.

When he came to a stream, he trotted over the footbridge and happened to glance into the water. He saw his own reflection.

Thinking it was another dog with a bigger bone, he growled and scowled at it. The reflection growled and scowled back.

"I'll get that bone too," thought the greedy dog, and he snapped his sharp teeth at the image in the water.

Alas, the hound dog's own bone fell with a splash, out of sight, the moment he opened his mouth to bite!

FREE RESPONSE
---

16. What do you think the theme of this story is? (RL.1.3)

1. READING: LITERATURE

MULTIPLE CHOICE

17. What did the dog see in the water? (RL.1.3)
- **A.** Another dog
- **B.** The footbridge
- **C.** Its own reflection
- **D.** Another bone

FILL IN THE BLANK

18. At the end of the story the dog's bone fell into _____.
(RL.1.3)

> **Directions:** Read the passage and answer the questions below.

JASON - THE OLYMPIC CHAMPION

Jason gripped his spear tightly and began to run. He fixed his gaze on the target: a large, prickly tree.

In Jason's mind he imagined it was a large bear, charging towards him in the forest, foaming at the mouth with anger.

Jason lived in Olympia, the town where the Olympic Games were held every four years. He loved to play sports like spear-throwing and sometimes watched his father training athletes after he had finished school.

He dreamed of being an Olympic champion one day.

1.1. KEY IDEAS AND DETAILS

1. READING: LITERATURE

FREE RESPONSE

19. Why do you think Jason imagines a large bear is charging towards him in the forest? (RL.1.3)

_____

_____

_____

_____

_____

_____

_____

_____

_____

_____

MULTIPLE CHOICE

20. What was Jason doing at the beginning of the story?
(RL.1.3)

    A. Chasing a large bear   **B.** Watching the athletes train
    C. Throwing his spear at a tree   **D.** Dreaming of being a champion

1.1. KEY IDEAS AND DETAILS

1.2. CRAFT AND STRUCTURE

1. READING: LITERATURE

1.2. Craft and Structure

Common Core State Standards: CCSS.ELA-LITERACY.RL.1.4, CCSS.ELA-LITERACY.RL.1.5, CCSS.ELA-LITERACY.RL.1.6

Skills:
- Identify words and phrases in stories or poems that suggest feelings or appeal to the senses
- Explain major differences between books that tell stories and books that give information, drawing on a wide reading of a range of text types
- Identify who is telling the story at various points in a text

> **Directions:** Read the passage and answer the questions below.

A Day at the Theme Park

Sophia went to a fun theme park with her family. She was excited when she got to the park. She saw many rides that she wanted to go on. The first ride Sophia went on was the bumper cars. The cars went so fast that she laughed. She was happy. The next ride she wanted to go on was the log ride. It was closed for the day. Sophia was now sad. She looked for another ride. She stood in line for the haunted house. She missed her turn. A young girl had cut in front of her. This made Sophia angry. At the end of the day, she got to go on the rollercoaster. This was her favorite ride of all. She was thrilled to go upside down and backward. When the ride was done, Sophia was glad that she spent the day at the theme park.

=== MULTIPLE CHOICE ===

1. **Which word in the reading tells you Sophia's feelings about going to the theme park?** (RL.1.4)

   A. fun   B. wanted   C. excited   D. park

1. READING: LITERATURE

2. **Which word in the reading tells you Sophia's feelings about going on the bumper cars?** (RL.1.4)

   A. fast **B.** happy **C.** laugh **D.** bumper

3. **Which word in the reading tells you Sophia's feelings about the log ride being closed for the day?** (RL.1.4)

   A. happy **B.** sad **C.** angry **D.** closed

4. **Which word in the reading tells you Sophia's feelings about missing her turn in line for the haunted house?** (RL.1.4)

   A. missed **B.** cut **C.** haunted **D.** angry

5. **Which word in the reading tells you Sophia's feelings about going on the rollercoaster?** (RL.1.4)

   A. upside down **B.** thrilled
   C. backwards **D.** favorite

6. **Which word in the reading tells you Sophia's feelings about spending the day at the theme park?** (RL.1.4)

   A. glad **B.** sad **C.** angry **D.** fun

> **Directions:** Read the passage and answer the questions below.

THE PLAYGROUND

Zack raced to the playground. He wanted to be the first to run across the bridge. Soon many other kids joined him. Some kids went down the slides. Others played on the merry-go-round. It was a sunny day at the playground. Zack and his new friends played all afternoon. They ran around and laughed with each other as they played.

NAME: _____ DATE: _____

1. READING: LITERATURE

== MULTIPLE CHOICE ==

7. **Does this reading tell you a story or does it give you information?** (RL.1.5)
   A. The reading tells me a story.
   B. The reading gives me information.

8. **How do you know what type of book the reading is from?** (RL.1.5)
   A. The reading shows an illustration or drawing of kids playing at a playground.
   B. The reading shows a real-life image of a playground.

> **Directions:** *Read the passage and answer the questions below.*

THE WATER PARK

Mia was excited. It was a hot summer day. She went to the water park with her best friend Patty. The two girls wanted to go down the water slide first.

"I'm scared," said Patty. She looked down the slide and saw how steep it was.

"You can hold my hand," said Mia. Patty smiled.

1.2. CRAFT AND STRUCTURE

== MULTIPLE CHOICE ==

9. **Does this reading tell you a story or does it give you information?** (RL.1.5)
   A. The reading tells me a story.
   B. The reading gives me information.

10. **How do you know what type of book the reading is from?** (RL.1.5)
    A. The reading tells me facts about water parks.
    B. The reading has characters speaking to one another.

www.prepaze.com   Copyrighted Material

1. READING: LITERATURE

> **Directions:** *Read the passage and answer the questions below.*

Best Friends

My best friend is named Emma. She and I are both in Mrs. Smith's first-grade class. We have desks right next to each other. At lunchtime, we always sit at the same table. We like to share our food. Emma gives me a bite of her peanut butter sandwich. I give her some of my chips. At recess, our favorite thing to do is swing on the monkey bars.

One day, Emma had a surprise for me. I saw a note on top of a small red box. They were sitting on my desk. The note read, "Mia, I made you a friendship bracelet." Inside the box was a yellow bracelet. Emma had made the bracelet for me! It was pretty. I walked over to Emma and gave her a big hug. "Thank you!" I said. Emma is my best friend forever.

1.2. CRAFT AND STRUCTURE

=== MULTIPLE CHOICE ===

11. Who is telling the story? (RL.1.6)

   A. The author **B.** Emma **C.** Mrs. Smith **D.** Mia

12. Which word in the reading tells you who is telling the story? (RL.1.6)

   A. Friend **B.** Emma **C.** Mrs. Smith **D.** Mia

13. Who wrote the note that said, "Mia, I made you a friendship bracelet"? (RL.1.6)

   A. The author **B.** Emma **C.** Mrs. Smith **D.** Mia

14. Who said, "Thank you"? (RL.1.6)

   A. The author **B.** Emma **C.** Mrs. Smith **D.** Mia

15. Who is Mrs. Smith? (RL.1.6)

   A. The author **B.** The best friend
   C. The first-grade teacher **D.** A student

1. READING: LITERATURE

16. Who is Emma? (RL.1.6)
- **A.** The author
- **B.** The best friend
- **C.** The first-grade teacher
- **D.** The principal

> **Directions:** Read the passage and answer the questions below.

Turtle Life Cycle

Turtles begin inside an egg. The baby turtles break out of their shells. They are called hatchlings. These baby turtles head for the water. They grow into young adults. The young adults will then grow into adult turtles. Female adult turtles lay eggs. They will start the life cycle again.

MULTIPLE CHOICE

17. Does this reading tell you a story or does it give you information? (RL.1.5)
- **A.** The reading tells me a story.
- **B.** The reading gives me information.

18. How do you know what type of book the reading is from? (RL.1.5)
- **A.** The reading tells me facts about the life cycle of turtles.
- **B.** The reading has a story plot.

TRUE OR FALSE

19. A reader would find this text in a storybook about magical turtles. (RL.1.5)
- **A.** True
- **B.** False

20. In a textbook, this reading would most likely have a picture of a baby turtle. (RL.1.5)
- **A.** True
- **B.** False

1.3. Integration of Knowledge and Ideas

1.2. CRAFT AND STRUCTURE

1. READING: LITERATURE

1.3. Integration of Knowledge and Ideas

Common Core State Standards: CCSS.ELA-LITERACY.RL.1.7, CCSS.ELA-LITERACY.RL.1.9

Skills:
- Use illustrations and details in a story to describe its characters, setting, or events
- Compare and contrast the adventures and experiences of characters in stories

> **Directions:** Read the passage and answer the questions below.

It was a hot day. Joe was chasing Billy with the water balloon. He was thinking about hitting him with it. Joe could picture the balloon splashing on Billy. Billy had a green water balloon. He was running too fast to throw it. The boys are having fun at the party.

=== FREE RESPONSE ===

1. **Which picture is most likely Joe?** (RL.1.7)

   _____

   _____

2. **Which picture is most likely Billy?** (RL.1.7)

   _____

   _____

1. READING: LITERATURE

3. **Why do the boys have the water balloons?** (RL.1.7)

   _____

   _____

   _____

4. **What is a detail that describes the setting?** (RL.1.7)

   _____

   _____

   _____

> **Directions:** *Read the passages and answer the questions below.*

PUSS IN BOOTS

Once upon a time, there lived a miller who had three sons.

When the man died he left the mill to his oldest son. The middle son got his donkey. The youngest son was given his only other possession, a cat.

The young man felt sad.

Seeing the young man sad, the cat went over and rubbed his head against the young man's leg.

The cat spoke.

The young man was surprised.

"Yes, I can talk," said the cat. "If you will but buy me a handsome pair of boots and a large leather bag I will make you a rich and happy man."

RAGGEDY ANN LEARNS A LESSON

Marcella liked to visit her Grandmother's old house. When she was at her Grandma's house, she played up in the attic.

...continued next page

1.3. INTEGRATION OF KNOWLEDGE AND IDEAS

1. READING: LITERATURE

Marcella found many old toys and things there.

One day, Marcella was up in the attic as usual. She was sad because she was alone. She was tired because she had played for a long time, so she sat down to rest. She looked around and saw a box in the back of the room.

"What could be in that box over there?" she thought. She stood up and climbed over some old chairs and tables. Finally, she got to the box.

She opened it, but it was too dark to see. Marcella brought the box over to the window where she could see better in the sunshine. She found a little white hat and put it on her head.

In an old bag, she found some dolls wearing old clothes. And there was a picture of a very pretty little girl with long hair. Then Marcella pulled out an old rag doll with only one button eye, a painted nose, and a smiling mouth. Her dress was made out of soft cloth. It was blue with pretty little flowers all over it.

TRUE OR FALSE

5. **The youngest son and Marcella are alike because they are both sad.** (RL.1.9)

   A. True   B. False

6. **Marcella gets a surprise in "Raggedy Ann." There are no character surprises in "Puss in Boots."** (RL.1.9)

   A. True   B. False

7. **The main character in "Puss in Boots" is a boy.** (RL.1.9)

   A. True   B. False

8. **The main character in "Raggedy Ann" is a boy.** (RL.1.9)

   A. True   B. False

9. **"Puss in Boots" could be real. "Raggedy Ann" could not be real.** (RL.1.9)

   A. True   B. False

1. READING: LITERATURE

> **Directions:** *Read the passage and answer the questions below.*

It was a hot day and the sun in the sky above, stared down upon the two boys on the sand. As Simon ran on the soft beach, he gripped his surf board tightly. The board was very precious to him as it was a birthday gift from his older brother, Tom.

Paddling the board out to sea, Simon was helped by the huge wind which was gently whipping the waves. With a huge leap, Simon moved through the water, just as an enormous creature rose below him, its jaws open wide. He tumbled from his board.

Suddenly his brother appeared, and pulled Simon onto his board. The two boys were afraid. They looked for the creature but saw nothing. Where had it gone?

1.3. INTEGRATION OF KNOWLEDGE AND IDEAS

=== MULTIPLE CHOICE ===

10. What does the text tell you about Simon? (RL.1.7)
   A. Simon has a younger brother.
   B. Simon is good at surfing.
   C. Simon has a brother called Tom.
   D. Simon lives by the sea.

11. How do Simon and Tom feel at the end of the text? (RL.1.7)
   A. They are sad.
   B. They are excited.
   C. They are afraid.
   D. They are annoyed.

12. Which word from the text shows the surf board was very special to Simon? (RL.1.7)
   A. Gift
   B. Precious
   C. Enormous
   D. Birthday

www.prepaze.com   Copyrighted Material

1. READING: LITERATURE

13. **What happens to Simon in the water?** (RL.1.7)
    A. He hurts his foot.
    B. He races Tom.
    C. He falls from his board.
    D. He fights the creature.

14. **Which word is used in the text to describe the creature?** (RL.1.7)
    A. Precious
    B. Soft
    C. Huge
    D. Enormous

> **Directions:** *Read the passages and answer the questions below.*

The Little Glass Slipper

Once there was a gentleman with a daughter who was sweet and kind. He married a proud woman with two daughters exactly like her.

After the wedding, his wife began to show her true colors. She made his daughter do all of the housework. She made her sleep in a tiny room with a straw bed.

The girl worked hard. After she finished her work she would go into the chimney-corner and rest in ashes. Her sisters called her a cinder maid or Cinderella.

The Prince invited everyone to a ball. Cinderella's sisters began choosing what to wear.

...continued next page

1. READING: LITERATURE

As they left for the ball, Cinderella began to cry. Her Godmother, who was a fairy, saw her tears and asked her what the matter was. "You wish you could go to the ball?"

"Yes," cried Cinderella.

Her Godmother said, "Run into the garden and bring me a pumpkin." Cinderella found a pumpkin and brought it to her. Her Godmother struck it with her wand and turned it into a fine coach, covered with gold.

She then found six mice and made a set of six horses. She turned a rat into a friendly coachman and six lizards into footmen.

The Godmother then said to Cinderella, "It is time to go."

"But I am wearing rags."

Her Godmother touched her with her wand and turned her clothes into a beautiful gown! "Now go! But, be home by midnight because at midnight all will return to the way it was."

PEAR BLOSSOM

There was a child named Pear Blossom. One morning, Pear Blossom's mother died. Her father cried, "Who will take care of Pear Blossom?"

He went to the village matchmaker. She knew of a widow with a daughter.

When Omoni and Peony saw how beautiful Pear Blossom was, they were jealous of her. Omoni made her work all day.

One day the village was having a festival. "Pear Blossom may go," said Omoni, "after she weeds the flowers."

When she reached the fields, Pear Blossom looked sad. Weeding it would take weeks.

A black ox came from the grass. It began to munch the weeds. Soon the ox was gone and the weeds were too.

"A thousand thanks!" she called to the ox.

Pear Blossom hurried to the festival.

1. READING: LITERATURE

TRUE OR FALSE

15. Cinderella and Pear Blossom get help from others. (RL.1.9)

　　A. True　　　　　　　　　　　B. False

16. Pear Blossom is lazy, but Cinderella is not. (RL.1.9)

　　A. True　　　　　　　　　　　B. False

17. Cinderella's dad is nice, but Pear Blossom's dad is mean. (RL.1.9)

　　A. True　　　　　　　　　　　B. False

MULTIPLE CHOICE

18. Who helps Cinderella? (RL.1.9)

　　A. The Fairy Godmother　　　　B. Her sisters
　　C. Her stepmom　　　　　　　　D. Her dad

19. Who helps Pear Blossom? (RL.1.9)

　　A. The black ox　　　　　　　　B. Her father
　　C. Peony　　　　　　　　　　　D. Omoni

20. How are the girls in the stories alike? (RL.1.9)

　　A. They both are lazy.　　　　　B. They both have a lot of money.
　　C. They both grow flowers.　　　D. They both have mean sisters.

1.3. INTEGRATION OF KNOWLEDGE AND IDEAS

1.4. RANGE OF READING AND LEVEL OF TEXT COMPLEXITY

1. READING: LITERATURE

1.4. Range of Reading and Level of Text Complexity

Common Core State Standards: CCSS.ELA-LITERACY.RL.1.10

Skills:
- With prompting and support, read prose and poetry of appropriate complexity for grade 1.

> **Directions:** *Read the poem and answer the questions below.*

THE SCHOOL BUS

The school bus is big, yellow, and loud.
Only two people in each seat are allowed.

I like to get on the bus early,
so I can save my friend a seat.
If we are calm and quiet,
our bus driver may give us a treat.

I sit and look out the window,
eating a healthy snack.
When the bus stops at my house,
I grab my coat and my red backpack.

═══ **MULTIPLE CHOICE** ═══

1. **Which word in the poem tells you the size of the bus?** (RL.1.10)

   A. school   **B.** big   **C.** yellow   **D.** loud

2. **Which word in the poem tells you the color of the backpack?** (RL.1.10)

   A. big   **B.** yellow   **C.** loud   **D.** red

1. READING: LITERATURE

3. **Which word in the poem rhymes with the seat?** (RL.1.10)
   A. Early   B. Quiet   C. Treat   D. Friend

4. **Which word in the poem rhymes with snack?** (RL.1.10)
   A. Window   B. House   C. Coat   D. Backpack

5. **Who is saying the poem?** (RL.1.10)
   A. A bus driver   B. A teacher   C. A student   D. A parent

6. **Why would the bus driver give a treat?** (RL.1.10)
   A. If the passenger is on the bus early
   B. If the passenger eats a healthy snack
   C. If the passenger saves their friend a seat
   D. If the passenger is calm and quiet

> **Directions:** Read the poem and answer the questions below.

TRAVELING FUN

Traveling is fun!
You can go on trips to places with a lot of sun

You can travel by boat or plane.
You can travel by car or train.

You can travel outside of your town,
or you can even leave your state.
Traveling can be really great!

Now pack up your bags and hit the road.
Remember to bring a brush and toothpaste.
Hurry and get ready to go!
There is no time to waste.

1. READING: LITERATURE

MULTIPLE CHOICE

7. **Which word in the poem rhymes with plane?** (RL.1.10)

   A. Boat   **B.** Car   **C.** Train   **D.** Travel

8. **Which word in the poem rhymes with toothpaste?** (RL.1.10)

   A. Road   **B.** Brush   **C.** Go   **D.** Waste

9. **Where does the poem say you can travel?** (RL.1.10)

   A. To the grocery store   **B.** To the library
   C. Outside your town   **D.** To the movies

10. **What does the poem tell you to bring?** (RL.1.10)

    A. Comb and clothes   **B.** Brush and toothpaste
    C. Pajamas and pillow   **D.** Shoes and socks

11. **Who is saying the poem?** (RL.1.10)

    A. The author   **B.** A driver
    C. A pilot   **D.** A conductor

12. **What is the poem about?** (RL.1.10)

    A. Flying on a plane   **B.** Traveling
    C. Going to school   **D.** Brushing your teeth

> **Directions:** *Read the poem and answer the questions below.*

THE BROWN BEAR

Our teacher took us on a field trip.
We got to go to the nearby zoo.
I was excited to be there with my class.
When we walked in, the welcome sign was red and blue.

My favorite animal I had yet to see.
Soon I saw it right in front of me.

...continued next page

1.4. RANGE OF READING AND LEVEL OF TEXT COMPLEXITY

1. READING: LITERATURE

> A big brown bear was walking around in its den.
> It would walk back and forth over and over again.
>
> "Here, brown bear," I yelled.
> "Look over here, please!"
> The bear turned its head.
> Then the bear let out a big sneeze.

TRUE OR FALSE

13. A student is saying the poem. (RL.1.10)

    A. True   **B.** False

14. The welcome sign was brown. (RL.1.10)

    A. True   **B.** False

15. The bear is the favorite animal in the poem. (RL.1.10)

    A. True   **B.** False

16. The zoo was close to the school. (RL.1.10)

    A. True   **B.** False

FREE RESPONSE

17. Who yelled, "Here, brown bear. Look over here, please"? How do you know? (RL.1.10)

_____

_____

_____

_____

1.4. RANGE OF READING AND LEVEL OF TEXT COMPLEXITY

1. READING: LITERATURE

18. What feeling was talked about in the poem? (RL.1.10)

_____

_____

_____

_____

_____

> **Directions:** *Read the poem and answer the questions below.*

THE RAIN CLOUDS

John and Jane went outside to play.
It was a nice, sunny day.

The two friends played catch and swam in the lake.
After some time, they stopped and took a break.

When the pair came back outside, the weather had changed.
Big rain clouds were in the sky above.
When it started to rain, Jane ran inside.
John did not go because he had to grab his baseball glove.

"Oh no," cried Jane.
"I want to play some more. I wish it would stop."
John walked to the window and looked outside.
All he could see were great big raindrops.

1.4. RANGE OF READING AND LEVEL OF TEXT COMPLEXITY

1. READING: LITERATURE

FREE RESPONSE

19. Who are the two friends? How else are they described in the poem? (RL.1.10)

20. How did the weather change? (RL.1.10)

1.5. Chapter Review

1. READING: LITERATURE

1.5. Chapter Review

> **Directions:** *Read the passage and answer the questions below.*

THE CROW AND THE PITCHER

In a spell of dry weather, when the birds could find very little to drink, a thirsty Crow found a pitcher with a little water in it. But the pitcher was high and had a narrow neck, and no matter how he tried, the crow could not reach the water. The poor thing felt as if he must die of thirst.

Then an idea came to him. Picking up some small pebbles, he dropped them into the pitcher one by one. With each pebble, the water rose a little higher until at last, it was near enough so he could drink.

=== FREE RESPONSE ===

1. **What is the lesson of this passage?** (RL.1.2)

_____

_____

_____

_____

_____

_____

_____

1. READING: LITERATURE

MULTIPLE CHOICE

2. **Why could the bird not find water?** (RL.1.2)
   - **A.** The weather was dry.
   - **B.** The pitcher was empty.
   - **C.** The pitcher was narrow.
   - **D.** There were no lakes close by.

> **Directions:** *Read the passage and answer the questions below.*

THE SELFISH CROCODILE

Deep in the mysterious forest, in the muddy river, lived a large Crocodile. He was thought to be a very selfish Crocodile. He didn't want any other animals and fish to drink or bathe in the river. He thought it was HIS river. As a result, it was usually a very quiet place.

Every day, he shouted to the animals of the magical forest, "Stay away from my river! It's MY river!! If you come into my river, I'll eat you all!" So there were no fish, no tadpoles, no frogs, no crabs, no crayfish in the river. All were afraid of the selfish Crocodile.

Even the forest animals kept away from the river as well. Whenever they were thirsty, they went a very long distance to drink in the other rivers and streams. It was so unfair.

1. READING: LITERATURE

=== FREE RESPONSE ===

3. **The final sentence in the passage states: 'It was so unfair'. Explain why this statement is true.** (RL.1.1)

_____

_____

_____

_____

_____

4. **What evidence from the passage suggests the river is located in an unusual place?** (RL.1.1)

_____

_____

_____

_____

_____

1.5. CHAPTER REVIEW

=== MULTIPLE CHOICE ===

5. **Exclamation marks are used each time the Crocodile speaks. What might they suggest about the Crocodile?** (RL.1.1)
   A. The Crocodile is lying.
   B. The Crocodile is shouting.
   C. The Crocodile is whispering.
   D. The Crocodile is frightened.

1. READING: LITERATURE

> **Directions:** *Read the passage and answer the questions below.*

It was a hot day. Joe was chasing Billy with the water balloon. He was thinking about hitting him with it. Joe could picture the balloon splashing on Billy. Billy had a green water balloon. He was running too fast to throw it. The boys are having fun at the party.

=== **FREE RESPONSE** ===

6. **Why can't Billy throw his balloon?** (RL.1.7)

   _____

   _____

   _____

7. **What color balloon is Joe carrying?** (RL.1.7)

   _____

   _____

   _____

1. READING: LITERATURE

> **Directions:** Read the passages and answer the questions below.

Little Red Riding Hood

Once upon a time there lived in a certain village a little country girl. She was the prettiest creature who was ever seen. Her mother was very fond of her. Her grandmother loved her even more. This good woman had a little red riding hood made for her. It suited the girl so well that everybody called her Little Red Riding Hood.

One day her mother, having made some cakes, said to her, "Go, my dear, and see how your grandmother is doing. She is sick. Take her a cake, and this little pot of butter."

Little Red Riding Hood set out immediately to go to her grandmother, who lived in another village. As she was going through the wood, she met with a wolf. He had a very great mind to eat her up. He dared not do it because of some woodcutters working nearby in the forest. He asked her where she was going.

The poor child did not know that it was dangerous to talk to a wolf. She said to him, "I am going to see my grandmother. I am taking her a cake and some butter."

The Little Red Hen

Little Red Hen lived in a barnyard. She spent almost all of her time walking about the barnyard. She was always busy looking for worms.

She loved fat, delicious worms. She felt they were necessary for her children's health. As often as she found a worm she would call "Chuck-chuck-chuck!" to her chickies.

When they were gathered about her, she would pass out tiny pieces of worm. A cat usually napped lazily in the barn door. The cat was lazy. The pig who lived in the pen was also lazy. He just wanted to eat and grow fat.

One day the Little Red Hen found a seed. It was a wheat seed, but the Little Red Hen was so used to bugs and worms, she did not know

...continued next page

1. READING: LITERATURE

what it was. She walked around asking other animals about it. Finally, she learned that it was a wheat seed.

The Little Red Hen asked other animals to plant it. They would not help her. She kept asking, "Will you plant the seed?"

But the Pig said, "Not I."

The Cat said, "Not I."

The Rat said, "Not I."

"Well, then," said the Little Red Hen, "I will." And she did.

=== FREE RESPONSE ===

8. **Was Little Red Riding Hood acting safely? Why or why not?** (RL.1.9)

_____
_____
_____
_____
_____

9. **What did the Wolf, the Rat, the Pig, and the Cat all have in common?** (RL.1.9)

_____
_____
_____
_____
_____

1. READING: LITERATURE

10. **Why was the Wolf afraid to hurt Little Red Riding Hood?** (RL.1.9)

   _____

   _____

   _____

11. **What does the Little Red Hen want to do with the seed?** (RL.1.9)

   _____

   _____

   _____

> **Directions:** *Read the passage and answer the questions below.*

My Big Red Balloon

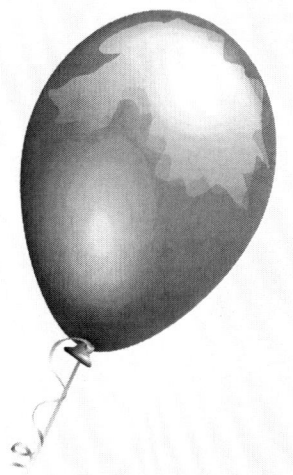

Last year my school had a huge party to celebrate it being a hundred years old. The party was great fun.

Our teacher carried out two large bags that had been hidden in the staffroom. They were as big as floating elephants. What was inside?

"These are the school's own birthday balloons," said the teacher. "We're going to send them flying as far as they can go to tell the world about our special day."

We were all given a balloon and each one had a label with our own name on it and the school's address. I signed it with my name, Jessica Smith.

As soon as everyone had finished writing their messages, we sent them, one by one, sailing off into the afternoon sky. I wondered who in the world would find mine.

...continued next page

1. READING: LITERATURE

Weeks went by, yet I didn't receive a reply about my red balloon. I was worried it had got lost in the sea or got caught amongst some great forest where no-one lived. Maybe I would never hear back about where my balloon had gone to.

One Friday, as I packed my school books into my bag at the end of the day, my teacher came rushing towards me.

"Guess what I have, Jessica?" she laughed with delight. "Someone has found your balloon and you'll never guess where it ended up!"

FREE RESPONSE

12. Why did the school hold a party? (RL.1.3)

13. Where is Jessica worried her red balloon might have ended up? List two places. (RL.1.3)

MULTIPLE CHOICE

14. Why do you think the school's address was on the balloon's label? (RL.1.3)
   A. So people could tell the school where they found the balloon.
   B. So the children knew what the school's address was.
   C. So people would know the school had their own balloons.
   D. So the children could write to their teachers.

NAME: _____ DATE: _____ 43

1. READING: LITERATURE

TRUE OR FALSE

15. Jessica's teacher is happy that Jessica's balloon has been found. (RL.1.3)

  A. True   **B.** False

> **Directions:** Read the passage and answer the questions below.

EATING APPLES

Mason loves to eat apples. His mom packs him red and green apples every day for lunch. Mason likes holding apples in his hand. The apples feel smooth on his skin. Before he eats them, Mason holds the apples up to his nose. He can smell the sweet scent of the apples. He likes to hold the stem of the apple while he eats it. Mason likes to bite down on apples and hear the loud crunch they make from his teeth. The apples taste crisp and juicy on his tongue. When he is eating the apples, Mason has to be careful. He does not want to chew any of the hard brown seeds inside the apple core. Mason likes to dip the apples in peanut butter for a snack. The peanut butter is crunchy, too. It helps to make the apple taste sweet and salty.

MULTIPLE CHOICE

16. Which word in the reading tells you how the apples feel on Mason's skin? (RL.1.4)

  A. red   **B.** holding   **C.** hand   **D.** smooth

17. Which phrase in the reading tells you how the apples smell? (RL.1.4)

  A. his nose   **B.** sweet scent
  C. eats them   **D.** hold the stem

18. Which phrase in the reading tells you the sound the apples make when Mason bites them with his teeth? (RL.1.4)

  A. bite down   **B.** his teeth
  C. loud crunch   **D.** sweet scent

1.5. CHAPTER REVIEW

www.prepaze.com   Copyrighted Material   prepaze

1. READING: LITERATURE

19. **Which phrase in the reading tells you how the apples taste on Mason's tongue?** (RL.1.4)

   A. crisp and juicy
   B. hard and juicy
   C. crisp and crunch
   D. sweet and juicy

> **Directions:** *Read the passage and answer the questions below.*

Pet Store

Michelle and her dad went to a pet store. Her dad said that she could pick out a new pet. Michelle was excited. She wanted to get a rabbit. Michelle walked all around the pet store looking for her new rabbit.

"Look over here at this one," said the pet store owner. "This rabbit would make a good pet for you."

Michelle looked at the black and white rabbit. "Oh, I like him," she said. "Dad, this one has white spots. It is really pretty."

Her dad walked over to the rabbit. "I think this rabbit will fit right in with our family," he said. "Let's get him and bring him home."

Michelle and her dad bought a few things for the rabbit, like food and supplies. They went to the counter to pay for their items.

"Here you go. You're all set, Mr. Martin," said the pet store owner.

Michelle and her dad thanked him. "What will you name your rabbit?" Michelle's dad asked.

"I will name him Fluffy," she said.

TRUE OR FALSE

20. **Michelle is telling the story.** (RL.1.6)

   A. True
   B. False

21. **Michelle named her pet rabbit Fluffy.** (RL.1.6)

   A. True
   B. False

22. **The pet store owner's name is Mr. Martin.** (RL.1.6)

   A. True
   B. False

1. READING: LITERATURE

> **Directions:** Read the poem and answer the questions below.

THE POND

Have you ever been to a pond to walk around?
Lots of things move in the water and make a sound.
There are ducks, lizards, and tadpoles.
There are bugs crawling in and out of holes.
The green critters are home at the pond.
You can see frogs on lily pads floating on top.
Wait for a minute or two and you will see them move.
If you watch closely, you can even see them hop.
Listen carefully and you will hear them speak.
"Ribbit, ribbit."
"Ribbit, ribbit."
"Ribbit, ribbit."

FREE RESPONSE

23. What is the setting of the poem? How do you know? (RL.1.10)

_____
_____
_____
_____
_____
_____
_____

1. READING: LITERATURE

24. **The poem says that things move in the water and make a sound. What things do you think the poem is talking about?** (RL.1.10)

25. **What word in the poem rhymes with hop? Name two more words that rhyme with hop.** (RL.1.10)

1.5. CHAPTER REVIEW

1. READING: LITERATURE

> **Directions:** Read the passage and answer the questions below.

ZEBRAS

Zebras are animals like horses and donkeys. Wild zebras live in Africa. Zebras have their own pattern of black and white stripes. Zebras can stand up while they sleep. They have good eyesight and hearing. When they are chased, zebras will zig-zag from side to side. This makes it difficult for predators to attack them.

=== MULTIPLE CHOICE ===

26. Does this reading tell you a story or does it give you information? (RL.1.5)
   A. The reading tells me a story.
   B. The reading gives me information.

27. How do you know what type of book the reading is from? (RL.1.5)
   A. The reading shows an illustration or drawing of a cartoon zebra.
   B. The reading shows a real-life image of a zebra.

1. READING: LITERATURE

> **Directions:** *Read the passage and answer the questions below.*

PERFORMANCE DAY

Jim and Jan were going to take the stage. It was their big day. Jan was ready to play the part of the fun dancer. Jim was ready to act out the part of the silly boy. He is trying to learn some dance moves. He has never danced before. Jan is trying to teach him some moves, but he does not look graceful like her. People coming to watch the play will be in for a real treat.

=== MULTIPLE CHOICE ===

28. What do the text *and* illustrations tell you about Jim? (RL.1.7)
  A. He is performing with short hair.
  B. He is shorter than Jan.
  C. He is younger than Jan.
  D. He is not a happy boy.

29. What do the text *and* illustrations tell you about Jan? (RL.1.7)
  A. She is not a dancer.
  B. She is a graceful dancer.
  C. She is too small to dance.
  D. She has green hair.

30. What do the text *and* illustrations tell you about the kids? (RL.1.7)
  A. They are both acting like they are hiking.
  B. They are wearing fake hair.
  C. They are nervous.
  D. They are happy.

2. READING: INFORMATIONAL TEXT

2.1. KEY IDEAS AND DETAILS — 50
- ❖ Text details
- ❖ Main idea
- ❖ Sequence

2.2. CRAFT AND STRUCTURE — 55
- ❖ Understanding vocabulary
- ❖ Locate information
- ❖ Author's point of view

2.3. INTEGRATION OF KNOWLEDGE AND IDEAS — 62
- ❖ Visual illustrations
- ❖ Text connections
- ❖ Compare/contrast key details

2.4. CHAPTER REVIEW — 68

2. READING: INFORMATIONAL TEXT

2.1. Key Ideas and Details

Common Core State Standards: CCSS.ELA-LITERACY.RI.1.1, CCSS.ELA-LITERACY.RI.1.2, CCSS.ELA-LITERACY.RI.1.3

Skills:
- Ask and answer questions about key details in a text
- Identify the main topic and retell key details of a text
- Describe the connection between two individuals, events, ideas, or pieces of information in a text

> **Directions:** Read the passage and answer the questions below.

CATERPILLARS

Caterpillars are insects. They have soft bodies. They have up to five pairs of legs. Caterpillars can grow very fast. They eat a lot of leaves. Caterpillars shed their skin. When they stop eating, they hang upside down from a twig or leaf. The caterpillar spins silk around its body. This makes a cocoon. Inside the cocoon, the caterpillar is changing. In a few weeks, it will come out of the cocoon. When it comes out, It will be a moth or a butterfly.

=== MULTIPLE CHOICE ===

1. **Which insect is the text about?** (RI.1.1)

    A. spider   **B.** ant   **C.** bee   **D.** caterpillar

2. **How many pairs of legs can caterpillars have?** (RI.1.1)

    A. ten   **B.** five   **C.** twelve   **D.** twenty

2. READING: INFORMATIONAL TEXT

3. **What do caterpillars eat?** (RI.1.1)
   - **A.** leaves
   - **B.** dirt
   - **C.** seeds
   - **D.** fruit

4. **What do caterpillars hang upside down from?** (RI.1.1)
   - **A.** A twig or a leaf
   - **B.** A rock
   - **C.** A log
   - **D.** A flower

5. **What do caterpillars spin around their bodies to make a cocoon?** (RI.1.1)
   - **A.** Bark
   - **B.** Dirt
   - **C.** Silk
   - **D.** Water

6. **What can caterpillars turn into?** (RI.1.1)
   - **A.** moth
   - **B.** butterfly
   - **C.** spider
   - **D.** a & b

> **Directions:** *Read the text and answer the questions below.*

ALLIGATORS AND CROCODILES

Alligators and crocodiles are both reptiles. They are close relatives. Both look very similar. If you have been to a zoo and seen these reptiles, you might have spotted a few differences. Alligators have a wider snout. It is in the shape of a U. Crocodiles have a pointed snout. It is in the shape of a V. When alligators close their mouths, all of their teeth are hidden. Their upper jaw is wider than the lower one. When crocodiles close their mouths, you can still see some of their teeth. Alligators live in freshwater marshes, lakes, and swamps. Crocodiles live in saltwater lakes, rivers, and swamps.

2.1. KEY IDEAS AND DETAILS

=== TRUE OR FALSE ===

> **Directions:** *Mark the following statements as either true or false.*

7. **Alligators and crocodiles are both reptiles.** (RI.1.3)
   - **A.** True
   - **B.** False

8. **Alligators have a snout in the shape of a V.** (RI.1.3)
   - **A.** True
   - **B.** False

2. READING: INFORMATIONAL TEXT

9. **Crocodiles have a pointed snout.** (RI.1.3)

   A. True   **B.** False

10. **When alligators close their mouth, you can still see some of their teeth.** (RI.1.3)

    A. True   **B.** False

> **Directions:** *Read the text and answer the questions below.*

GEORGE WASHINGTON

George Washington was the first president of the United States. He was 57 years old when he became president. He was president for two terms. He led the country from 1789 to 1797.

Washington was the only president to not live in the White House. He was very tall. He stood over six feet high. He also had false teeth. They were made of ivory. His wife's name was Martha. Today you can see Washington's picture on the one dollar bill and quarter.

=== MULTIPLE CHOICE ===

11. **What is the main topic?** (RI.1.2)
    - **A.** Presidents of the United States
    - **B.** George Washington as our first president
    - **C.** The White House
    - **D.** The First Lady Martha Washington

12. **How old was George Washington when he became president?** (RI.1.2)

    A. 50   **B.** 55   **C.** 57   **D.** 60

13. **How many terms was George Washington president?** (RI.1.2)

    A. one   **B.** two   **C.** three   **D.** four

2.1. KEY IDEAS AND DETAILS

2. READING: INFORMATIONAL TEXT

14. How many years did George Washington live in the White House? (RI.1.2)

- **A.** two years
- **B.** four years
- **C.** eight years
- **D.** He did not live in the White House.

> **Directions:** *Read the text and answer the questions below.*

SEALS & WALRUSES

The seal is a mammal. It lives on both land and water. Seals have their babies on land. They can live in both cold and warm waters. Seals can weigh a lot. They use their thick fur coat and layer of blubber to stay warm. Seals eat both fish and meat. They can find their food by using their whiskers. They can be white, silver, or brown.

The walrus is also a mammal. They have their babies on ice. They live in mostly cold water. Walruses can also weigh a lot. They use their layer of blubber to keep warm. Walruses eat both fish and meat. They can find their food by using their whiskers, too. They are brown in color.

=== **FREE RESPONSE** ===

15. Where do seals have their babies? Where do walruses have their babies? (RI.1.3)

_____

_____

_____

16. Where do both seals and walruses live? (RI.1.3)

_____

_____

_____

2.1. KEY IDEAS AND DETAILS

2. READING: INFORMATIONAL TEXT

17. How do both seals and walruses keep warm? (RI.1.3)

_____

_____

_____

_____

> **Directions:** Read the text and answer the questions below.

Healthy Eating

Eating healthy is a good thing to do. It can give you energy during the day. Eating food that is good for us helps us with many things. We can learn better. We can play longer without being tired. Fruits and vegetables are healthy foods. You can eat as many as you want. They fill you up so you are less likely to eat junk food. You will have less room in your stomach for candy bars or chips. You may even go to the doctor less because you become stronger from eating healthy food.

=== TRUE OR FALSE ===

18. The main topic of the text is that eating healthy food is good for us. (RI.1.2)

    A. True   **B.** False

19. Healthy foods give us energy during the day. (RI.1.2)

    A. True   **B.** False

20. Eating healthy foods makes us tired faster. (RI.1.2)

    A. True   **B.** False

2.2. CRAFT AND STRUCTURE

2. READING: INFORMATIONAL TEXT

2.2. Craft and Structure

Common Core State Standards: CCSS.ELA-LITERACY.RI.1.4, CCSS.ELA-LITERACY.RI.1.5

Skills:
- Ask and answer questions to help determine or clarify the meaning of words and phrases in a text
- Know and use various text features (e.g., headings, tables of contents, glossaries, electronic menus, icons) to locate key facts or information in a text

> **Directions:** *Read the text and answer the questions below.*

PLANETS CIRCLING THE SUN

Did you know that there are eight planets in the solar system? Can you name them all? There is Mercury, Venus, Earth, Mars, Jupiter, Saturn, Uranus, and Neptune. These planets **orbit** or circle around the sun. Everything in the solar system moves around the sun. Moons, comets, dust, and gases orbit the sun, too. The third planet from the sun is Earth. It takes the Earth 365 days to go around the sun one time! That is why we have 365 days in one year.

=== **TRUE OR FALSE** ===

1. **There are eight planets in the solar system.** (RI.1.4)

    A. True **B.** False

2. **Jupiter is a planet.** (RI.1.4)

    A. True **B.** False

3. **Everything in the solar system moves around Earth.** (RI.1.4)

    A. True **B.** False

2. READING: INFORMATIONAL TEXT

4. Earth is the fourth planet from the sun. (RI.1.4)

   A. True **B.** False

=== FREE RESPONSE ===

5. What does the word orbit mean? (RI.1.4)

_____

_____

_____

6. How do you know what orbit means? What clues from the text help you? (RI.1.4)

_____

_____

_____

2.2. CRAFT AND STRUCTURE

GLOSSARIES

Some books have a list of special words that are in a glossary. This part of the book is found at the end. This is where you can find out what these words mean.

> **Directions:** *Read the glossary from a book about butterflies.*

Abdomen	The back part of an insect's body; it contains their heart and stomach.
Caterpillar	This is the second stage in a butterfly's life; also called larva. The butterfly is worm-like.

...continued next page

2. READING: INFORMATIONAL TEXT

Chrysalis	The third stage in a butterfly's life; also called pupa. It is inside a hard case.
Hindwings	The wings located at the back of the butterfly. They are close to the abdomen.
Metamorphosis	The change that takes place inside the chrysalis from caterpillar to adult butterfly. There are three stages.
Pupa	The third stage of a butterfly's life. It is known as a chrysalis.

=== MULTIPLE CHOICE ===

7. **The third stage in a butterfly's life is known as** _____. (RI.1.5)
   - **A.** chrysalis
   - **B.** metamorphosis
   - **C.** abdomen
   - **D.** larva

8. **Chrysalis is the same as** _____. (RI.1.5)
   - **A.** pupa
   - **B.** worm-like
   - **C.** abdomen
   - **D.** larva

9. **The three changes a butterfly goes through is known as** _____. (RI.1.5)
   - **A.** chrysalis
   - **B.** metamorphosis
   - **C.** abdomen
   - **D.** larva

10. **This glossary is most likely found in a book about** _____. (RI.1.5)
    - **A.** flowers
    - **B.** reptiles
    - **C.** wildlife
    - **D.** butterflies

11. **Which one of these items is NOT located inside a butterfly's abdomen?** (RI.1.5)
    - **A.** heart
    - **B.** stomach
    - **C.** hindwings
    - **D.** All of these are in the abdomen.

2.2. CRAFT AND STRUCTURE

2. READING: INFORMATIONAL TEXT

> **Directions:** Read the text and answer the questions below.

TURTLE FACTS

Turtles are known as reptiles. Like other reptiles, they lay eggs. They are cold-blooded or **ectothermic**. They take on the temperature of their environment. When they are outside in the heat, they become hot, too. When they are in a cold place, they become cold, too. Turtles need to be warm. This helps them to eat and move around. You can find turtles that live in hot places or warm **climates**. One of the best things about turtles is their shell. They use it to hide from **predators** or other animals that may want to eat them. All turtles have shells. They cannot take them off. The shell is important to a turtle.

― FREE RESPONSE ―

12. What do reptiles lay? (RI.1.4)

_____
_____
_____
_____

13. What does ectothermic mean? (RI.1.4)

_____
_____
_____
_____

2. READING: INFORMATIONAL TEXT

14. Why do turtles need to be warm? (RI.1.4)

15. What does the word climate mean? (RI.1.4)

2.2. CRAFT AND STRUCTURE

2. READING: INFORMATIONAL TEXT

> **Directions:** Use the table of contents to answer the following questions.

WILDLIFE IN KENTUCKY

Table of Contents

Chapter 1: Deer 1
Chapter 2: Raccoons 7
Chapter 3: Squirrels 13
Chapter 4: Rabbits 19
Chapter 5: Opossums 24

16. Which chapter begins on page 7? (RI.1.5)

_____
_____
_____

17. How many total chapters are there in the book? (RI.1.5)

_____
_____
_____

2. READING: INFORMATIONAL TEXT

18. **Which chapter should you read to learn about rabbits?** (RI.1.5)

   _____

   _____

   _____

   _____

19. **If you want to read ALL the information about deer, what pages will you need to read?** (RI.1.5)

   _____

   _____

   _____

   _____

20. **Which chapter has information about raccoons?** (RI.1.5)

   _____

   _____

   _____

   _____

2.3. INTEGRATION OF KNOWLEDGE AND IDEAS

2. READING: INFORMATIONAL TEXT

2.3. Integration of Knowledge and Ideas

Common Core State Standards: CCSS.ELA-LITERACY.RI.1.7, CCSS.ELA-LITERACY.RI.1.8, CCSS.ELA-LITERACY.RI.1.9

Skills:
- Use the illustrations and details in a text to describe its key ideas
- Identify the reasons an author gives to support points in a text
- Identify basic similarities in and differences between two texts on the same topic (e.g., in illustrations, descriptions, or procedures)

> **Directions:** Read the texts and answer the questions below.

BATS

Have you seen a bat flying in the sky? They often fly together in swarms. They look like a big ribbon flying in the sky. Bats come out at night. They look for food at night. Bats have to fly when it is dark because the sun dries out their wings.

TRUE OR FALSE

1. **Bats can be seen flying during the day.** (RI.1.7)

   A. True					B. False

2. **Bats have to look for food at night because the sun dries out their wings.** (RI.1.7)

   A. True					B. False

The bats use their ears to find food in the dark. Yes, they use their ears, not their eyes. The bats make a sound. Then they listen for the sound to come back. This is how they can tell how far away something is. They have to have good hearing to do this. They use their big ears to help them find their food in the dark.

2. READING: INFORMATIONAL TEXT

3. **Bats use their eyes to find their food in the dark.** (RI.1.7)

   A. True   B. False

4. **Bats can tell how far away their food is by making and listening for sounds.** (RI.1.7)

   A. True   B. False

> **Directions:** *Read the texts and answer the questions below.*

SAVING PAPER

We use a lot of paper every day. Do you ever think about where paper comes from? Paper is made from trees. Trees are cut down to make the paper we use. Trees are good for the Earth. They help us breathe clean air. They give animals a place to live and food to eat.

=== MULTIPLE CHOICE ===

5. **Why do we cut down trees to make paper?** (RI.1.8)
   A. Because trees are big
   B. Because trees help us
   C. Because paper is made from trees
   D. Because we use trees and paper every day

6. **Why are trees good for the Earth?** (RI.1.8)
   A. They help us breathe.   B. They give animals food.
   C. They give animals a home.   D. All of the above

We need to not waste paper. There are many ways we can do this. We can recycle paper when we are done with it. We can reuse paper, too. We can write something new on a blank piece of the paper.

2.3. INTEGRATION OF KNOWLEDGE AND IDEAS

2. READING: INFORMATIONAL TEXT

7. **Why does the author say we should recycle or reuse paper?** (RI.1.8)
   A. Because we need to help animals
   B. Because we need to not waste paper
   C. Because it is the right thing to do
   D. Because it is easy

> **Directions:** *Read the texts and answer the questions below.*

Summer Fun

In summer, the weather is warm. We can go outside and play in the sun. We can wear our swimsuits and go swimming in a pool. We can play in the sand on a beach. In the summer, we can go camping with family and friends. There we can go fishing or on a bike ride.

Winter Fun

In winter, the weather is cold. We can go outside and play in the snow. We wear our winter clothes to keep us warm. In winter, we can go skiing on a mountain. We can go sledding down a hill. We can build snowmen.

=== TRUE OR FALSE ===

8. **We wear different clothes in the summer and the winter.** (RI.1.9)

   A. True   B. False

9. **The weather becomes cold in the summer and warm in the winter.** (RI.1.9)

   A. True   B. False

The sun is out longer in summer. This means that the days are longer, too. We have more time to go outside and play games.

The sun is not out as long in winter. The days are shorter. It gets darker earlier so we spend more time indoors.

2. READING: INFORMATIONAL TEXT

10. We can see outside longer during summer. (RI.1.9)

   A. True   **B.** False

    In summer, we can light fireworks. We can cook food outside on a grill. We have picnics in the park. We play outdoor sports like baseball.

    In winter, we cook food inside on the stove or the oven. We find fun things to do inside because it is too cold to stay outside for too long. We play indoor sports like basketball.

11. We do fewer things outside in the winter. (RI.1.9)

   A. True   **B.** False

12. We play sports like baseball and basketball in different seasons. (RI.1.9)

   A. True   **B.** False

> **Directions:** *Read the texts and answer the questions below.*

VEGETABLES

    Have you seen vegetables in different colors? Many vegetables are green. These help us build strong bones. Red and orange vegetables help our eyes and teeth. Our heart needs blue and purple vegetables to keep healthy.

    Vegetables have many vitamins in them. You can find vitamin C in beans. This vitamin helps you have a healthy heart. Vitamin A is found in carrots. It helps you see better. Vitamin E in potatoes helps us heal faster.

=== MULTIPLE CHOICE ===

13. What is different about both texts? (RI.1.9)

   A. One talks about vegetables and the other talks about fruits.

   B. One talks about vegetables and the other talks about junk food.

   C. One talks about the different colors of vegetables and one talks about the different vitamins in vegetables.

   D. One talks about your heart and one talks about your eyes.

2.3. INTEGRATION OF KNOWLEDGE AND IDEAS

2. READING: INFORMATIONAL TEXT

14. **Orange vegetables like carrots with vitamin A help our _____.** (RI.1.9)

    A. bones **B.** ears **C.** hearts **D.** eyes

15. **Why do both texts say we should eat different vegetables? Choose the best answer.** (RI.1.9)

    A. Because they are different colors
    B. Because they have lots of vitamins
    C. Because different vegetables help keep different parts of our bodies healthy
    D. Because different vegetables have different tastes

> **Directions:** *Read the text and answer the questions below.*

SAVING PAPER

We can cut back on how much paper we use each day. We can use smaller pieces of paper to draw on. We can use cloth towels in place of paper towels. We can also use cloth napkins. We can print out less paper. At home, we can use plates that we wash. Then we will not need to throw away paper plates.

=== MULTIPLE CHOICE ===

16. **How can we cut back on paper waste at lunchtime?** (RI.1.8)

    A. We can eat less food.
    B. We can use paper napkins.
    C. We can use cloth napkins.
    D. We can recycle.

17. **How can we reuse our plates?** (RI.1.8)

    A. We can throw them away.
    B. We can wash them.
    C. We can use paper plates.
    D. We can use fewer plates.

18. **What is the author's main point?** (RI.1.8)

    A. We need to save our trees by saving paper.
    B. We need to use smaller pieces of paper.
    C. We need to recycle.
    D. We need to wash our dishes.

2. READING: INFORMATIONAL TEXT

> **Directions:** Read the text, look at the image, and answer the questions below.

BATS

Bats also need to have a furry body to keep them warm in cold caves. The caves keep the bats safe as they sleep during the day. The bats use their strong feet and claws to hold onto rocks while they sleep. The bats sleep upside down. This helps them hide from other animals.

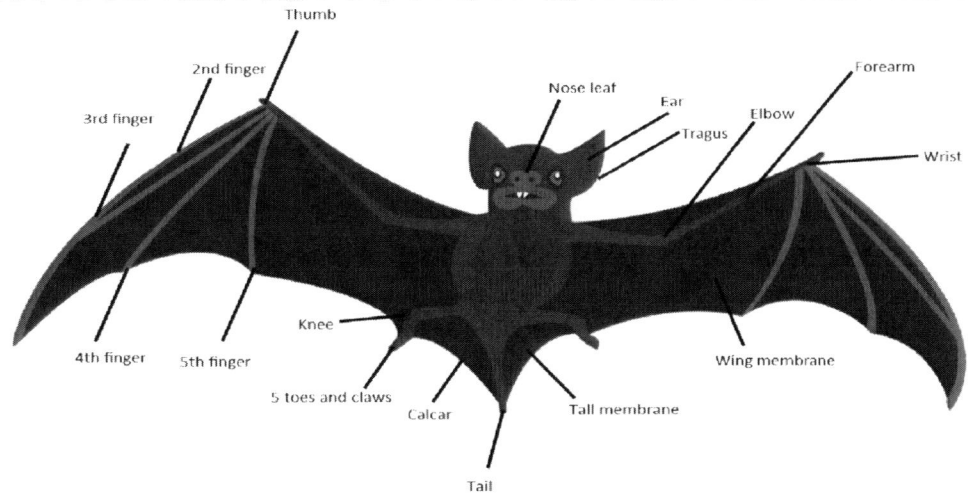

=== TRUE OR FALSE ===

19. The key idea of the text is that bats use their body parts to help them hide, keep warm, and find food. (RI.1.7)

  A. True   **B.** False

20. The illustration shows the reader how bats sleep upside down. (RI.1.7)

  A. True   **B.** False

2.4. CHAPTER REVIEW

2.3. INTEGRATION OF KNOWLEDGE AND IDEAS

2. READING: INFORMATIONAL TEXT

2.4. Chapter Review

> **Directions:** *Read the passage and answer the questions below.*

PUMPKIN LIFE CYCLE

When we go to a pumpkin patch we see lots of pumpkins. We can also find them on farms and in gardens. Pumpkins grow in different sizes. Some are big. Some are small. How does a pumpkin grow? Pumpkins have a life cycle.

=== MULTIPLE CHOICE ===

1. **Where can you find a pumpkin?** (RI.1.7)
   - **A.** pumpkin patch
   - **B.** farm
   - **C.** garden
   - **D.** all of the above

2. **How do pumpkins grow?** (RI.1.7)
   - **A.** They grow to be big.
   - **B.** They grow to be small.
   - **C.** They grow in different sizes.
   - **D.** They grow through a life cycle.

> **Directions:** *Read the passage and answer the questions below.*

WATER IS IMPORTANT

Water is important to our lives. We use water every day. Think about all of the times you use water. We use water to take showers. We use it to brush our teeth. We use water to flush the toilet. We also use water in our communities. Fire stations, parks, and swimming pools all need water. Water is used to grow food, too.

2. READING: INFORMATIONAL TEXT

TRUE OR FALSE

3. **The author's main point is that water is important to our lives.** (RI.1.8)

   A. True   B. False

4. **We use water at home and in our community.** (RI.1.8)

   A. True   B. False

   Most of the water on Earth is salt water. We need fresh water to live. Because of this, we need to make sure we do not waste water. There are many ways we can do this. We can take shorter showers. We can take fewer baths. If we turn off the faucet when brushing our teeth, we can save 8 gallons of water.

5. **We do not need to save water because most of the water on Earth is fresh water.** (RI.1.8)

   A. True   B. False

6. **We can save water by taking longer showers and more baths.** (RI.1.8)

   A. True   B. False

> **Directions:** *Read the passage and answer the questions below.*

BALD EAGLE

The bald eagle only lives in North America. These birds have white feathers on their heads. They are not bald. Their name comes from an English word meaning white. Bald eagles can fly over 10,000 feet high. They have great eyesight. They can see fish up to a mile away. When they spot a fish, the bald eagles can fly very fast. They can fly 100 miles per hour! When they fly down to the water, the bald eagle picks up the fish with its feet. Then they fly off to eat their food.

2. READING: INFORMATIONAL TEXT

=== MULTIPLE CHOICE ===

7. **Where does the bald eagle live?** (RI.1.1)
   - **A.** South America
   - **B.** North America
   - **C.** Europe
   - **D.** Asia

8. **What do bald eagles have on their heads?** (RI.1.1)
   - **A.** brown feathers
   - **B.** black feathers
   - **C.** white feathers
   - **D.** no feathers

9. **How high can bald eagles fly up to?** (RI.1.1)
   - **A.** 100 feet
   - **B.** 500 feet
   - **C.** 1,000 feet
   - **D.** 10,000 feet

10. **What do bald eagles use their great eyesight to do?** (RI.1.1)
    - **A.** See fish up to a mile away
    - **B.** Build nests
    - **C.** Eat food
    - **D.** Swim

> **Directions:** *Read the text and answer the questions below.*

FROG LIFE CYCLE

Frogs go through a life cycle. An adult female frog lays frog eggs. Frog eggs float in a pond. The eggs are covered with jelly. This helps keep them safe. They are in a **cluster** called an egg mass or **frogspawn**. This group also helps **protect** the eggs. It makes it harder for other animals to eat them. Ducks, fish, and insects may eat the eggs. Then **tadpoles** hatch from the eggs. They eat and grow in the pond. They do not look like frogs yet. They look more like little fish. Tadpoles have a tail. They have **gills** that they use to breathe. The tadpoles turn into **froglets**. The froglet's tail will shrink. They grow back or hind legs first and then their front legs or arms. They will now have lungs for breathing air. In the last stage, they become an adult frog.

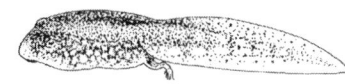
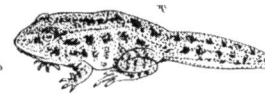

2. READING: INFORMATIONAL TEXT

MULTIPLE CHOICE

11. **What does the word cluster mean?** (RI.1.4)
    A. group   B. safe   C. eggs   D. mess

12. **What is frogspawn?** (RI.1.4)
    A. tail
    B. pond
    C. adult frog
    D. egg mass or group of frog eggs

13. **What does the word protect mean?** (RI.1.4)
    A. fight   B. eat   C. keep safe   D. float

> **Directions:** *Read the text and answer the questions below.*

FIREFIGHTERS AND POLICE OFFICERS

Firefighters and police officers are our community helpers. Both work to help people. They help us in an emergency. Both police officers and firefighters help people in car accidents. Firefighters put out fires. Police officers help people when there is a fire, too. Firefighters work for the fire department. They work out of a fire station. They fight fires in houses and buildings. Police officers work for the police department. They work out of a police station. They make sure people follow the law. They keep people safe.

MULTIPLE CHOICE

14. **Firefighters and police officers are our _____.** (RI.1.3)
    A. friends   B. neighbors
    C. community helpers   D. workers

15. **Both firefighters and police officers work to _____ people.** (RI.1.3)
    A. help   B. teach   C. heal   D. call

2. READING: INFORMATIONAL TEXT

16. Firefighters work out of a fire _____. (RI.1.3)

A. house **B.** building **C.** station **D.** school

> **Directions:** Use the index below to answer the following questions.

An index is found at the back of a book. It lists the words from the book and the pages where you can find those words.

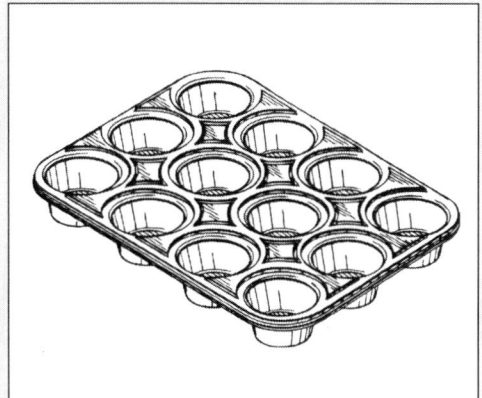

Index
Baking Pans 7
Mixing bowls 9
Forks 10
Measuring cups 11
Spoons 13

=== FREE RESPONSE ===

17. On what page would you turn to read more about baking pans? (RI.1.5)

_____
_____
_____

18. What topic is covered on page 11? (RI.1.5)

_____
_____
_____

2. READING: INFORMATIONAL TEXT

19. On what page would you turn to learn more about spoons? (RI.1.5)

_____
_____
_____

20. What topic is covered on page 10? (RI.1.5)

_____
_____
_____

> **Directions:** *Read the text and answer the questions below.*

Lightning Storms

Have you ever seen flashes of light in the sky? And then heard a loud thunder sound? That happens when there is a lightning storm. These storms can have strong winds. They can also have heavy rain or hail. Lightning storms are made when warm air rises and is mixed with cooler air. Lightning is very powerful. If a tree is struck by lightning, it will feel the heat and a magnetic force. This is very dangerous. When you see lightning in the sky, stay indoors to be safe.

=== MULTIPLE CHOICE ===

21. What is the main topic? (RI.1.2)
- A. Rainstorms
- B. Hail storms
- C. Lightning storms
- D. Hurricanes

22. What happens during a lightning storm? (RI.1.2)
- A. Light flashes in the sky.
- B. It snows.
- C. The sun comes out.
- D. It is quiet.

2. READING: INFORMATIONAL TEXT

23. How do lightning storms form? (RI.1.2)
- **A.** Snow mixes with ice.
- **B.** Warm air mixes with cooler air.
- **C.** Rain mixes with hail.
- **D.** The sun heats the ground.

24. Lightning is very _____. (RI.1.2)
- **A.** strange
- **B.** slow
- **C.** weak
- **D.** powerful

> **Directions:** *Read the text and answer the questions below.*

Pets

Having a pet teaches you many things. You learn how they need to exercise to stay healthy. Some pets we take for a walk. Some pets run around. Hamsters have a wheel that they run inside of to keep their bodies moving.

At a pet store, the workers must make sure the pets stay clean. There is a part of the store where the pets are groomed. Their fur coat is brushed. They are washed with special soap and water.

25. What is similar about the two texts? (RI.1.9)

_____
_____
_____
_____
_____
_____
_____
_____

2. READING: INFORMATIONAL TEXT

26. What is different about the two texts? (RI.1.9)

_____
_____
_____
_____
_____
_____
_____
_____

> **Directions:** Read the text and answer the questions below.

PUMPKINS

Yellow flowers grow on the vine. The flowers turn into small green pumpkins. These pumpkins will turn orange. These are the pumpkins we see at the grocery store. If we plant pumpkin seeds, more pumpkins will grow. They will be ready to pick in fall.

2. READING: INFORMATIONAL TEXT

=== MULTIPLE CHOICE ===

27. What color do pumpkins begin as? (RI.1.7)
   A. yellow flowers   **B.** green pumpkins
   C. orange pumpkins   **D.** white pumpkins

28. Why do we go to pumpkin patches in fall? (RI.1.7)
   A. Because that is when we plant them
   B. Because we need them in time for Halloween
   C. Because that is when they are ready to be picked
   D. Because they are orange

> **Directions:** *Read the text and answer the questions below.*

PETS

Pets can be a lot of fun. We can take them to the park and play games. We can sleep with them on the couch. We can take pictures of them. We take our pets on trips with us.

In a pet store, it can be fun to watch people playing with the pets. People come into the store and get excited when they see the pets. They want to take pictures of them.

29. How can we have fun with pets? (RI.1.9)

_____

_____

_____

_____

_____

2. READING: INFORMATIONAL TEXT

30. What do people do when they see pets in the pet store? (RI.1.9)

_____

_____

_____

_____

_____

2.4. CHAPTER REVIEW

3. READING: FOUNDATIONAL SKILLS

3.1. PRINT CONCEPTS   80
- Organization and basic features of print

3.2. PHONOLOGICAL AWARENESS   86
- Syllables and Sounds

3.3. CHAPTER REVIEW   94

3. READING: FOUNDATIONAL SKILLS

3.1. Print Concepts

Common Core State Standards: CCSS.ELA-LITERACY.RF.1.1

Skills:
- Demonstrate an understanding of the organization and basic features of print

> **Directions:** *Read the passage. Then answer the questions that follow.*

A TRIP TO THE ICE CREAM SHOP

David and his friend Charlie wanted a treat. They went to an ice cream shop. The friends <u>sat</u> at a table. Each boy asked for two scoops of vanilla ice cream.

=== MULTIPLE CHOICE ===

1. **What is the first word in the second sentence?** (RF.1.1)
   - **A.** David
   - **B.** They
   - **C.** The
   - **D.** Each

David got his ice cream in a cone. Charlie got his ice cream in a bowl. David's ice cream started to drip. It was slowly moving down the edge of his cone. Charlie used a spoon to <u>eat</u> his ice cream.

2. **Why do David and Charlie have capital letters?** (RF.1.1)
   - **A.** Because their names are at the beginning of a sentence
   - **B.** Because that is how they spell their names
   - **C.** Because their names are proper nouns
   - **D.** Because their names are at the beginning of the alphabet

3. READING: FOUNDATIONAL SKILLS

David finished eating his ice cream first. "I'm full!" said David. "I think I ate too much." Charlie just sat there laughing at his friend. Charlie kept eating his ice cream.

3. **What ending punctuation mark is used after the sentence "I'm full"?** (RF.1.1)

   A. A period (.)
   B. An apostrophe (')
   C. A question mark (?)
   D. An exclamation point (!)

4. **How can you tell the character David is speaking?** (RF.1.1)

   A. Because he says he is speaking
   B. Because his name is written first
   C. Because Charlie never speaks
   D. Because quotation marks (") tell the reader what David says

Charlie took his last bite. "I'm ready to go now," he said. "Are you, David?" David shook his head. The two friends left the shop and walked back home.

5. **What ending punctuation mark is used after the sentence "Are you, David"?** (RF.1.1)

   A. A period (.)
   B. A comma (,)
   C. A question mark (?)
   D. An exclamation point (!)

3.1. PRINT CONCEPTS

> **Directions:** Read the passage. Then answer the questions that follow.

A TRIP TO THE LAKE

Jake and his sister, Grace, went to the lake.

When they got there, Grace took out her kite.

She flew it in the wind. Jake ran into the water.

3. READING: FOUNDATIONAL SKILLS

TRUE OR FALSE

6. The first sentence uses two commas. (RF.1.1)

    A. True   **B.** False

> Jake jumped <u>off</u> a dock. He landed in the water feet first. He called out to his sister. "Grace!" he cried. "Come on in the water with me." Grace put down her kite. She ran into the lake.

7. The fourth sentence uses an exclamation point (!) after the word Grace. (RF.1.1)

    A. True   **B.** False

> Grace let out a big scream. "The water is so cold!" she yelled. Jake started to laugh. "I know," he said. Grace was not happy. "I want to get <u>out</u> of the water," she said.

8. The reading passage above uses one question mark. (RF.1.1)

    A. True   **B.** False

> Grace got out of the lake. She ran back to their car for a snack. She picked up an <u>apple</u>. She ate and watched her <u>brother</u> play in the lake.

9. The word <u>brother</u> should have a capital letter. (RF.1.1)

    A. True   **B.** False

10. The ending punctuation mark for the last sentence is a period (.). (RF.1.1)

    A. True   **B.** False

3.1. PRINT CONCEPTS

3. READING: FOUNDATIONAL SKILLS

> **Directions:** *Read the passage. Then answer the questions that follow.*

THE WEATHER

The weather changes every day. We look outside to see if it is cloudy, sunny, or rainy. The weather helps us make choices. If it is snowing, we may make a hot pot of soup. If it is warm, we may want to cook hot dogs.

=== FILL IN THE BLANK ===

11. To end a sentence, we use a punctuation _____. (RF.1.1)

12. We use _____ letters at the beginning of sentences. (RF.1.1)

How do you choose what to wear? You may wear a coat when it is cold outside. You may wear shorts in the heat. You can put on a swimming suit and go swimming in a pool on a hot summer day.

13. The first sentence uses a _____ as the ending punctuation mark. (RF.1.1)

The weather changes which jobs we can do. A painter cannot paint outside in the rain! An ice cream truck driver only works when it is hot outside.

14. The second sentence uses a(n) _____ as the ending punctuation mark. (RF.1.1)

15. There are _____ question marks in the text. (RF.1.1)

3. READING: FOUNDATIONAL SKILLS

The weather changes which games we play, too. We play ball outside when it is sunny. We play video games indoors when it is cold.

16. _____, _____, and _____ are **capitalized.** (RF.1.1)

> **Directions:** Read the passage. Then answer the questions that follow.

SCIENCE TOOLS

We use science tools to help us know things. If we want to measure something, we use a measuring <u>cup</u>. We <u>can</u> use a ruler to find a length. We can use a scale to find a weight.

Something may be too small to see. We can use a hand lens or a <u>microscope</u> to see something very tiny. Have you ever used a microscope?

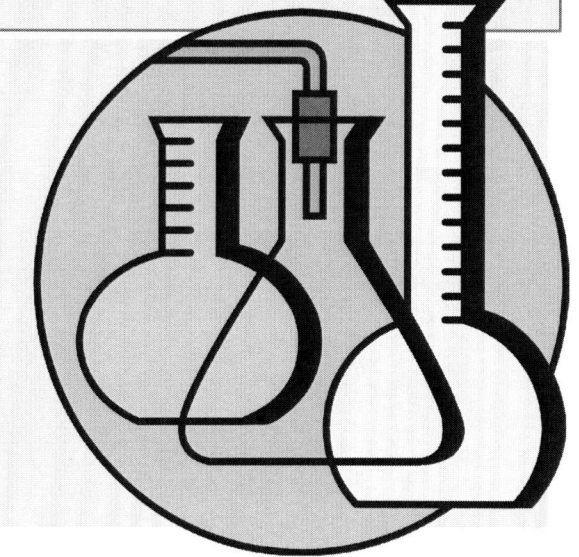

═══ **FREE RESPONSE** ═══

17. **Why does the last sentence use a question mark?** (RF.1.1)

_____

_____

_____

3. READING: FOUNDATIONAL SKILLS

Sometimes we need to know how much heat an object has. We <u>read</u> a thermometer to tell us how hot or cold it is. <u>Magnets</u> are used to see if something is magnetic like a paper clip.

18. Why is there not an exclamation point at the end of the sentences? (RF.1.1)

_____

_____

_____

19. Why is the word <u>magnets</u> capitalized? (RF.1.1)

_____

_____

_____

Other <u>science</u> tools keep us safe while we work. We may use <u>goggles</u>, gloves, and aprons. We can wear goggles for our eyes and gloves for our hands. We can wear an apron to keep our clothes clean, too.

20. Why does the second sentence use commas? (RF.1.1)

_____

_____

_____

3.2. PHONOLOGICAL AWARENESS

3.1. PRINT CONCEPTS

3. READING: FOUNDATIONAL SKILLS

3.2. Phonological Awareness

Common Core State Standards: CCSS.ELA-LITERACY.RF.1.2

Skills:
- Demonstrate an understanding of spoken words, syllables, and sounds (phonemes)

> **Directions:** *Read the passage. Then answer the questions that follow.*

A TRIP TO THE ICE CREAM SHOP

David and his friend Charlie wanted a treat. They went to an ice cream shop. The friends <u>sat</u> at a table. Each boy asked for two scoops of vanilla ice cream.

=== MULTIPLE CHOICE ===

1. **Does the underlined word "sat", have a short or long vowel sound?** (RF.1.2)

   A. Short vowel   **B.** Long vowel

David got his ice cream in a cone. Charlie got his ice cream in a bowl. David's ice cream started to drip. It was slowly moving down the edge of his cone. Charlie used a spoon to <u>eat</u> his ice cream.

2. **Which word has a long *i* vowel sound?** (RF.1.2)

   A. his   **B.** ice   **C.** in   **D.** drip

3. **Which word has a short e vowel sound?** (RF.1.2)

   A. Charlie   **B.** cream   **C.** edge   **D.** eat

3. READING: FOUNDATIONAL SKILLS

4. **Does the underlined word "_eat_", have a short or long vowel sound?** (RF.1.2)

   A. Short vowel   **B.** Long vowel

   David finished eating his ice cream first. "I'm full!" said David. "I think I ate too much." Charlie just sat there laughing at his friend. Charlie kept eating his ice cream.

   Charlie took his last bite. "I'm ready to go now," he said. "Are you, David?" David shook his head. The two friends left the shop and walked back home.

5. **Which word has a long i vowel sound?** (RF.1.2)

   A. his   **B.** bite   **C.** said   **D.** friends

> **Directions:** *Read the passage. Then answer the questions that follow.*

A Trip to the Lake

Jake and his sister, Grace, went to the lake. When they got there, Grace took out her kite. She flew it in the wind. Jake ran into the water.

TRUE OR FALSE

6. **The word lake has a short vowel sound.** (RF.1.2)

   A. True   **B.** False

7. **The word kite has a long vowel sound.** (RF.1.2)

   A. True   **B.** False

3. READING: FOUNDATIONAL SKILLS

Jake jumped <u>off</u> a dock. He landed in the water feet first. He called out to his sister. "Grace!" he cried. "Come on in the water with me." Grace put down her kite. She ran into the lake.

8. **The word <u>off</u> has a long vowel sound.** (RF.1.2)

   A. True   B. False

Grace let out a big scream. "The water is so cold!" she yelled. Jake started to laugh. "I know," he said. Grace was not happy. "I want to get <u>out</u> of the water," she said.

9. **The word <u>out</u> has a short vowel sound.** (RF.1.2)

   A. True   B. False

Grace got out of the lake. She ran back to their car for a snack. She picked up an <u>apple</u>. She ate and watched her <u>brother</u> play in the lake.

10. **The word <u>apple</u> has a long vowel sound.** (RF.1.2)

    A. True   B. False

➢ **Directions:** *Read the passage. Then answer the questions that follow.*

The Weather

The weather changes every day. We look outside to see if it is cloudy, sunny, or rainy. The weather helps us make choices. If it is snowing, we may make a hot pot of soup. If it is warm, we may want to cook hot dogs.

3. READING: FOUNDATIONAL SKILLS

FILL IN THE BLANK

11. Look at the picture. Fill in the letters of the word below. (RF.1.2)

___ ___ ___

How do you choose what to wear? You may wear a coat when it is cold outside. You may wear shorts in the heat. You can put on a swimming suit and go swimming in a pool on a hot summer day.

12. Find the one-syllable word in the box below. Write your answer here:

_____ (RF.1.2)

outside	swimming
summer	coat

The weather changes which jobs we can do. A painter cannot paint outside in the rain! An ice cream truck driver only works when it is hot outside.

13. Find the one-syllable word in the box below. Write your answer here:

_____ (RF.1.2)

weather	painter
rain	driver

The weather changes which games we play, too. We play ball outside when it is sunny. We play video games indoors when it is cold.

14. Look at the picture. Fill in the letters of the word below. (RF.1.2)

___ ___ ___ ___

3. READING: FOUNDATIONAL SKILLS

> **Directions:** *Read the passage. Then answer the questions that follow.*

SCIENCE TOOLS

We use science tools to help us know things. If we want to measure something, we use a measuring <u>cup</u>. We <u>can</u> use a ruler to find a length. We can use a scale to find a weight.

=== **FREE RESPONSE** ===

3.2. PHONOLOGICAL AWARENESS

15. **Read the word "*cup*" in the second sentence. What is another word that has the same sound as "*cup*"?** (RF.1.2)

    _____

    _____

    _____

    _____

    _____

    _____

16. **Read the word <u>can</u> in the third sentence. What is another word that has the same sound as can?** (RF.1.2)

    _____

    _____

    _____

    _____

    _____

3. READING: FOUNDATIONAL SKILLS

Something may be too small to see. We can use a hand lens or a <u>microscope</u> to see something very tiny. Have you ever used a microscope?

17. **Look at the pictures below. Circle the word that has three syllables.** (RF.1.2)

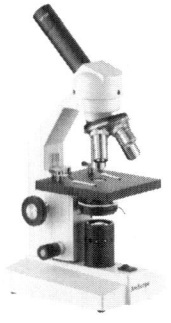
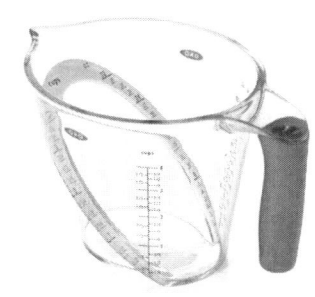

microscope   cup   scale

Write how you found your answer.

_____
_____
_____
_____
_____
_____
_____

3. READING: FOUNDATIONAL SKILLS

Sometimes we need to know how much heat an object has. We read a thermometer to tell us how hot or cold it is. Magnets are used to see if something is magnetic like a paper clip.

18. Look at the pictures below. Circle the word that has a short vowel sound. (RF.1.2)

hot

cold

Write how you found your answer.

_____
_____
_____
_____
_____
_____
_____

3. READING: FOUNDATIONAL SKILLS

Other <u>science</u> tools keep us safe while we work. We may use <u>goggles</u>, gloves, and aprons. We can wear goggles for our eyes and gloves for our hands. We can wear an apron to keep our clothes clean, too.

19. Look at the pictures below. Circle the word that has one syllable. (RF.1.2)

 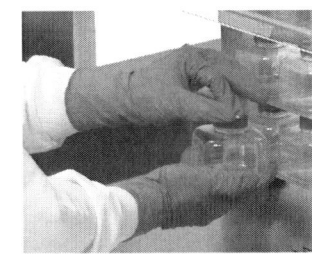 

goggles   gloves   aprons

Write how you found your answer.

_____
_____
_____
_____

20. Say the word <u>goggles</u>. Why is it important that we say each word correctly? (RF.1.2)

_____
_____
_____
_____

3.3. Chapter Review

3.2. PHONOLOGICAL AWARENESS

3. READING: FOUNDATIONAL SKILLS

3.3. Chapter Review

> **Directions:** *Read the passage. Then answer the questions that follow.*

SKIING DOWN A MOUNTAIN

Sandy and her friend Sara went skiing. Each girl put on her boots. Sandy wore a red <u>ski</u> coat. Sara wore a black ski coat. They both liked the sport. It was fun to play in the snow.

=== MULTIPLE CHOICE ===

1. **Does the underlined word <u>ski</u> have a short or long vowel sound?** (RF.1.2)

   A. Short vowel   **B.** Long vowel

2. **What is the first word in the second sentence?** (RF.1.1)

   A. Sandy   **B.** Each   **C.** Sara   **D.** They

Sandy put on her yellow hat. She pulled it down to cover her ears. Sara told her friend that they should follow a map. Sandy wanted to ski somewhere flat. She was afraid to go down a steep hill. Sandy went slowly down the mountain. Sara pulled her <u>red</u> goggles down on her face. The snow was deep.

3. **Which word has a short e vowel sound?** (RF.1.2)

   A. ears   **B.** steep   **C.** went   **D.** deep

4. **Which word has a long a vowel sound?** (RF.1.2)

   A. face   **B.** flat   **C.** hat   **D.** map

5. **Does the underlined word <u>red</u> have a short or long vowel sound?** (RF.1.2)

   A. Short vowel   **B.** Long vowel

3. READING: FOUNDATIONAL SKILLS

6. **Why do Sandy and Sara have capital letters?** (RF.1.1)
   A. Because their names are at the beginning of a sentence
   B. Because that is how they spell their names
   C. Because their names are proper nouns
   D. Because their names are at the beginning of the alphabet

"Wait!" shouted Sara. "I think this hill is too hard for us." Sandy looked down the mountain. It had a big drop. The friends turned around. They chose to go down a different hill.

7. **What ending punctuation mark is used after the word "Wait"?** (RF.1.1)
   A. A period (.)
   B. An apostrophe (')
   C. A question mark (?)
   D. An exclamation point (!)

8. **How can you tell the character Sara is speaking?** (RF.1.1)
   A. Because she says she is speaking
   B. Because her name is written first
   C. Because Sandy never speaks
   D. Because quotation marks (") tell the reader what Sara says

Sandy found a new hill for the pair to ski down. Sara went down first. Sara was going too fast. She lost her balance and fell on a piece of ice. "Ouch, that hurt!" Sara yelled. "Can you see a mark on my elbow?" she asked Sandy. Sandy helped her friend stand up.

9. **Which word has a long i vowel sound?** (RF.1.2)
   A. hill
   B. ski
   C. ice
   D. first

10. **What ending punctuation mark is used after the sentence "Can you see a mark on my elbow"?** (RF.1.1)
    A. A period (.)
    B. A comma (,)
    C. A question mark (?)
    D. An exclamation point (!)

3.3. CHAPTER REVIEW

3. READING: FOUNDATIONAL SKILLS

> **Directions:** Read the passage. Then answer the questions that follow.

THE CLASS PET

Ms. Miller told the class they were going to get a <u>pet</u>. The students cheered. Ms. Miller asked the class to guess what kind of pet it would be. The students guessed a dog, a <u>cat</u>, a rabbit, or a snake.

=== TRUE OR FALSE ===

11. **The word <u>pet</u> has a short vowel sound.** (RF.1.2)
    A. True   B. False

12. **The word <u>cat</u> has a long vowel sound.** (RF.1.2)
    A. True   B. False

13. **The last sentence uses three commas.** (RF.1.1)
    A. True   B. False

"You are right, Johnny!" Ms. Miller said. She pointed to the <u>boy</u> in the back row. Johnny had guessed that the class pet was a rabbit. The teacher walked into the hallway.

14. **The first sentence uses an exclamation point (!) after the word Johnny.** (RF.1.1)
    A. True   B. False

15. **The word <u>boy</u> has a long vowel sound.** (RF.1.2)
    A. True   B. False

Ms. Miller returned from the hallway. She was holding a large <u>cage</u>. The rabbit was inside the cage. The rabbit jumped. The kids screamed. "Wow!" said Johnny. "I was right." He turned to his friend Tom. "Is that what you guessed, Tom?"

16. **The word <u>cage</u> has a short vowel sound.** (RF.1.2)
    A. True   B. False

3. READING: FOUNDATIONAL SKILLS

17. The reading passage above uses one question mark. (RF.1.1)

  A. True   **B.** False

  The rabbit was <u>brown</u>. It had white ears. Ms. Miller asked the class who wanted to feed the <u>new</u> pet. "I do!" shouted Johnny.

18. The word <u>brown</u> has a long vowel sound. (RF.1.2)

  A. True   **B.** False

19. The word <u>new</u> should have a capital letter. (RF.1.1)

  A. True   **B.** False

20. The ending punctuation mark for the last sentence is an exclamation point (!). (RF.1.1)

  A. True   **B.** False

> **Directions:** *Read the passage. Then answer the questions that follow.*

THE PARK

  We wanted to go to the park. My mom and I packed a bag full of snacks. I grabbed a blanket. We could use the blanket to sit on. We took a cab to get to the park.

=== FILL IN THE BLANK ===

21. Look at the picture. Fill in the letters of the word below. (RF.1.2)

___ ___ ___

3. READING: FOUNDATIONAL SKILLS

The park was so much fun! We found a spot of grass to lay down the blanket. I helped my mom unpack the bag full of snacks. We ate bananas, yogurt, and sandwiches.

22. **The first sentence uses a(n) _____ as the ending punctuation mark.** (RF.1.1)

> **Directions:** Use the table below to answer questions 23 and 24.

blanket	sandwiches
bag	bananas
drink	water
head	pack

23. **Find the one-syllable word in the box below.**

    Write your answer here: _____ (RF.1.2)

24. **Find the two-syllable word in the box below.**

    Write your answer here: _____ (RF.1.2)

I looked in the bag for more snacks. "Mom, did you pack anything to drink?" My mom shook her head. "I must have forgotten to bring some water."

25. **The second sentence uses a(n) _____ as the ending punctuation mark.** (RF.1.1)

26. **There are _____ periods in the text above.** (RF.1.1)

3. READING: FOUNDATIONAL SKILLS

I looked around the park for something to drink. There was a man selling water from a box nearby. We walked over to the man after we were done eating our snacks to buy some water.

27. _____, _____, and _____ are capitalized in the passage above. (RF.1.1)

28. Look at the picture. Fill in the letters of the word below. (RF.1.2)

___ ___ ___

> **Directions:** *Read the passage. Then answer the questions that follow.*

THE GARDEN

There are lots of plants in a garden. You can also <u>see</u> dirt and tiny rocks. You <u>may</u> find weeds or flowers.

3. READING: FOUNDATIONAL SKILLS

=== **FREE RESPONSE** ===

29. Read the word <u>see</u> in the second sentence. What is another word that has the same sound as see? (RF.1.2)

    _____

30. Read the word <u>may</u> in the third sentence. What is another word that has the same sound as may? (RF.1.2)

    _____

4. WRITING

4.1. TEXT TYPES AND PURPOSES — 102
- Opinion pieces
- Informative/explanatory writing
- Narrative writing

4.2. CHAPTER REVIEW — 109

4. WRITING

4.1. Text Types and Purposes

Common Core State Standards: CCSS.ELA-LITERACY.W.1.1, CCSS.ELA-LITERACY.W.1.2, CCSS.ELA-LITERACY.W.1.3

Skills:
- Write opinion pieces in which they introduce the topic or name the book they are writing about, state an opinion, supply a reason for the opinion and provide some sense of closure
- Write informative/explanatory texts in which they name a topic, supply some facts about the topic, and provide some sense of closure
- Write narratives in which they recount two or more appropriately sequenced events, include some details regarding what happened, use temporal words to signal event order, and provide some sense of closure

> **Directions:** Read the passage and answer the questions below.

FAMILY TRADITIONS

What things do you do with your family? Sometimes we do things that are special to our family. We may do them over and over again. This is called a tradition. Family traditions are important.

=== TRUE OR FALSE ===

1. **The author introduces the topic on family traditions.** (W.1.1)

   A. True   B. False

2. **The author states an opinion.** (W.1.1)

   A. True   B. False

3. **The author's opinion is that we do not need family traditions.** (W.1.1)

   A. True   B. False

4. WRITING

> **Directions:** *Read the passage and answer the questions below.*

King Penguins

King penguins are birds, but they do not fly. They can walk, hop, and swim. They are very good swimmers. King penguins use their wings to help them as they swim in the water.

=== MULTIPLE CHOICE ===

4. **The author introduces the topic on** (W.1.2)
   - **A.** Birds
   - **B.** Water
   - **C.** King penguins
   - **D.** Swimming

King penguins hop from rock to rock. They can slide on their bellies on the ice and snow. They eat fish. To find the fish, king penguins can dive up to 900 feet deep.

5. **Which is not a fact from the text?** (W.1.2)
   - **A.** King penguins hop from rock to rock.
   - **B.** King penguins can slide on their bellies on the ice and snow.
   - **C.** King penguins are cute birds.
   - **D.** King penguins can dive up to 900 feet deep looking for fish.

6. **Read the sentence: "They eat fish." The author is:** (W.1.2)
   - **A.** Giving their opinion
   - **B.** Telling the reader a fact about king penguins
   - **C.** Writing the introduction
   - **D.** Writing the conclusion

4.1. TEXT TYPES AND PURPOSES

4. WRITING

FREE RESPONSE

7. **If you are asked to write an informative passage about penguins, what facts would you write about?** (W.1.2)

   _____
   _____
   _____
   _____
   _____
   _____
   _____

8. **If you are asked to write an informative passage about an arctic animal, which one would you choose to write about?** (W.1.2)

   _____
   _____
   _____

4.1. TEXT TYPES AND PURPOSES

> **Directions:** Read the passage and answer the questions below.

The Grocery Store

Ted and his mom went to the grocery store. They needed to buy some food. When they got to the store, Ted got a cart. He pushed the cart and walked behind his mom.

4. WRITING

TRUE OR FALSE

9. The author introduces a story about a trip to the grocery store. (W.1.3)
   A. True
   B. False

10. The author is teaching the reader about different foods in the grocery store. (W.1.3)
   A. True
   B. False

   Ted was busy looking at the different cereal boxes. He then pushed the cart into a pile of soda cans. "Oh no!" cried Ted. Boxes of the soda cans fell to the floor.
   "Clean up on aisle 2," said the store manager.

11. The passage above is a narrative. (W.1.3)
   A. True
   B. False

12. The story is telling the reader a fact about soda cans. (W.1.3)
   A. True
   B. False

   Ted helped the store manager. He picked up the boxes that fell. There was soda all over the floor. Ted took a mop and started cleaning. His mom saw what happened. She was happy that Ted was helping clean up. Ted was ready to leave the grocery store and go back home.

MULTIPLE CHOICE

13. The author is: (W.1.3)
   A. Giving their opinion about why you should be careful in a grocery store
   B. Giving facts about what it's like to be a store manager
   C. Writing the introduction
   D. Telling a story

4.1. TEXT TYPES AND PURPOSES

4. WRITING

14. The conclusion is: (W.1.3)
- **A.** Ted was ready to leave the grocery store and go back home.
- **B.** His mom saw what happened.
- **C.** Ted took a mop and started cleaning.
- **D.** Ted helped the store manager.

> **Directions:** *Read the passage and answer the questions below.*

King Penguins

As parents, king penguins work together to care for their babies. The mother lays an egg. Then she goes to find food. The father holds the egg on his feet under his belly. This keeps the egg warm. King penguins work to help and care for each other.

=== FREE RESPONSE ===

15. If you are asked to write a passage about different types of penguins, what kind of passage would it be? Why? (W.1.2)

_____
_____
_____
_____
_____
_____
_____

4. WRITING

16. You are asked to write a passage about penguins at the zoo. Write the first two lines of the passage in the space below. (W.1.2)

17. What is the conclusion in the passage above? (W.1.2)

4. WRITING

> **Directions:** Read the passage and answer the questions below.

FAMILY TRADITIONS

A family tradition can be having dinner together. Everyone sits around a table. Each person talks about their day. Together they eat a warm meal. A family tradition can be watching Saturday morning cartoons. A family tradition can be taking a trip. These traditions can bring a family closer together.

=== **TRUE OR FALSE** ===

18. **The passage above is a narrative.** (W.1.1)

    A. True **B.** False

19. **If you wrote a passage about your favorite family tradition, that would be an opinion piece.** (W.1.1)

    A. True **B.** False

20. **The last sentence reads, "These traditions can bring a family closer together." This is a closing statement.** (W.1.1)

    A. True **B.** False

4.2. CHAPTER REVIEW

4. WRITING

4.2. Chapter Review

> **Directions:** *Read the passage and answer the questions below.*

READING BOOKS

Reading books is a good way to be a better student. If you read a lot of books, you can learn many things. You can learn about other people. You can learn about animals.

=== TRUE OR FALSE ===

1. **The author introduces the topic on reading about animals.** (W.1.1)

   A. True   **B.** False

2. **The author's opinion is that reading books is a good thing for us to do.** (W.1.1)

   A. True   **B.** False

   Reading books can also teach you new words. Many books will have words you have not learned. You can read the new word and find out what it means. You will also know how it is spelled. By learning new words, you can be a better writer, too.

3. **A reason for the author's opinion is that reading books can make us better spellers.** (W.1.1)

   A. True   **B.** False

4. **The passage above is informative. It teaches the reader about books.** (W.1.1)

   A. True   **B.** False

4. WRITING

> **Directions:** *Read the passage and answer the questions below.*

FIREFIGHTERS

Firefighters work in our community. Their job is to put out fires. They also help people. Firefighters work in a building called a fire station. They do many things. They put out fires in houses and buildings. They also fight wildfires in forests.

=== TRUE OR FALSE ===

5. **The author introduces the topic of how to put out fires.** (W.1.2)

    A. True **B.** False

6. **The author teaches the reader about what firefighters do.** (W.1.2)

    A. True **B.** False

Firefighters use tools to help them. They use ladders to reach fires in tall buildings. They have axes to pull up the floor. Water hoses and fire hydrants help, too. They help the firefighters pump water onto the flames.

7. **The text says that firefighters use ladders to reach fires in tall buildings. This is a fact.** (W.1.2)

    A. True **B.** False

8. **If the text said that firefighters are funny, this would be a fact.** (W.1.2)

    A. True **B.** False

> **Directions:** *Read the passage and answer the questions below.*

READING BOOKS

Reading books can also teach you lessons. You can learn about sharing with others. You can learn about making good choices. In conclusion, reading books will help you be a better student.

4. WRITING

MULTIPLE CHOICE

9. **The author is:** (W.1.1)
   A. Changing their opinion
   B. Giving another reason for their opinion
   C. Writing the introduction
   D. Telling a story

10. **The conclusion is:** (W.1.1)
    A. Reading books can also teach you lessons.
    B. You can learn about sharing with others.
    C. You can learn about making good choices.
    D. Reading books will help you be a better student.

> **Directions:** Read the passage and answer the questions below.

THE BIRTHDAY PARTY

It was Amy's birthday. She was so happy! She was having a birthday party to celebrate. Amy asked her friends from school to come to her party. First, Amy cleaned her room. Then she helped her mom bake some cookies.

TRUE OR FALSE

11. **The story is about Amy's friends from school.** (W.1.3)
    A. True
    B. False

12. **The passage above is an informative text.** (W.1.3)
    A. True
    B. False

13. **The words "first" and "then" tell the reader the order the events happen in the story.** (W.1.3)
    A. True
    B. False

4. WRITING

> Soon Amy heard the doorbell ring. She ran to answer the door. Her friends were all there. "Come on in," Amy said. The party had started. Her friends gave her lots of gifts. "Thank you all," she said. Amy opened the gifts. Then she blew out the six candles on her birthday cake. Amy had a great birthday party.

14. **There are three events happening in the passage above.** (W.1.3)

  A. True   **B.** False

15. **A detail in the passage is that Amy is celebrating her sixth birthday.** (W.1.3)

  A. True   **B.** False

16. **The last sentence reads, "Amy had a great birthday party." This is a closing statement.** (W.1.3)

  A. True   **B.** False

> **Directions:** *Read the passage and answer the questions below.*

FIREFIGHTERS

Firefighters work to help us when something goes wrong. They show up to car accidents. They help find missing people. Firefighters do many things in our community to help people.

=== MULTIPLE CHOICE ===

17. **The author is:** (W.1.2)
  A. Giving their opinion about why firefighters are important
  B. Giving facts about what firefighters do
  C. Writing the introduction
  D. Telling a story

4. WRITING

18. **The conclusion is:** (W.1.2)
    A. Firefighters work to help us when something goes wrong.
    B. They show up to car accidents.
    C. They help find missing people.
    D. Firefighters do many things in our community to help people.

> **Directions:** Read the passage and answer the questions below.

ROLLER COASTERS

If you go to an amusement park, you can go on many rides. One ride that is fun is the roller coaster. On this ride, you sit down in a seat and wear a seat belt. When the ride takes off, it goes really fast.

=== MULTIPLE CHOICE ===

19. **The author introduces the topic on:** (W.1.1)
    A. Amusement parks
    B. Rides
    C. Seat buckles
    D. Roller coasters

20. **The author's opinion is:** (W.1.1)
    A. Amusement parks are crowded
    B. Rides can make you dizzy
    C. Roller coasters are fun
    D. Roller coasters are scary

Roller coasters are fun because they go so fast. They make you feel like you are in a racecar. You are moving fast around corners. Sometimes you get to go upside down. On a roller coaster, you feel the wind race past you. All of these things make roller coasters a fun ride!

21. **What is a reason the author gives for why roller coasters are fun?** (W.1.1)
    A. They move slowly.
    B. They make you feel like you are in a racecar.
    C. They stop on corners.
    D. They make you feel sick.

4. WRITING

FREE RESPONSE

22. If you are asked to write an opinion passage about roller coasters, what would your opinion be? (W.1.1)

_____

_____

_____

_____

_____

_____

_____

> **Directions:** Read the passage and answer the questions below.

MAGNETS

Have you played with a magnet? Maybe you stick magnets to your refrigerator. They can hold up pictures. Magnets are tools that push and pull objects. Take a paperclip and put it next to a magnet. Watch what happens. The paperclip will be pulled toward the magnet.

TRUE OR FALSE

23. The author is writing an informative passage. (W.1.2)

　A. True　　　　　　　　**B.** False

24. The topic of the text is on science tools. (W.1.2)

　A. True　　　　　　　　**B.** False

25. The author states facts about magnets. (W.1.2)

　A. True　　　　　　　　**B.** False

4. WRITING

A magnet only pulls some things toward it. Metals like iron and nickel are pulled toward a magnet. Things made out of glass or plastic will not pull toward a magnet. Things made out of wood will push away from a magnet. There are many things that magnets can push and pull.

26. The text says, "Metals like iron and nickel are pulled toward a magnet." This is a fact. (W.1.2)

  A. True
  B. False

> **Directions:** Read the passage and answer the questions below.

Swimming Lessons

Peter did not like to swim. He was scared of the water. His parents told him he needed to learn how to swim. They signed him up for swimming lessons. Peter was not happy.

=== **MULTIPLE CHOICE** ===

27. The event in the story is: (W.1.3)
  A. Peter goes to school
  B. Peter takes a test
  C. Peter takes swimming lessons
  D. Peter falls in a pool

28. The author is trying to: (W.1.3)
  A. Give their opinion about swimming lessons
  B. Tell the reader to take swimming lessons
  C. Tell a story about Peter taking swimming lessons
  D. Teach the reader about water safety

On the first day, Peter had to learn how to kick. He held on to the side of the pool. He kicked his legs up and down. The water splashed. "I like this," said Peter. Peter got water in his eyes. He stopped kicking. Peter rubbed his eyes. His eyes had turned red.

4. WRITING

29. **Read the sentence: "He kicked his legs up and down."
The author is:** (W.1.3)
   - **A.** Giving their opinion
   - **B.** Telling the reader a fact about water
   - **C.** Writing the introduction
   - **D.** Telling the reader a detail about how Peter was kicking his legs

=== **FREE RESPONSE** ===

30. **If you are asked to write a narrative passage about swimming lessons, what event would happen in your story?** (W.1.3)

_____

_____

_____

_____

_____

_____

5. LANGUAGE

5.1. CONVENTIONS OF STANDARD ENGLISH   118
- ❖ Forms of Nouns
- ❖ Past, Present and Future tense
- ❖ Adjectives and Pronouns
- ❖ Other Grammar Topics

5.2. VOCABULARY ACQUISITION AND USE   122
- ❖ Multiple-meaning Words and Phrases
- ❖ Distinguish Words Differing in Manner and Intensity

5.3. CHAPTER REVIEW   127

5. LANGUAGE

5.1. Conventions of Standard English

Common Core State Standards: CCSS.ELA-LITERACY.L.1.1, CCSS.ELA-LITERACY.L.1.2

Skills:
- Demonstrate command of the conventions of standard English grammar and usage when writing or speaking
- Demonstrate command of the conventions of standard English capitalization, punctuation, and spelling when writing

> **Directions:** Write the letter that correctly completes each word. Some words <u>will</u> require capital letters. Be sure to use correct letter formation.

1. _____ an you help me? (L.1.1)

> **Directions:** Choose the correct possessive noun to complete each sentence.

5. LANGUAGE

2. _____ **puppy is so cute.** (L.1.1)

   A. Emily's   **B.** Emilys   **C.** Emilies   **D.** Emilys'

> **Directions:** Circle the proper nouns in the following sentence.

3. **My friend, Max, is running late.** (L.1.1)

> **Directions:** Read each sentence. Circle **ALL** the words that need to begin with capital letters. Rewrite the sentence in the space provided.

4. **sam is a boy.** (L.1.2)

   _____

5. **Tomorrow is december 19, 2017.** (L.1.2)

   _____

> **Directions:** Circle the common nouns in the following sentence.

6. **We need to go to the store.** (L.1.1)

> **Directions:** Choose the correct verb to complete the following sentence.

7. **The dog _____ across the lawn all the time.** (L.1.1)

   A. ran   **B.** run   **C.** runs   **D.** running

5.1. CONVENTIONS OF STANDARD ENGLISH

5. LANGUAGE

> **Directions:** Choose the correct pronoun to replace the underlined words in the following sentence.

8. <u>Wyatt and Bryson</u> are sick. (L.1.1)

    A. They   **B.** She   **C.** He   **D.** It

> **Directions:** Circle the verbs in the following sentence.

9. My dog sits in my lap. (L.1.1)

> **Directions:** Read each sentence. Add end punctuation and capital letters where they are needed. Rewrite the sentence in the space provided.

10. sally has a cat (L.1.2)

_____

11. her cat has yellow fur (L.1.2)

_____

> **Directions:** Read each sentence. Add commas where they are needed.

12. The dog was born on March 21 2015. (L.1.2)

13. Its favorite toys are bones balls and stuffed animals. (L.1.2)

> **Directions:** Write the conjunction from the ( ) that best completes the following sentence.

14. Jasmine wore a blue dress _____ Jeremiah wore a blue tie. (and, so) (L.1.1)

5.1. CONVENTIONS OF STANDARD ENGLISH

NAME: _____ DATE: _____

5. LANGUAGE

> **Directions:** Circle the prepositions in each sentence.

15. **I put the ice cream in the freezer.** (L.1.1)

16. **Please put down the cell phone.** (L.1.1)

> **Directions:** Look at the list of the words. Choose the word that matches the pattern.

17. **cheese, chips, chew** (L.1.2)
    A. catch **B.** shark **C.** crash **D.** whisper

18. **ship, shark, wish** (L.1.2)
    A. crash **B.** wheel **C.** when **D.** math

> **Directions:** Look at each sentence. Choose the digraph blend that completes each underlined word in the sentence.

DIGRAPH BLENDS
sh   wh   ch   gh   th

19. **The little girl drew a _____ost.** (L.1.2)

20. **The _____ip is setting sail.** (L.1.2)

5.2. VOCABULARY ACQUISITION AND USE

5. LANGUAGE

5.2. Vocabulary Acquisition and Use

Common Core State Standards: CCSS.ELA-LITERACY.L.1.4, CCSS.ELA-LITERACY.L.1.5, CCSS.ELA-LITERACY.L.1.6

Skills:

- Determine or clarify the meaning of unknown and multiple-meaning words and phrases based on grade 1 reading and content, choosing flexibly from an array of strategies
- With guidance and support from adults, demonstrate the understanding of word relationships and nuances in word meanings
- Use words and phrases acquired through conversations, reading and being read to, and responding to texts, including using frequently occurring conjunctions to signal simple relationships (e.g., because)

> **Directions:** Choose the word that **BEST** completes each sentence. Make sure that the selected word completes your sentence in a way that makes sense!

MULTIPLE CHOICE

1. The story made everyone _____. Their smiles were as big as their faces. (L.1.4)

    A. mad   **B.** joyous   **C.** sleepy   **D.** sad

2. My shoes are _____. I need to have my mom wash them. (L.1.4)

    A. clean   **B.** filthy   **C.** new   **D.** broken

NAME: .... DATE: ....

5. LANGUAGE

> **Directions:** Write a sentence that correctly uses the given word.

3. **energy** (L.1.4)

   _____

   _____

   _____

> **Directions:** Read the words in the box below and use them to answer the questions.

pear	carrot	apple	lettuce	grape	purple
yellow	bunny	blue	pig	dog	potato

4. **What is one category that some of the words could be put into?** (L.1.5)
   - **A.** Colors
   - **B.** Dogs
   - **C.** Apples
   - **D.** Carrots

5. **Which word would not fit into a category on fruits?** (L.1.5)
   - **A.** Pear
   - **B.** Apple
   - **C.** Potato
   - **D.** Grape

6. **Which word would not fit into a category on vegetables?** (L.1.5)
   - **A.** Carrot
   - **B.** Lettuce
   - **C.** Potato
   - **D.** Bunny

7. **Which word would not fit into a category on animals?** (L.1.5)
   - **A.** Dog
   - **B.** Blue
   - **C.** Bunny
   - **D.** Pig

8. **Read the sentence: Dogs would also fit into a category on pets _____ these animals can live in people's homes. What is the missing word?** (L.1.6)
   - **A.** But
   - **B.** Because
   - **C.** How
   - **D.** Or

5.2. VOCABULARY ACQUISITION AND USE

5. LANGUAGE

9. **Read the sentence: Blue, purple, _____ yellow fit into a category on colors. What is the missing word?** (L.1.6)

   A. If   **B.** Because   **C.** And   **D.** But

10. **Read the sentence: I love to eat breakfast. I like to eat pancakes, _____ I do not like to put syrup on them. I like to drink orange juice and eat toast, too. What is the missing word?** (L.1.6)

    A. And   **B.** So   **C.** Or   **D.** But

11. **Read the sentence: My favorite thing about school is playing games at recess _____ I get to see my friends. We play tag, hopscotch, and jump rope. What is the missing word?** (L.1.6)

    A. Because   **B.** But   **C.** Or   **D.** Why

> **Directions:** *Read the words in the box below and use them to answer the questions.*

socks	jeans	boots
shirts	pants	gloves

12. **What category could the words above fit into?** (L.1.5)

    A. House   **B.** Clothes   **C.** Colors   **D.** School

13. **What phrase best describes jeans?** (L.1.5)
    A. Shoes we wear on our feet
    B. Helmet we wear on our head
    C. Pants we wear with pockets
    D. Mittens we wear to keep our hands warm

NAME: _____ DATE: _____

5. LANGUAGE

> **Directions:** *Read the passage and answer the questions below.*

Ducks live in ponds, streams, and lakes. They have webbed feet. Their feet help them move in the water. Ducks have good vision. They can see in color.

===== MULTIPLE CHOICE =====

14. A duck can be described as what? (L.1.5)
- **A.** a bird that swims
- **B.** a rooster
- **C.** a yellow animal
- **D.** a fast runner

15. The word *webbed* is used to describe what? (L.1.6)
- **A.** the duck's eyes
- **B.** the duck's beak
- **C.** the duck's feet
- **D.** the duck's body

> **Directions:** *Read the passage and answer the questions below.*

Tigers are wild cats. They have stripes on their fur. They are good swimmers. They cool off in pools or streams. Tigers can jump high. They can roar very loudly.

===== MULTIPLE CHOICE =====

16. A tiger can be described as what? (L.1.5)
- **A.** a big wild dog
- **B.** a wild cat with stripes
- **C.** a small animal
- **D.** a funny animal

17. The word *stripes* is used to describe what? (L.1.6)
- **A.** the lines on the tiger's fur
- **B.** the tiger's roar
- **C.** the tiger's size
- **D.** the tiger's feet

5.2. VOCABULARY ACQUISITION AND USE

5. LANGUAGE

> **Directions:** Read each sentence. Choose the prefix from the word bank to complete the sentence.

Word List

re-	un-	dis-
non-	pre-	mis-

18. We _____ did the assignment for the third time. (L.1.4)

> **Directions:** Read each sentence. Choose the suffix from the word bank to complete the sentence.

Word List

-ing	-less	-ful
-scope	-er	-est

19. Why are you wear_____ those boots? (L.1.4)

> **Directions:** Circle the root word from the following word.

20. **Papers** (L.1.4)

5.3. Chapter Review

5. LANGUAGE

5.3. Chapter Review

> **Directions:** Choose the correct possessive noun to complete the following sentence.

1. The _____ shirt is green. (L.1.1)

   A. boys'   **B.** boy's   **C.** boys   **D.** boy'

> **Directions:** Circle the proper nouns in the following sentence.

2. He is driving back from New York. (L.1.1)

> **Directions:** Choose the correct verb to complete the following sentence.

3. We enjoy _____ on the trampoline. (L.1.1)

   A. jump   **B.** jumps   **C.** jumping   **D.** jumped

> **Directions:** Choose the word that **BEST** completes each sentence. Make sure that the selected word completes your sentence in a way that makes sense!

4. I am _____. I cannot wait until dinner is ready to eat. (L.1.4)

   A. Ravenous   **B.** Sick   **C.** Thirsty   **D.** Sad

5. The hill is _____. Do not ride your bike down it. (L.1.4)

   A. dangerous   **B.** safe   **C.** short   **D.** empty

5. LANGUAGE

FILL IN THE BLANK

> **Directions:** Read the words in the box below and use them to answer the questions.

peek	walk	run	stare	glare
skip	hop	glance	scowl	jog

6. Write the verbs from the list above that mean *to look*. (L.1.5)

   _____, _____, _____, _____, _____

7. Write the verbs from the list above that mean *to move*. (L.1.5)

   _____, _____, _____, _____, _____

8. A verb that means *to jump* is _____. (L.1.5)

9. A verb that means *to see* is _____. (L.1.5)

> **Directions:** Read each sentence. Circle **ALL** the words that need to begin with capital letters. Rewrite the sentence in the space provided.

10. emily was born on april 15, 2011. (L.1.2)

    _____

5.3. CHAPTER REVIEW

NAME: _____ DATE: _____ 129

5. LANGUAGE

> **Directions:** *Read the sentence. Add end punctuation and capital letters where they are needed. Rewrite the sentence in the space provided.*

11. **its birthday is june 10th** (L.1.2)

   _____

> **Directions:** *Read the following sentence. Add commas where they are needed.*

12. **Buttons Zipper and Splash live with the new dog.** (L.1.2)

> **Directions:** *Write a sentence that correctly uses the given word.*

13. **found** (L.1.4)

   _____

> **Directions:** *Read the following sentence. Choose the prefix from the word bank to complete the underlined word.*

Word List

re-	un-	dis-
non-	pre-	mis-

14. She _____ <u>missed</u> me from school early. (L.1.4)

5.3. CHAPTER REVIEW

5. LANGUAGE

> **Directions:** Read the following sentence. Choose the suffix from the word bank to complete the underlined word.

Word List

-ing	-less	-ful
-scope	-er	-est

15. I was <u>speech</u>_____ after I heard the news. (L.1.4)

> **Directions:** Choose the correct pronoun to replace the underlined words in the following sentence.

16. <u>The dog</u> has a red collar. (L.1.1)

   A. He   **B.** She   **C.** They   **D.** It

> **Directions:** Circle the verbs in the following sentence.

17. **Robin wears ballet shoes.** (L.1.1)

> **Directions:** Write the conjunction from the ( ) that best completes the following sentence.

18. I missed school _____ I have a fever. (because, and) (L.1.1)

> **Directions:** Read the passage below and answer the questions that follow.

A teacher had a box. The box was full of different things. Inside there was a ruler, a pencil, a book, and an umbrella. The teacher asked the students to grab one thing from the box.

5. LANGUAGE

MULTIPLE CHOICE

19. **A ruler is used to do what?** (L.1.5)
    A. to sing with
    B. to write with
    C. to clean with
    D. to measure with

20. **In the passage above, what is another word that could be used for thing?** (L.1.6)
    A. shoe
    B. brush
    C. item
    D. marker

21. **An umbrella is used to do what?** (L.1.5)
    A. keep dry from the rain
    B. clean our shoes
    C. make noise
    D. do our homework

22. **In the passage above, what is another word that could be used for asked?** (L.1.6)
    A. yelled
    B. told
    C. wished
    D. sung

23. **A book is used to do what?** (L.1.5)
    A. sleep with
    B. read
    C. paint with
    D. eat with

24. **A pencil is used to do what?** (L.1.5)
    A. cook with
    B. play with
    C. write with
    D. clean with

> **Directions:** Look at the list of the words. Choose the word that matches the pattern.

25. **when, why, whine** (L.1.2)
    A. thumb
    B. math
    C. teach
    D. wheel

5.3. CHAPTER REVIEW

5. LANGUAGE

> **Directions:** Read the following sentence. Add end punctuation and capital letters where they are needed. Rewrite the sentence in the space provided.

26. her brother, alex, does not like the cat (L.1.2)

_____

> **Directions:** Look at the list of the words. Choose the word that matches the pattern.

27. **thirty, math, thunder** (L.1.2)

    A. thumb   **B.** crash   **C.** store   **D.** stay

> **Directions:** Circle the root word from each word.

28. speaking (L.1.4)

===== FREE RESPONSE =====

29. Write a sentence about why you like school. Use the word *because* in your sentence. (L.1.6)

_____

_____

30. Write a sentence about your two favorite books to read. Use the word *and* in your sentence. (L.1.6)

_____

_____

END OF YEAR ASSESSMENT

END OF YEAR ASSESSMENT

> **Directions:** *Read the passages and answer the questions below.*

PLAYING IN THE SNOW

Eddie loved to play in the snow. He would put on his jacket, gloves, and boots so he could run outside. Eddie would roll around in the snow. He picked it up and threw the snow at his friends. Eddie kept warm in the cold snow because he wore his winter clothes.

WINTER CLOTHES

During winter, it can get very cold outside. We need to wear clothes that will keep us warm. We can wear thick coats, gloves, and hats. The hats need to cover our ears. We lose a lot of body heat through our heads. By wearing a hat and scarf, we can keep our bodies warm.

--- FREE RESPONSE ---

1. **Which reading is the non-fiction text?** (RL.1.5)

   _____
   _____
   _____

2. **How do you know which one is the non-fiction text?** (RL.1.5)

   _____
   _____
   _____

END OF YEAR ASSESSMENT

> **Directions:** *Read the passage and answer the questions below.*

THE LITTLE LAME PRINCE

The little Prince had never seen anything like it. Despite feeling disappointed, he looked at the cloak curiously. He spread it out and then arranged it on his shoulders. It felt very warm and comfortable but it was so ragged - the most ragged thing that the little prince had ever seen in his life.

"And what use will it be to me?" said he sadly. "I have no need of outdoor clothes, as I never go outside as my legs are too weak. Why was this given to me, I wonder? What in the world am I to do with it?"

Nevertheless, because she was his godmother and had given him the cloak, he folded it carefully and put it away. Even though it was ragged, he hid it in a safe corner of his top cupboard, where no-one would look.

=== FREE RESPONSE ===

3. **What do you learn about the little Prince in this passage?** (RL.1.2)

_____

_____

_____

_____

_____

=== FILL IN THE BLANK ===

4. **The little Prince could not go outside because**
_____. (RL.1.2)

END OF YEAR ASSESSMENT

> **Directions:** Read the text and answer the questions below.

COMMUNITY HELPERS: DENTISTS

Dentists are doctors who help us with our teeth. Dentists help us keep our teeth strong and healthy. We should go to a dentist's office twice a year. Here we will have a checkup or exam on our teeth. The dentist will ask us questions about our teeth. They want to know if we have any problems. The dentist will then look at our teeth and gums. Before we see the dentist, our teeth will be cleaned. They will be brushed and flossed. Dentists use small tools to look inside our mouths. They can use tiny mirrors that help them see our teeth. As we grow, our teeth grow. Our baby teeth fall out. Permanent teeth grow in their place. Dentists look to see that our teeth are growing how they should be.

=== **FREE RESPONSE** ===

5. What do dentists help us with? (RI.1.1)

_____
_____
_____
_____

6. What is a checkup? (RI.1.1)

_____
_____
_____
_____

END OF YEAR ASSESSMENT

> **Directions:** *Read the text and answer the questions below.*

Turtle Facts

Turtles are known as reptiles. Like other reptiles, they lay eggs. They are cold-blooded or **ectothermic**. They take on the temperature of their environment. When they are outside in the heat, they become hot, too. When they are in a cold place, they become cold, too. Turtles need to be warm. This helps them to eat and move around. You can find turtles that live in hot places or warm **climates**. One of the best things about turtles is their shell. They use it to hide from **predators** or other animals that may want to eat them. All turtles have shells. They cannot take them off. The shell is important to a turtle.

=== FREE RESPONSE ===

7. **What does the word predator mean?** (RI.1.4)

_____

_____

_____

> **Directions:** *Read the words in the box below and use them to answer the questions.*

large	tiny	petite	mini	massive
little	huge	gigantic	teeny	enormous

8. **Write the adjectives from the box above that mean *big*.** (L.1.5)

   _____, _____, _____, _____, _____

9. **Write the adjectives from the box above that mean *small*.** (L.1.5)

   _____, _____, _____, _____, _____

END OF YEAR ASSESSMENT

> **Directions:** *Read the passage and answer the questions below.*

THE CROW AND THE PITCHER

In a spell of dry weather, when the birds could find very little to drink, a thirsty Crow found a pitcher with a little water in it.

But the pitcher was high and had a narrow neck, and no matter how he tried, the Crow could not reach the water. The poor thing felt as if he must die of thirst.

Then an idea came to him. Picking up some small pebbles, he dropped them into the pitcher one by one.

With each pebble, the water rose a little higher until at last it was near enough so he could drink.

=== FREE RESPONSE ===

10. What was the Crow's idea? (RL.1.1)

_____

_____

_____

=== MULTIPLE CHOICE ===

11. What happened when the bird put pebbles in the pitcher? (RL.1.1)
   A. It filled the empty pitcher.
   B. It made the water dirty.
   C. It made the waterline rise.
   D. It made the waterline fall.

END OF YEAR ASSESSMENT

> **Directions:** *Read the text and answer the questions below.*

Healthy Eating

Eating healthy is a good thing to do. It can give you energy during the day. Eating food that is good for us helps us with many things. We can learn better. We can play longer without being tired. Fruits and vegetables are healthy foods. You can eat as many as you want.

They fill you up so you are less likely to eat junk food. You will have less room in your stomach for candy bars or chips. You may even go to the doctor less because you become stronger from eating healthy food.

=== TRUE OR FALSE ===

12. Candy bars and chips are healthy foods. (RI.1.2)

    A. True   **B.** False

=== FREE RESPONSE ===

13. Why will you eat less junk food if you eat healthy food? (RI.1.2)

_____

_____

_____

_____

_____

_____

_____

END OF YEAR ASSESSMENT

> **Directions:** Read the text and answer the questions below.

Performance Day

Jim and Jill were going to take the stage. It was their big day. Jill was ready to play the part of the fun dancer. Jim was ready to act out the part of the silly boy. He is trying to learn some dance moves. He has never danced before. Jill is trying to teach him some moves, but he does not look graceful like her. People coming to watch the play will be in for a real treat.

=== MULTIPLE CHOICE ===

14. **What does this tell you about Jill?** (RL.1.7)

    A. Jill is helpful.
    B. Jill is not nice.
    C. Jill cannot dance.
    D. Jill is an only child.

15. **What does this tell you about Jim?** (RL.1.7)

    A. Jim is willing to try new things.
    B. Jim is lazy.
    C. Jim will not dance.
    D. Jim does not have a sister.

> **Directions:** Read the passage and answer the questions below.

The Lion and the Mouse

A great Lion was sleeping under a tree when a little Mouse accidentally ran across his nose. The Lion woke up and, quick as a flash, grabbed the tiny little Mouse in his huge paw. The Mouse was terrified, thinking that the Lion was about to kill him.

"Please spare me," begged the Mouse. "I didn't mean to wake you. If you let me go, one day I might be able to help you."

The Lion felt sorry for the Mouse and released him. But he thought to himself how unlikely it was that such a tiny Mouse would ever be able to help a powerful beast like himself.

...continued next page

NAME: .... DATE: ....

END OF YEAR ASSESSMENT

The very next day, the Lion was hunting in the forest when he walked into a hunter's trap. The Lion's angry roars of pain filled the forest, and the Mouse pricked up his tiny little ears. He recognized the voice of the lion and remembered that he had spared his life and so went to find him.

"Don't worry, my friend," said the Mouse to the Lion. "I will soon have you free from these ropes." He set to work, chewing at the ropes with his sharp teeth until he had cut through it.

The Lion was free. He learned that kindness can always be repaid, even by little friends!

=== FREE RESPONSE ===

16. **In the story, how did the Lion and the Mouse show kindness towards each other?** (RL.1.3)

_____

_____

_____

_____

_____

_____

_____

_____

END OF YEAR ASSESSMENT

=== FILL IN THE BLANK ===

17. _____ is one of the themes of this story. (RL.1.3)

18. Why does the Lion think the Mouse will never be able to help him? (RF.1.2)

END OF YEAR ASSESSMENT

> **Directions:** *Read the passage and answer the questions below.*

Plants need air, water, and soil to grow. Like us, plants need food to live. When we plant a garden, we must remember to water the plants each day. We have to pick out any weeds that grow in the garden, too.

19. Why is there not a question mark at the end of the sentences? (RF.1.1)

_____

_____

_____

20. Look at the pictures below. Circle the word that has a long vowel sound. (RF.1.2)

pea

apple

Write how you found your answer.

_____

_____

_____

_____

_____

21. **Look at the pictures below. Circle the word that has two syllables.** (RF.1.2)

 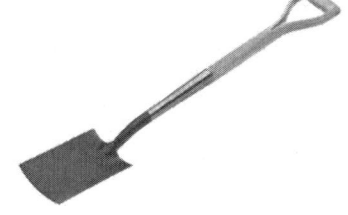 

gloves   shovel   hose

Write how you found your answer.

_____
_____
_____
_____
_____
_____
_____
_____

END OF YEAR ASSESSMENT

> **Directions:** Read the following sentence. Circle **ALL** the words that need to begin with capital letters. Rewrite the sentence in the space provided.

22. tommy, timmy, and tina are triplets who were born on tuesday, december 1st. (L.1.2)

_____

_____

_____

> **Directions:** Look at the list of words. Choose the word that matches the pattern.

23. **start, stay, storm** (L.1.2)

    A. chest   **B.** story   **C.** sheep   **D.** snow

> **Directions:** Complete the following sentences with your choice of word.

24. Finish the sentence: The huge monster was _____. (L.1.6)

25. Finish the sentence: The little box was full of _____. (L.1.6)

END OF YEAR ASSESSMENT

> **Directions:** *Read the passage and answer the questions below.*

THE ZOO

Mrs. Taylor's first grade class went to the zoo. When they got to the zoo, the kids ran inside. They were so excited to see the animals. They had been learning about them in class.

Emily smiled when she saw the elephants. They were her favorite animals. Emily watched them as they ate lettuce and fruits. The elephants sprayed water out of their trunks. The students laughed at the funny trick. Emily got too close to the gate and got wet!

The students walked over to see the alligators next. "Do not lean too far on the fence," said Mrs. Taylor. "You can see the alligators in their pen if you stand by me." The alligators were hard to see. The biggest one was hiding. It was under the pond water.

The students heard a loud roar. Emily and her classmates ran over to see where it was coming from. A pair of lions roared at the crowd. The crowd began to clap and cheer. When the lions went back into their den, a zookeeper came in to feed the lions some red meat.

FREE RESPONSE

26. Why did the kids in Mrs. Taylor's first grade class run inside when they got to the zoo? (RL.1.4)

_____

_____

_____

27. Why did the students laugh at the elephants? (RL.1.4)

_____

_____

_____

END OF YEAR ASSESSMENT

> **Directions:** Read the passage and answer the questions below.

THE LITTLE GLASS SLIPPER

Once there was a gentleman with a daughter who was sweet and kind. He married a proud woman with two daughters exactly like her.

After the wedding his wife began to show her true colors. She made his daughter do all of the housework. She made her sleep in a tiny room with a straw bed.

The girl worked hard. After she finished her work she would go into the chimney-corner and rest in ashes. Her sisters called her a cinder maid, or Cinderella.

The Prince invited everyone to a ball. Cinderella's sisters began choosing what to wear.

As they left for the ball, Cinderella began to cry. Her Godmother, who was a fairy, saw her tears and asked her what the matter was. "You wish you could go to the ball?"

"Yes," cried Cinderella.

Her Godmother said, "Run into the garden and bring me a pumpkin." Cinderella found a pumpkin and brought it to her. Her Godmother struck it with her wand and turned it into a fine coach, covered with gold.

She then found six mice and made a set of six horses. She turned a rat into a friendly coachman and six lizards into footmen.

The fairy then said to Cinderella, "It is time to go?"

"But I am wearing rags."

Her Godmother touched her with her wand, and turned her clothes into a beautiful gown! "Now go! But, be home by midnight because at midnight all will return to the way it was."

PEAR BLOSSOM

There was a child named Pear Blossom. One morning, Pear Blossom's mother died. Her father cried, "Who will take care of Pear Blossom?"

He went to the village matchmaker. She knew of a widow with a daughter.

...continued next page

END OF YEAR ASSESSMENT

When Omoni and Peony saw how beautiful Pear Blossom was, they were jealous of her. Omoni made her work all day.

One day the village was having a festival. "Pear Blossom may go," said Omoni, "after she weeds the flowers."

When she reached the fields, Pear Blossom looked sad. Weeding it would take weeks.

A black ox came from the grass. It began to munch the weeds. Soon the ox was gone and the weeds were too.

"A thousand thanks!" she called to the ox.

Pear Blossom hurried to the festival.

TRUE OR FALSE

28. Both girls get to go to special events. (RL.1.9)

    A. True   **B.** False

29. People are jealous of Cinderella, but not of Pear Blossom. (RL.1.9)

    A. True   **B.** False

> **Directions:** Read the passage and answer the question below.

Yellow flowers grow on the vine. The flowers turn into small green pumpkins. These pumpkins will turn orange. These are the pumpkins we see at the grocery store. If we plant pumpkin seeds, more pumpkins will grow. They will be ready to pick in fall.

30. What does the illustration show you? (RI.1.7)

    A. a vine   **B.** a pumpkin   **C.** a leaf   **D.** a flower on a vine

END OF YEAR ASSESSMENT

> **Directions:** Write the letter that correctly completes each word. Some words <u>will</u> require capital letters. Be sure to use correct letter formation.

31. I see a _____ at in the field. (L.1.1)

> **Directions:** Choose the correct possessive noun to complete the following sentence.

32. We are going to _____ house later today. (L.1.1)
    A. grandma
    B. grandmas'
    C. grandma's
    D. grandmas

> **Directions:** Choose the word that **BEST** completes the following sentence. Make sure that the selected word completes your sentence in a way that makes sense!

33. Did you see the cat _____ the ornament? Glass is everywhere! (L.1.4)
    A. Shatter
    B. Touch
    C. Smell
    D. Lick

END OF YEAR ASSESSMENT

> **Directions:** Read the passage and answer the questions below.

The School Band

It was the start to a new school year. I was happy to see my students and get them playing again. Last year, the school band won an award. We finished in first place. I hope we can win this year, too. I wait for the students to get quiet so I can start class.

"Hello. Welcome to music class," I said.

"Good morning, Ms. Kerry," the students said back.

I begin to pass out the instruments to each student. "Can I play the flute this year?" asked Chris.

"Yes, you can," I said. I handed him the flute to play.

Another student raised their hand. "Can I play the drums?" asked Lisa. "I'm really good. I played them all summer."

I nodded my head. I handed her a pair of drumsticks. Then I felt a tap on my shoulder.

"I'll play the guitar," said Joe.

"Yes, you can," I said.

Soon all of the students had their instruments to play. "Ms. Kerry," said Chris, "Let's win first place again."

All the students smiled. "Yes! Let's win!" they cheered.

=== **FREE RESPONSE** ===

34. Who is telling the story? How do you know? (RL.1.6)

_____

_____

_____

_____

NAME: _____ DATE: _____

END OF YEAR ASSESSMENT

35. What does the storyteller want to do? (RL.1.6)

_____
_____
_____
_____
_____

> **Directions:** *Read the text and answer the questions below.*

BIKES

Do you like to ride your bike? Many people own a bike. Learning to ride a bike is one of the first things we do as a kid. Riding bikes can be fun. You can ride your bike with your friends. You can ride around town on a bike path. You can ride on a trail. You can ride your bike around a campground. You can ride your bike in a race. Bike riding is a sport.

=== **FREE RESPONSE** ===

36. Where can you ride a bike? (RI.1.8)

_____
_____
_____
_____
_____
_____

END OF YEAR ASSESSMENT

> **Directions:** Read the text and answer the questions below.

ROLLER COASTERS

Most amusement parks have roller coasters. Sometimes they have long lines because so many people want to go on them. People may wait for hours. If you like fun rides that move fast, you should go on a roller coaster.

=== FREE RESPONSE ===

37. **If you are asked to write a passage about why roller coasters are fun, what kind of passage would it be? Why?** (W.1.1)

_____

_____

_____

> **Directions:** Read the text and answer the questions below.

SWIMMING LESSONS

Peter did not like to swim. He was scared of the water. His parents told him he needed to learn how to swim. They signed him up for swimming lessons. Peter was not happy.

On the first day, Peter had to learn how to kick. He held on to the side of the pool. He kicked his legs up and down. The water splashed. "I like this," said Peter. Peter got water in his eyes. He stopped kicking. Peter rubbed his eyes. His eyes had turned red.

END OF YEAR ASSESSMENT

FREE RESPONSE

38. You are asked to write a narrative passage about swimming. Write the introduction. (W.1.3)

_____

_____

_____

_____

_____

_____

_____

> **Directions:** Read the text and answer the question below.

MAGNETS

A magnet only pulls some things toward it. Metals like iron and nickel are pulled toward a magnet. Things made out of glass or plastic will not pull toward a magnet. Things made out of wood will push away from a magnet. There are many things that magnets can push and pull.

TRUE OR FALSE

39. The text says, "Things made out of wood will push away from a magnet." This is an opinion. (W.1.2)

   A. True   **B.** False

END OF YEAR ASSESSMENT

> **Directions:** Read the texts and answer the question below.

Taking Care of a Pet

Do you have a pet? Having a pet can be a big responsibility. We have to take care of them to help them live longer. You need to feed them the right food. If they eat something bad for them, they can get sick just like humans can.

Working at a Pet Store

Have you been to a pet store? There are so many different animals there. Each animal needs someone to take care of them so they can live a long life. They need to be fed the right food for their diet. Different animals eat different things. Some have food that is made special for them.

=== **FREE RESPONSE** ===

40. What is similar about the two texts? (RI.1.9)

_____

_____

_____

_____

_____

_____

_____

_____

END OF YEAR ASSESSMENT

> **Directions:** Use the table of contents to answer the following question.

WILDLIFE IN KENTUCKY
Table of Contents

Chapter 1: Deer 1

Chapter 2: Raccoons 7

Chapter 3: Squirrels 13

Chapter 4: Rabbits 19

Chapter 5: Opossums 24

41. What is this book called? (RI.1.5)

_____

> **Directions:** Read the text and answer the questions below.

SEALS & WALRUSES

The seal is a mammal. It lives on both land and water. Seals have their babies on land. They can live in both cold and warm waters. Seals can weigh a lot. They use their thick fur coat and layer of blubber to stay warm. Seals eat both fish and meat. They can find their food by using their whiskers. They can be white, silver, or brown.

The walrus is also a mammal. They have their babies on ice. They live in mostly cold water. Walruses can also weigh a lot. They use their layer of blubber to keep warm. Walruses eat both fish and meat. They can find their food by using their whiskers, too. They are brown in color.

END OF YEAR ASSESSMENT

FREE RESPONSE

42. What do both seals and walruses eat? (RI.1.3)

_____

_____

43. How do both seals and walruses find their food? (RI.1.3)

_____

_____

> **Directions:** Read the poem and answer the questions below.

THE RAIN CLOUDS

John and Jane went outside to play.
It was a nice, sunny day.
The two friends played catch and swam in the lake.
After some time, they stopped and took a break.

When the pair came back outside, the weather had changed.
Big rain clouds were in the sky above.
When it started to rain, Jane ran inside.
John did not go because he had to grab his baseball glove.

"Oh no," cried Jane.
"I want to play some more. I wish it would stop."
John walked to the window and looked outside.
All he could see were great big raindrops.

NAME: .... DATE: ....

END OF YEAR ASSESSMENT

=== **FREE RESPONSE** ===

44. Why did John and Jane stop playing at first? (RL.1.10)

_____

_____

_____

_____

_____

45. Why did John not go inside with Jane when it started to rain? (RL.1.10)

_____

_____

_____

_____

_____

ANSWER KEY

1. **Reading: Literature**
   1.1. Key Ideas and Details 160
   1.2. Craft and Structure 161
   1.3. Integration of Knowledge
        and Ideas 162
   1.4. Range of Reading and
        Level of Text Complexity 163
   1.5. Chapter Review 164

2. **Reading: Informational Text**
   2.1. Key Ideas and Details 166
   2.2. Craft and Structure 167
   2.3. Integration of
        Knowledge and Ideas 168
   2.4. Chapter Review 169

3. **Reading: Foundational Skills**
   3.1. Print Concepts 171
   3.2. Phonological Awareness 172
   3.3. Chapter Review 173

4. **Writing**
   4.1. Text Types and Purposes 174
   4.2. Chapter Review 175

5. **Language**
   5.1. Conventions of Standard English ... 177
   5.2. Vocabulary Acquisition and Use 178
   5.3. Chapter Review 179

End of Year Assessment 180

ANSWER KEY

1. READING: LITERATURE

1.1. Key Ideas and Details

1. Answer: Answers will vary.
Explanation: Answers must include a reasonable explanation such as, "I would ask my friend why Hare took a nap and why Hare was making fun of Tortoise."

2. Answer: Answers will vary.
Explanation: Answers must include a reasonable explanation such as, "Hare chose to take a nap because he thought it would show Tortoise how silly it was to race him. He thought he could take a nap, wake up, and still win."

3. Answer: Answers will vary.
Explanation: Answers must include a reasonable explanation such as, "The passage teaches us that it is better to be slow and steady than fast and reckless."

4. Answer: B
Explanation: Hare is making fun of Tortoise being slow by asking if he ever gets anywhere.

5. Answer: Fox
Explanation: Fox judged the race.

6. Answer: Steady
Explanation: The Tortoise is slow and steady.

7. Answer: Hare
Explanation: Everyone thought Hare would win the race.

8. Answer: False
Explanation: Tortoise felt confident. He is the one that suggested the race.

9. Answer: Answers will vary.
Explanation: Answers must include a reasonable explanation such as, "The lesson of this passage is that if you are not honest people may not believe you when you are being honest."

10. Answer: Answers will vary.
Explanation: Answers must include a reasonable explanation such as, "The main character in this passage is a Shepherd Boy. His job is to tend sheep in a pasture by a field. He thinks his job is boring so he tries to amuse himself by playing a trick on the townspeople."

11. Answer: Pasture
Explanation: The story is set in the pasture where the Shepherd Boy works.

12. Answer: False
Explanation: The townspeople ignored the Boy because they did not believe there was really a Wolf.

13. Answer: Answers will vary.
Explanation: Answers must include a reasonable description such as, "The Crocodile lived in a muddy river, set within a mysterious and magical forest. It was usually a very quiet area."

14. Answer: Answers will vary.
Explanation: Answers must include a reasonable explanation such as, "The Crocodile is described as a very selfish creature, therefore it may not want anyone else to go into the river as it may want all of the food and water for itself."

15. Answer: C
Explanation: The forest animals were afraid of the Crocodile which is why they did not go into the river.

16. Answer: Answers will vary.
Explanation: Answers must include a reasonable explanation such as, "The theme of the story is to be happy with what you have and not to be greedy.

ANSWER KEY

The story serves as a reminder not to behave in this way.

17. Answer: C
Explanation: The hound dog sees its own reflection in the water, though it thinks it is another dog and therefore tries to steal its bone.

18. Answer: the water
Explanation: The hound dog open its mouth and the bone falls into the water.

19. Answer: Answers will vary.
Explanation: Answers must include a reasonable explanation such as, "Jason would like to be an Olympic athlete and therefore he imagines that the tree is a bear so that he can prepare and train himself to fight against other strong opponents."

20. Answer: C
Explanation: Jason was throwing his spear at a tree, though he was imagining it was a large bear.

1.2. Craft and Structure

1. Answer: C
Explanation: The reading says she was excited when she got to the park.

2. Answer: B
Explanation: The reading says she was happy after the cars went so fast that she laughed.

3. Answer: B
Explanation: The reading says she was now sad after the log ride was closed.

4. Answer: D
Explanation: The reading says she was angry when a young girl cut in front of Sophia, making her miss her turn for the haunted house.

5. Answer: B
Explanation: The reading says she was thrilled to go upside down and backwards on the rollercoaster.

6. Answer: A
Explanation: The reading says she was glad she spent the day at the theme park.

7. Answer: A
Explanation: The reading tells a story because it talks about how kids are playing at a playground.

8. Answer: A
Explanation: The reading shows a cartoon illustration of kids playing at a playground.

9. Answer: A
Explanation: The reading tells a story because it has characters speaking and a setting at a water park.

10. Answer: B
Explanation: The reading has two characters speaking to each other, Mia and Patty.

11. Answer: D
Explanation: In the reading, the note is written for Mia; she is the one telling the story.

12. Answer: D
Explanation: The word "Mia" appears in the note.

13. Answer: B
Explanation: The reading says that Emma left the note.

1. READING: LITERATURE

ANSWER KEY

14. Answer: D
Explanation: The reading says that the person telling the story (Mia) said "thank you" to Emma.

15. Answer: C
Explanation: The reading says, "Mrs. Smith's first grade class," so she is the teacher.

16. Answer: B
Explanation: The reading says, "Emma is my best friend forever," so she is the best friend of Mia.

17. Answer: B
Explanation: The reading gives the reader information about the turtle life cycle.

18. Answer: A
Explanation: The reading tells facts about the life cycle of turtles – egg, hatchlings, young adults, and adult turtles, which lay eggs.

19. Answer: B
Explanation: The text would not be found in a storybook. It has facts about turtles. It is not a story about magical turtles.

20. Answer: A
Explanation: This reading would most likely be found in a textbook with a picture of a baby turtle or hatchling to show the reader what the stages of the life cycle look like.

1.3. Integration of Knowledge and Ideas

1. Answer: 1
Explanation: Joe is chasing Billy. This means that Joe would be behind Billy. Joe is the first position, which means he is #1.

2. Answer: 2
Explanation: Billy is being chased. The passage also mentions water splashing. There is water splashing on person #2.

3. Answer: The boys are at a party.
Explanation: The last sentence says that the boys are at a party. They have water balloons as part of the party celebrations.

4. Answer: It was a hot day.
Explanation: The setting refers to the location. It may describe the place, the time of day, or some other detail, such as the weather.

5. Answer: A
Explanation: The passages mention that Marcella is sad because she is alone. The youngest son is sad because he only received a cat.

6. Answer: B
Explanation: Both characters get surprises. The cat can talk which shocks the son. The little girl is surprised because of the doll.

7. Answer: A
Explanation: The youngest son is the main character.

8. Answer: B
Explanation: Marcella is a girl. She is playing in the attic.

9. Answer: B
Explanation: The cat from "Puss in Boots" makes the story not real. Cats cannot talk.

10. Answer: C
Explanation: The text reveals that Simon has an older brother called Tom.

11. Answer: C
Explanation: The text reveals that both Simon and Tom are afraid as an enormous creature has appeared in the water.

1. READING: LITERATURE

ANSWER KEY

12. Answer: B
Explanation: The word 'precious' is used to describe the surf board which Tom gave to his brother Simon for his birthday. The word suggests the board is very special to Simon.

13. Answer: C
Explanation: The text reveals that Simon falls from his board when he sees the creature.

14. Answer: D
Explanation: The word 'enormous' is used to describe the creature in the water.

15. Answer: A
Explanation: Cinderella gets help from the mice and her fairy godmother. Pear Blossom gets help from a black ox.

16. Answer: B
Explanation: Both girls are hard workers. Cinderella has to do a lot of cleaning. Pear Blossom has to weed the area.

17. Answer: B
Explanation: Cinderella's dad is not mentioned enough to know how he really acts. Pear Blossom's father cries and worries about his daughter, so he is not mean.

18. Answer: A
Explanation: The Fairy Godmother helps Cinderella. She would not be able to go to the ball.

19. Answer: A
Explanation: The black ox helps Pear Blossom. He shows up and eats all the weeds for her.

20. Answer: D
Explanation: The girls both have mean sisters.

1.4. Range of Reading and Level of Text Complexity

1. Answer: B
Explanation: The word "big" describes the size of the bus.

2. Answer: D
Explanation: The word "red" tells the reader the color of the backpack.

3. Answer: C
Explanation: The student should be able to identify that the word "treat" rhymes with "seat."

4. Answer: D
Explanation: The student should be able to identify that the word "backpack" rhymes with "snack."

5. Answer: C
Explanation: A student is saying the poem because they are describing what it's like to ride the bus and talk about having a backpack with them. These clues help the reader to know that the person saying the poem is a student.

6. Answer: D
Explanation: The poem says the bus driver may give a treat if the passenger is calm and quiet.

7. Answer: C
Explanation: The student should be able to identify that the word "train" rhymes with "plane."

8. Answer: D
Explanation: The student should be able to identify that the word "waste" rhymes with "toothpaste."

9. Answer: C
Explanation: The poem says that you can travel outside of your town.

ANSWER KEY

10. Answer: B

Explanation: The poem says to remember to bring a brush and toothpaste.

11. Answer: A

Explanation: The author is telling the poem. There are no clues to suggest that the poem is written in first person or from a character's point of view.

12. Answer: B

Explanation: The poem is about traveling. The reader can tell the subject of the poem by the title.

13. Answer: A

Explanation: The student should be able to recognize that a student is saying the poem by clues from the text (our teacher, field trip, my class).

14. Answer: B

Explanation: The poem says the welcome sign was red and blue.

15. Answer: A

Explanation: The poem says that the favorite animal was in front of the student, a big brown bear.

16. Answer: A

Explanation: The poem says the zoo was nearby, which suggests that it is close to the school.

17. Answer: The student saying the poem. Answers will vary.

Explanation: The poem says, "Here, brown bear," I yelled. "Look over here, please!" This lets the reader know that the person saying the poem (the student) is talking to the bear.

18. Answer: Excitement

Explanation: The poem says the student was excited to be there with their class.

19. Answer: The two friends are John and Jane. Answers may vary.

Explanation: The poem describes them as a pair. Jane wishes the rain would stop. John looks out the window at the raindrops.

20. Answer: The poem says it was a nice, sunny day. The weather changed and it started to rain.

Explanation: The student should identify the sun and the rain clouds.

1.5. Chapter Review

1. Answer: Answers will vary.

Explanation: Answers must include a reasonable explanation such as, "The lesson of this passage is that you can find a way to solve your problems if you are creative."

2. Answer: A

Explanation: The bird could not find water because of the dry weather.

3. Answer: Answers will vary.

Explanation: Answers must include a reasonable explanation such as, "The statement is unfair as the Crocodile in the text is very selfish and should not expect to have the river to itself. It is unfair as the other animals and fish should also be able to use the river."

4. Answer: Answers will vary.

Explanation: Answers must include a reasonable explanation such as, "The river is described as being in a mysterious and magical forest. This might suggest that it is an usual place."

5. Answer: B

Explanation: The exclamation marks might suggest the Crocodile is shouting.

ANSWER KEY

6. Answer: Billy can't throw his balloon because he is running too fast.
Explanation: The passage says, "He was running too fast to throw it."

7. Answer: Joe is carrying a red balloon.
Explanation: Look at the picture. Joe is in position 1. He has a balloon in his hand.

8. Answer: She was not acting safe. Spending time with a wolf is never a good idea.
Explanation: The text talks about the wolf's inability to eat her, only because the woodcutters were close by. This shows how unsafe it is.

9. Answer: These characters were all trying to get something from nothing. The Wolf was trying to get food from Little Red Riding Hood. The animals all expected the Little Red Hen to take care of them.
Explanation: Same as answer.

10. Answer: The Wolf is afraid to hurt Little Red Riding Hood because he knows woodcutters were nearby.
Explanation: Same as answer.

11. Answer: She wants to plant the seed. Once she learns what it is, she knows it will be a good way to get wheat for herself and the other animals.
Explanation: Same as answer.

12. Answer: The school was one hundred years old which is why there was a party.
Explanation: Same as answer.

13. Answer: Jessica is worried her balloon might end up lost in the sea or caught amongst some great forest.
Explanation: Same as answer.

14. Answer: A
Explanation: Same as answer.

15. Answer: True
Explanation: Jessica's teacher is happy that Jessica's balloon has been found as she laughs and is described as speaking with 'delight'.

16. Answer: D
Explanation: The reading says the apples feel smooth on Mason's skin.

17. Answer: B
Explanation: The reading says Mason can smell the sweet scent of the apples.

18. Answer: C
Explanation: The reading says Mason hears the loud crunch the apples make from his teeth.

19. Answer: A
Explanation: The reading says the apples taste crisp and juicy on his tongue.

20. Answer: B
Explanation: The author of the story is telling the story, not Michelle.

21. Answer: A
Explanation: Michelle did name her pet rabbit Fluffy.

22. Answer: B
Explanation: Mr. Martin is Michelle's dad. The pet store owner does not have a name in the story.

23. Answer: The pond is the setting of the poem. Answers will vary.
Explanation: The poem gives the reader clues about the setting (pond, water, ducks, lizards, tadpoles, frogs, lily pads).

24. Answer: Answers will vary.
Explanation: The student should identify that things that move and make sound are the ducks, lizards, tadpoles, bugs, and frogs.

1. READING: LITERATURE

www.prepaze.com

ANSWER KEY

25. Answer: Top. Answers will vary.
Explanation: The student should identify two additional words that rhyme with hop: chop, cop, crop, drop, flop, mop, pop, shop, stop, slop, swap

26. Answer: B
Explanation: The reading gives the reader information about zebras.

27. Answer: B
Explanation: The reading shows a real-life image of a zebra in the wild.

28. Answer: A
Explanation: He has blue hair. The picture shows Jim with his blue hair.

29. Answer: B
Explanation: The picture shows Jan dancing. The text also talks about her experience as a dancer.

30. Answer: D
Explanation: The pictures show that the kids are happy with big smiles.

2. READING: INFORMATIONAL TEXT

2.1. Key Ideas and Details

1. Answer: D
Explanation: The text is about caterpillars. The student should understand this from the facts included in the text as well as the title.

2. Answer: B
Explanation: The text says that caterpillars can have up to five pairs of legs.

3. Answer: A
Explanation: The text says that caterpillars eat a lot of leaves.

4. Answer: A
Explanation: The text says that caterpillars hang upside down from a twig or leaf.

5. Answer: C
Explanation: The text says that caterpillars spin silk around their bodies.

6. Answer: D
Explanation: The text says that caterpillars will become a moth or a butterfly. Both choices are correct.

7. Answer: A
Explanation: The text says alligators and crocodiles are both reptiles.

8. Answer: B
Explanation: The text says alligators have a snout in the shape of a U.

9. Answer: A
Explanation: The text says crocodiles have a pointed snout.

10. Answer: B
Explanation: The text says that when crocodiles, not alligators, close their mouths, you can still see some of their teeth.

11. Answer: B
Explanation: The text is about George Washington as our first president. The student should understand this from the facts included in the text as well as the title.

12. Answer: C
Explanation: The text says that George Washington was 57 years old when he became president.

13. Answer: B
Explanation: The text says that Washington was president for two terms.

14. Answer: D
Explanation: The text says that Washington was the only president to not live in the White House.

ANSWER KEY

15. **Answer: Seals have their babies on land. Walruses have their babies on ice.**
Explanation: The student should recognize this answer from the text.

16. **Answer: Seals live in both cold and warm waters. Walruses live in mostly cold water.**
Explanation: The student should recognize that seals live in both cold and warm waters, while walruses only live in cold water.

17. **Answer: Seals use their thick fur coat and blubber to stay warm. Walruses use their layer of blubber to keep warm.**
Explanation: The student should recognize that both seals and walruses use their blubber to keep warm.

18. **Answer: A**
Explanation: The text is about eating healthy food that is good for us. The student should understand this from the facts included in the text as well as the title.

19. **Answer: A**
Explanation: The text says that eating healthy can give us energy during the day.

20. **Answer: B**
Explanation: The text says that eating healthy foods make us play longer without being tired.

2.2. Craft and Structure

1. **Answer: A**
Explanation: The text says there are eight planets in the solar system.

2. **Answer: A**
Explanation: The text lists Jupiter as a planet.

3. **Answer: B**
Explanation: The text says everything in the solar system moves around the sun, not Earth.

4. **Answer: B**
Explanation: The text says Earth is the third planet from the sun, not the fourth.

5. **Answer: The word orbit means to circle around.**
Explanation: The student should recognize the definition in the text where it states, "these planets *orbit* or circle around the sun."

6. **Answer: Answers may vary.**
Explanation: The student should recognize the definition in the text where it states, "these planets *orbit* or circle around the sun."

7. **Answer: A**
Explanation: The glossary defines the chrysalis as the third stage in a butterfly's life.

8. **Answer: A**
Explanation: Pupa is defined as the third stage in the butterfly's life. It even says that it is the same as chrysalis.

9. **Answer: B**
Explanation: The glossary defines metamorphosis as the change the butterfly goes through.

10. **Answer: D**
Explanation: All of these definitions relate to a butterfly. The book must be about butterflies.

11. **Answer: C**
Explanation: The hindwings are defined and noted to be at the back of the butterfly.

12. **Answer: Reptiles lay eggs.**
Explanation: The student should recognize that turtles and other reptiles lay eggs.

2. READING: INFORMATIONAL TEXT

ANSWER KEY

13. Answer: Ectothermic means cold blooded.
Explanation: The student should find the definition in the text.

14. Answer: Answers may vary.
Explanation: The student should say that turtles need to be warm because this helps them to eat and move around, giving them energy.

15. Answer: Climate means the temperature or weather conditions of a place.
Explanation: The student should be able to recognize this definition from the text.

16. Answer: Raccoons, Chapter 2
Explanation: Chapter 2 is about raccoons. It begins on page 7.

17. Answer: 5 Chapters
Explanation: There are five chapters in the book.

18. Answer: Chapter 4
Explanation: Chapter 4 is about rabbits. It starts on page 19.

19. Answer: Pages 1-6
Explanation: Pages 1-6 are about deer.

20. Answer: Chapter 2
Explanation: Chapter 2 is about raccoons.

2.3. Integration of Knowledge and Ideas

1. Answer: B
Explanation: Bats fly at night, not during the day.

2. Answer: A
Explanation: Because the sun dries out their wings, the bats have to find their food at night when they can fly.

3. Answer: B
Explanation: Bats use their ears to find food, not their eyes.

4. Answer: A
Explanation: The text says bats make a sound and when it comes back to them, then they can tell how far away something is.

5. Answer: C
Explanation: The text explains that paper is made from trees so that is why we cut them down.

6. Answer: D
Explanation: The student should understand that all of the choices are correct.

7. Answer: B
Explanation: The author is making the point that we need to not waste paper so we should recycle or reuse it.

8. Answer: A
Explanation: The student should understand that because of the different temperatures in summer and winter, we wear different clothes.

9. Answer: B
Explanation: The opposite is true – it is warm in the summer and cold in the winter.

10. Answer: A
Explanation: Because the days are longer, we can see outside longer during summer.

11. Answer: A
Explanation: Because it is too cold to stay outside for too long in the winter, we do fewer things outside.

12. Answer: A
Explanation: We play baseball outside in summer and basketball inside in winter.

ANSWER KEY

13. Answer: C
Explanation: The student should understand the difference between the two texts – one is about the colors of vegetables, one is about the vitamins in the vegetables.

14. Answer: D
Explanation: The student should recognize this answer from both texts.

15. Answer: C
Explanation: The student should understand that this is best answer choice.

16. Answer: C
Explanation: The author would suggest that we use cloth napkins.

17. Answer: B
Explanation: The author would suggest that we wash our plates.

18. Answer: A
Explanation: The student should understand that this is the author's main point – save trees by saving paper.

19. Answer: A
Explanation: The student should recognize this as the key idea of the text.

20. Answer: B
Explanation: The illustration shows the body parts of a bat.

2.4. Chapter Review

1. Answer: D
Explanation: The text lists a pumpkin patch, farm, and garden as places where you can find pumpkins. The student should recognize that all of the choices are correct.

2. Answer: D
Explanation: The student should understand the question is asking "how" pumpkins grow. Pumpkins grow by going through a life cycle.

3. Answer: A
Explanation: The author states that water is important to our lives and then explains why with reasons.

4. Answer: A
Explanation: The text explains where we use water in our homes and our community.

5. Answer: B
Explanation: We do need to save water because most of the water on Earth is salt water. We need fresh water to live.

6. Answer: B
Explanation: The opposite is true – we need to take shorter showers and fewer baths.

7. Answer: B
Explanation: The text says that the bald eagle only lives in North America.

8. Answer: C
Explanation: The text says that bald eagles are not bald. They have white feathers on their heads.

9. Answer: D
Explanation: The text says bald eagles can fly over 10,000 feet.

10. Answer: A
Explanation: The text says bald eagles have great eyesight and can see fish up to a mile away.

11. Answer: A
Explanation: The text refers to the egg mass as a cluster and a group, letting the reader know a cluster is a group of something.

2. READING: INFORMATIONAL TEXT

ANSWER KEY

12. Answer: D
Explanation: The text says frogspawn is an egg mass or cluster/group of frog eggs.

13. Answer: C
Explanation: The text says the group protects the eggs by making it harder for other animals to eat them. "Keep safe" is the best possible answer choice.

14. Answer: C
Explanation: The text says that firefighters and police officers are our community helpers.

15. Answer: A
Explanation: The text says that firefighters and police officers work to help people.

16. Answer: C
Explanation: The text says firefighters work out of a fire station.

17. Answer: 7
Explanation: The index shows that page 7 is where baking pans are listed.

18. Answer: Measuring Cups
Explanation: The measuring cups are listed on page 11.

19. Answer: 13
Explanation: Spoons are covered on page 13.

20. Answer: Forks
Explanation: Page 10 has forks listed.

21. Answer: C
Explanation: The text is about lightning storms. The student should understand this from the facts included in the text as well as the title.

22. Answer: A
Explanation: The text says that during a lightning storm light flashes in the sky and loud thunder is heard.

23. Answer: B
Explanation: The text says that lightning storms are made when warm air rises and is mixed with cooler air.

24. Answer: D
Explanation: The text says that lightning is very powerful.

25. Answer: Answers will vary.
Explanation: The student should say what is the same in the two texts – both talk about caring for pets.

26. Answer: Answers will vary.
Explanation: The student should say what is different in the two texts – one talks about exercise, the other talks about grooming and keeping the pets clean.

27. Answer: B
Explanation: The student should understand that pumpkins start out as small green pumpkins.

28. Answer: C
Explanation: The student should understand the pumpkins are grown and ready to be picked in fall.

29. Answer: Answers will vary.
Explanation: The student should give an example for one or both of the texts – park, pictures, play games.

30. Answer: Answers will vary.
Explanation: The student can say that people play with the pets, take pictures of them, and get excited.

ANSWER KEY

3. READING: FOUNDATIONAL SKILLS

3.1. Print Concepts

1. Answer: B
Explanation: The student should recognize where the first word is in a sentence.

2. Answer: C
Explanation: The student should understand that a person's name is a proper noun and should always be capitalized.

3. Answer: D
Explanation: The student should recognize that the ! symbol is an exclamation point.

4. Answer: D
Explanation: The student should recognize what quotation marks mean in a sentence and how to tell that a character is speaking.

5. Answer: C
Explanation: The student should recognize that the ? symbol is a question mark.

6. Answer: A
Explanation: The student should recognize what a comma (,) symbol looks like.

7. Answer: A
Explanation: The student should recognize the exclamation point symbol.

8. Answer: B
Explanation: The student should recognize that there are no question marks in the text.

9. Answer: B
Explanation: The student should understand which letters to capitalize. *brother* is not a proper noun and does not begin a sentence so it should not be capitalized.

10. Answer: A
Explanation: The student should recognize that the last sentence uses a period as the ending punctuation mark.

11. Answer: Mark
Explanation: The student should know that a punctuation *mark* ends a sentence.

12. Answer: Capital
Explanation: The student should know that letters are capitalized at the beginning of sentences.

13. Answer: Question mark
Explanation: The student should be able to identify what a question mark symbol looks like.

14. Answer: Exclamation point
Explanation: The student should be able to identify what an exclamation point symbol looks like.

15. Answer: Zero
Explanation: The student should understand that there are no question marks in the text.

16. Answer: The, We, and We
Explanation: The student should recognize that the first word of each sentence is capitalized.

17. Answer: Answers will vary.
Explanation: The student should recognize that the sentence is asking a question to the reader so it would need a question mark as the ending punctuation.

ANSWER KEY

18. Answer: Answers will vary.

Explanation: The student should explain when to use exclamation points. Because none of the sentences express excitement, it does not make sense to use them.

19. Answer: It is capitalized because it is the first word in a sentence.

Explanation: The student should understand that all words are capitalized at the beginning of a sentence.

20. Answer: Answers will vary.

Explanation: The student should explain that commas are used to list three science tools we use to keep us safe.

3.2. Phonological Awareness

1. Answer: A

Explanation: The "a" vowel makes a short "a" sound.

2. Answer: B

Explanation: The "i" vowel in the word ice makes a long "i" sound.

3. Answer: C

Explanation: The "e" vowel in the word edge makes a short "e" sound.

4. Answer: B

Explanation: The "ea" vowel in eat makes a long "e" sound.

5. Answer: B

Explanation: The "i" vowel in the word bite makes a long "i" sound.

6. Answer: B

Explanation: The "a" vowel makes a long "a" sound.

7. Answer: A

Explanation: The "i" vowel makes a long "i" sound.

8. Answer: B

Explanation: The "o" vowel makes a short "o" sound.

9. Answer: A

Explanation: The "o" vowel makes a short "o" sound.

10. Answer: B

Explanation: The "a" vowel makes a short "a" sound.

11. Answer: Pot

Explanation: The student should know how to spell the word *pot* that matches the picture and the passage.

12. Answer: Coat

Explanation: The student should recognize the word coat as having only one syllable.

13. Answer: Rain

Explanation: The student should recognize the word rain as having only one syllable.

14. Answer: Ball

Explanation: The student should know how to spell the word *ball* that matches the picture and the passage.

15. Answer: Answers will vary.

Explanation: The student should write another word that has the same sound as cup (Ex: pup).

16. Answer: Answers will vary.

Explanation: The student should write another word that has the same sound as can (Ex: man).

17. Answer: Microscope; Answers will vary.

Explanation: The student should explain that when they hear a vowel as a separate sound that is a syllable. The words cup and scale only have one syllable while microscope has three.

ANSWER KEY

18. Answer: Hot; Answers will vary.
Explanation: The student should be able to explain that cold has a long "o" sound while hot has a short "o" sound.

19. Answer: Gloves; Answers will vary.
Explanation: The student should explain that when they hear a vowel as a separate sound that is a syllable. The words goggles and aprons have two syllables while gloves has only one syllable.

20. Answer: Answers will vary.
Explanation: The student should explain that words need to be pronounced or said correctly so that the listener can understand what the speaker is telling them.

3.3. Chapter Review

1. Answer: A
Explanation: The "i" vowel makes a short "i" sound.

2. Answer: B
Explanation: The student should recognize where the first word is in a sentence.

3. Answer: C
Explanation: The "e" vowel in the word went makes a short "e" sound.

4. Answer: A
Explanation: The "a" vowel in the word face makes a long "a" sound.

5. Answer: A
Explanation: The "e" vowel makes a short "e" sound.

6. Answer: C
Explanation: The student should understand that a person's name is a proper noun and should always be capitalized.

7. Answer: D
Explanation: The student should recognize that the ! symbol is an exclamation point.

8. Answer: D
Explanation: The student should recognize what quotation marks mean in a sentence and how to tell that a character is speaking.

9. Answer: C
Explanation: The "i" vowel in the word ice makes a long "i" sound.

10. Answer: C
Explanation: The student should recognize that the ? symbol is a question mark.

11. Answer: A
Explanation: The "e" vowel makes a short "e" sound.

12. Answer: B
Explanation: The "a" vowel makes a short "a" sound.

13. Answer: A
Explanation: The student should recognize what a comma (,) symbol looks like.

14. Answer: A
Explanation: The student should recognize the exclamation point symbol.

15. Answer: A
Explanation: The "o" vowel makes a long "o" sound.

16. Answer: B
Explanation: The "a" vowel makes a long "a" sound.

17. Answer: A
Explanation: The student should recognize that there is one question mark in the text.

3. READING: FOUNDATIONAL SKILLS

ANSWER KEY

18. Answer: B
Explanation: The "o" vowel makes a short "o" sound.

19. Answer: B
Explanation: The student should understand which letters to capitalize. *new* is not a proper noun and does not begin a sentence so it should not be capitalized.

20. Answer: B
Explanation: The student should recognize that the last sentence uses a period as the ending punctuation mark.

21. Answer: Cab
Explanation: The student should know how to spell the word *cab* that matches the picture and the passage.

22. Answer: Exclamation Point
Explanation: The student should be able to identify what an exclamation point symbol looks like.

23. Answer: Bag
Explanation: The student should recognize the word bag as having only one syllable.

24. Answer: Water
Explanation: The student should recognize the word water as having two syllables.

25. Answer: Question Mark
Explanation: The student should be able to identify what a question mark symbol looks like.

26. Answer: Three
Explanation: The student should understand that there are three periods in the text.

27. Answer: I, There, and We
Explanation: The student should recognize that the first word of each sentence is capitalized.

28. Answer: Box
Explanation: The student should know how to spell the word *box* that matches the picture and the passage.

29. Answer: Answers will vary.
Explanation: The student should write another word that has the same sound as see (Ex: me, free, tree).

30. Answer: Answers will vary.
Explanation: The student should write another word that has the same sound as may (Ex: day, way, say, pay).

4. WRITING

4.1. Text Types and Purposes

1. Answer: A
Explanation: The student should recognize the topic of the reading is about family traditions.

2. Answer: A
Explanation: The student should be able to recognize that the author is giving their opinion when they say that family traditions are important.

3. Answer: B
Explanation: The author's opinion is that family traditions are important.

4. Answer: C
Explanation: The student should recognize the topic of the text is on king penguins based on the content and title.

5. Answer: C
Explanation: The student should understand that saying king penguins are cute birds is not a fact but an opinion that is not included in the text.

6. Answer: B
Explanation: The student should recognize this as a fact about king penguins.

ANSWER KEY

7. Answer: Answers will vary.
Explanation: The student will list what facts they would want to write about in an informative passage about penguins.

8. Answer: Answers will vary.
Explanation: The student will explain which arctic animal they would want to write an informative passage about.

9. Answer: A
Explanation: The story is about a mother and son's trip to the grocery store.

10. Answer: B
Explanation: The student should understand the author is not teaching them something but is telling them a story.

11. Answer: A
Explanation: The student should recognize the passage is a narrative.

12. Answer: B
Explanation: The student should understand the story is not telling the reader facts but instead is recounting an event in the grocery store.

13. Answer: D
Explanation: The student needs to know that the author is telling a story.

14. Answer: A
Explanation: The student should recognize that this sentence is the conclusion that ends the story.

15. Answer: Informative; Answers will vary.
Explanation: The student will explain why this would be an informative passage.

16. Answer: Answers will vary.
Explanation: The student will write the first two lines of an informative passage about penguins at the zoo.

17. Answer: "King penguins work to help and care for each other."
Explanation: The student will be able to identify this sentence as the concluding statement.

18. Answer: B
Explanation: The passage above is an opinion piece, not a narrative.

19. Answer: A
Explanation: The student should understand that because they are choosing their favorite family tradition and giving reasons to support their opinion, that would be an opinion piece.

20. Answer: A
Explanation: The student should recognize this as a closing statement.

4.2. Chapter Review

1. Answer: B
Explanation: The topic of the text is about reading books to become a better student, not to learn about animals.

2. Answer: A
Explanation: The student should understand the author's opinion is that reading books can make us a better student, which makes it a good thing for us to do.

3. Answer: A
Explanation: The student should recognize that by becoming better spellers, we can be better students.

4. Answer: B
Explanation: The passage is not informative, it is an opinion piece.

5. Answer: B
Explanation: The topic of the text is about what firefighters do, not how to put out fires.

ANSWER KEY

6. Answer: A
Explanation: The student should understand the author is teaching them something, in this case what firefighters do.

7. Answer: A
Explanation: The student should recognize that this statement is a fact.

8. Answer: B
Explanation: The student should understand that saying firefighters are funny is not a fact but an opinion.

9. Answer: B
Explanation: When the author says that books can teach you lessons, the author is giving another reason for their opinion.

10. Answer: D
Explanation: The student should recognize that the conclusion is the last sentence of the text with the lead in "In conclusion, …"

11. Answer: B
Explanation: The student should recognize that the story is about Amy's birthday party based on the content and title.

12. Answer: B
Explanation: The student should recognize the passage above as a narrative.

13. Answer: A
Explanation: The student should recognize the temporal words that signal event order.

14. Answer: B
Explanation: The student should be able to recognize that there is only one event happening in the passage.

15. Answer: A
Explanation: The student should be able to understand that Amy is celebrating her sixth birthday because there are six candles on her birthday cake.

16. Answer: A
Explanation: The student should recognize this as a closing statement.

17. Answer: B
Explanation: The student needs to know that the author is giving facts about what firefighters do.

18. Answer: D
Explanation: The student should recognize that the conclusion is the last sentence of the text that summarizes the information.

19. Answer: D
Explanation: The student should recognize the topic of the text is on roller coasters based on the content and title.

20. Answer: C
Explanation: The student should be able to understand that the author's opinion is that roller coasters are fun.

21. Answer: B
Explanation: The student should understand that a reason for why roller coasters are fun is because of their fast speed that is like being in a racecar.

22. Answer: Answers will vary.
Explanation: The student will write their opinion about roller coasters.

23. Answer: A
Explanation: The student should recognize that the text is an informative passage.

24. Answer: B
Explanation: The student should recognize the topic of the reading is about magnets, not science tools in general.

25. Answer: A
Explanation: The student should recognize that the author is stating facts about magnets, not giving their opinion.

ANSWER KEY

26. Answer: A
Explanation: The student should be able to recognize this statement as a fact.

27. Answer: C
Explanation: The student should recognize the event in the story based on the content and title.

28. Answer: C
Explanation: The student should be able to understand that the author is trying to tell a story about a character, Peter, who takes swimming lessons.

29. Answer: D
Explanation: The student should recognize this as a detail in the text.

30. Answer: Answers will vary.
Explanation: The student will write about an event that happens in their story on swimming lessons.

5. LANGUAGE

5.1. Conventions of Standard English

1. Answer: Can
Explanation: Can (the 'c' in can should be capitalized.)

2. Answer: A
Explanation: The puppy belongs to Emily, so an 's is needed to make Emily's possessive.

3. Answer: Max
Explanation: Max refers to a specific person.

4. Answer: Sam
Explanation: People's names should be capitalized. These are proper nouns.

5. Answer: December
Explanation: Dates should be capitalized. This includes the months of the year. These are proper nouns.

6. Answer: store
Explanation: Store is a common noun. It refers to a general store.

7. Answer: C
Explanation: "Runs" is plural because the dog is singular.

8. Answer: They
Explanation: The pronoun "They" is needed to replace the two boys' names in the sentence.

9. Answer: Sits
Explanation: The dog's action in this sentence is sitting. Sits is the correct form of the verb.

10. Answer: Sally has a cat.
Explanation: People's names should be capitalized. A statement should end with a period.

11. Answer: Her cat has yellow fur.
Explanation: The beginning of a sentence should be capitalized. A statement should end with a period.

12. Answer: March 21, 2015
Explanation: A comma is needed to separate the day of the month from the year.

13. Answer: Bones, balls, and stuffed animals
Explanation: Commas are used to separate items in a series. When there are three items, two commas are needed.

14. Answer: and
Explanation: The conjunction 'and' links the two details. Jeremiah did not wear the shirt because she wore the dress, which is why 'so' is not the answer.

ANSWER KEY

15. Answer: in
Explanation: Prepositions are used to indicate location. The ice cream is 'in' the freezer. This shows you where the ice cream is located.

16. Answer: down
Explanation: Prepositions are used to indicate location. By putting the phone 'down' a change in the phone's location is occurring.

17. Answer: A
Explanation: All of the words contain the digraph blend 'ch'.

18. Answer: A
Explanation: All of the words contain the digraph blend 'sh'.

19. Answer: ghost
Explanation: The little girl drew a ghost.
Explanation: Using the digraph "gh" is the only combination that creates a word which accurately completes the sentence.

20. Answer: ship
Explanation: The ship is setting sail.
Explanation: Using the digraph "sh" is the only combination that creates a word which accurately completes the sentence.

5.2. Vocabulary Acquisition and Use

1. Answer: B
Explanation: Since everyone had big smiles, they must be joyous.

2. Answer: B
Explanation: If the shoes need to be washed, filthy is the only word that makes sense.

3. Answer: Answers will vary.
Explanation: I have a lot of energy, so I cannot stop running.

4. Answer: A
Explanation: The category some of the words could be put into would be "colors".

5. Answer: C
Explanation: Potato would not be included in a category on fruits.

6. Answer: D
Explanation: Bunny would not be included in a category on vegetables.

7. Answer: B
Explanation: Blue would not be included in a category on animals.

8. Answer: B
Explanation: The missing word is "because". It is the only word that correctly completes the sentence.

9. Answer: C
Explanation: The missing word is "and". It is the only word that correctly completes the sentence.

10. Answer: D
Explanation: The best word choice is "but" to complete the sentence.

11. Answer: A
Explanation: The missing word is "because." It is the only word that correctly completes the sentence.

12. Answer: B
Explanation: The only category the words could fit into is "clothes."

13. Answer: C
Explanation: The student should recognize the attribute used to describe jeans.

14. Answer: A
Explanation: The student should recognize the attribute used to describe a duck.

ANSWER KEY

15. Answer: C
Explanation: The student should recognize the meaning of the word "webbed" from the context of the sentence.

16. Answer: B
Explanation: The student should recognize this as an attribute of tigers.

17. Answer: A
Explanation: The student should recognize the meaning of the word "stripes" from the context of the sentence.

18. Answer: Redid
Explanation: The prefix 're' means again. Redid means to do it again.

19. Answer: Wearing
Explanation: The suffix 'ing' means the act of something. Wearing means the act of wearing something.

20. Answer: Paper
Explanation: The 's' has been added to make 'paper' plural.

5.3. Chapter Review

1. Answer: B
Explanation: There is one shirt, so there is one boy. Making this singular noun possessive requires an 's.

2. Answer: New York
Explanation: New York is the name of a specific place.

3. Answer: C
Explanation: "Jumping" is singular because we is plural.

4. Answer: A
Explanation: If the person is eagerly awaiting dinner, they must be hungry. The words sick, thirsty, nor sad would go with them wanting dinner.

5. Answer: A
Explanation: If the instructions are to not bike down it, it must be dangerous. None of the other words would fit with that warning.

6. Answer: peek; glance; stare; scowl; glare
Explanation: The student should recognize these words as verbs meaning *to look*.

7. Answer: Skip; walk; hop; run; jog
Explanation: The student should recognize these words as verbs meaning *to move*.

8. Answer: Answers will vary.
Explanation: The student will write in a verb that means *to jump*. (Ex: leap)

9. Answer: Answers will vary.
Explanation: The student will write in a verb that means *to see*. (Ex: look)

10. Answer: Emily, April
Explanation: People's names and months of the year should be capitalized. These are proper nouns.

11. Answer: Its birthday is June 10th.
Explanation: The beginning of a sentence should be capitalized. Months of the year should be capitalized. These are proper nouns. A statement should end with a period.

12. Answer: Buttons, Zipper, and Splash
Explanation: Commas are used to separate items in a series. When there are three items, two commas are needed.

13. Answer: Answers may vary.
Explanation: I found my favorite toy outside.

14. Answer: Dismissed
Explanation: The prefix 'dis' means not or the opposite of. Dismissed means the opposite of missed.

5. LANGUAGE

www.prepaze.com   Copyrighted Material

ANSWER KEY

15. Answer: Speechless
Explanation: The suffix 'less' means without. Speechless means without speech.

16. Answer: It
Explanation: The pronoun "It" is needed to replace the non-human item in the sentence.

17. Answer: Wears
Explanation: What is Robin doing? She is wearing ballet shoes. Wears is the correct form of the verb.

18. Answer: Because
Explanation: The person missed school as a result of having a fever. Because shows this cause and effect relationship.

19. Answer: D
Explanation: The student should know that the real-life connection of a ruler is to measure with.

20. Answer: C
Explanation: The student should recognize the meaning of the word and understand other words that are related to it.

21. Answer: A
Explanation: The student should know that the real-life connection of an umbrella is to keep dry from the rain.

22. Answer: B
Explanation: The student should recognize the meaning of the word "asked" and see that "told" is the best possible choice.

23. Answer: B
Explanation: The student should know that the real-life connection or use of a book is to read it.

24. Answer: C
Explanation: The student should know that the real-life connection of a pencil is to write with.

25. Answer: D
Explanation: All of the words contain the digraph blend 'wh'.

26. Answer: Her brother, Alex, does not like the cat.
Explanation: The beginning of a sentence should be capitalized. People's names should be capitalized. These are proper nouns. A statement should end with a period.

27. Answer: A
Explanation: All of the words contain the digraph blend 'th'.

28. Answer: speak
Explanation: The 'ing' has been added to indicate the current action.

29. Answer: Answers will vary.
Explanation: The student will write a sentence about why they like school and use the word *because* in their sentence.

30. Answer: Answers will vary.
Explanation: The student will write a sentence about their two favorite books and use the word *and* in their sentence.

END OF YEAR ASSESSMENT

1. Answer: "Winter Clothes" is the non-fiction text.
Explanation: "Winter Clothes" is the non-fiction text while "Playing in the Snow" is the fiction text.

2. Answer: Answers will vary.
Explanation: The student should explain that the non-fiction text talks about why we need to wear warm clothes in winter. It is not a story like the fiction text.

ANSWER KEY

3. Answer: Answers will vary.
Explanation: Answers must include a reasonable explanation such as, "In this text we learn that the little Prince has been given a cloak by his godmother, though he does not know what to do with it. He also cannot go outside as his legs are weak."

4. Answer: His legs are too weak
Explanation: The text states that the prince's legs are too weak to go outside.

5. Answer: Answers will vary.
Explanation: The student should say something about the dentist helping us with our teeth. The text says that dentists help us keep our teeth strong and healthy.

6. Answer: A checkup is an exam on our teeth.
Explanation: The student should see that the text is defining a checkup as an exam on our teeth.

7. Answer: A predator is an animal that eats another animal.
Explanation: The student should be able to recognize this definition from the text.

8. Answer: large; huge; gigantic; massive; enormous
Explanation: The student should recognize these words as adjectives meaning *big*.

9. Answer: little; tiny; petite; mini; teeny
Explanation: The student should recognize these words as adjectives meaning *small*.

10. Answer: Answers will vary.
Explanation: Answers must include a reasonable explanation such as, "The bird's idea is to fill the pitcher with pebbles to make the water level go up. Then the bird will be able to reach it."

11. Answer: C
Explanation: Putting pebbles in made the water rise.

12. Answer: B
Explanation: The text says that candy bars and chips are junk food.

13. Answer: Answers will vary.
Explanation: The student should understand that eating healthy foods fill up our stomachs so we are not as hungry for junk food.

14. Answer: A
Explanation: Jill is helpful. She is helping Jim learn some new dance moves.

15. Answer: A
Explanation: Jim is willing to try new things. He is learning dance, and he has blue hair, which is also a new thing for him.

16. Answer: Answers will vary.
Explanation: Answers must include a reasonable explanation such as, "The Lion shows kindness to the Mouse by sparing his life and setting it free. The Mouse shows kindness to the Lion by chewing through the rope and setting it free.

17. Answer: Answers will vary
Explanation: Answers might be 'showing kindness to others' or a similar explanation.

18. Answer: Answers will vary.
Explanation: Answers must be along the lines of "The Lion thinks that the Mouse is too small and weak to ever be able to help it."

19. Answer: Answers will vary.
Explanation: The student should explain when to use question marks. Because none of the sentences are asking a question, it does not make sense to use them.

20. Answer: Pea; Answers will vary.
Explanation: The student should be able to explain that pea has a long "e" sound while apple has a short "a" sound.

21. Answer: Shovel; Answers will vary.
Explanation: The student should explain that when they hear a vowel as a separate

END OF YEAR ASSESSMENT

ANSWER KEY

sound that is a syllable. The words gloves and hose have one syllable while shovel has two syllables.

22. Answer: Tommy, Timmy, Tina, Tuesday, December
Explanation: People's names, days, of the week, and months of the year should be capitalized. These are proper nouns.

23. Answer: B
Explanation: All of the words begin with the digraph blend 'st'.

24. Answer: Answers will vary.
Explanation: The student will complete the sentence. (Ex: right behind us)

25. Answer: Answers will vary.
Explanation: The student will complete the sentence. (Ex: candy)

26. Answer: Answers will vary.
Explanation: The kids ran inside because they were excited to see the animals they had been learning about in class.

27. Answer: The students laughed at the elephants' funny trick.
Explanation: The reading says that the elephants sprayed water out of their trucks.

28. Answer: True
Explanation: With the help of others, both girls get to go to special events.

29. Answer: False
Explanation: Both girls are treated badly because other people are jealous of them.

30. Answer: D
Explanation: The illustration is of a flower growing on a pumpkin vine.

31. Answer: cat
Explanation: cat (the 'c' in cat should be lowercase.)

32. Answer: C
Explanation: There is one house, so there is one grandma. Making this singular noun possessive requires an 's.

33. Answer: A
Explanation: If there is glass everywhere, the ornament must be broken. Since that would not relate to touching, smelling, or licking the ornament, shatter is the only obvious choice.

34. Answer: Ms. Kerry is telling the story. Answers will vary.
Explanation: The student should explain that the reading gives the reader clues to know that Ms. Kerry is the storyteller (she waits for the students, she tells them good morning).

35. Answer: The storyteller, Ms. Kerry, wants the band to win first place for a second year in a row.
Explanation: The reading says that the school band won first place last year. She says that she hopes they can win this year, too.

36. Answer: Answers will vary.
Explanation: The student should list some examples in the text — bike path, trail, campground, in a race.

37. Answer: Opinion; Answers will vary.
Explanation: The student will explain why this topic is for an opinion writing piece.

38. Answer: Answers will vary.
Explanation: The student will write an introduction to their story.

39. Answer: B
Explanation: The student should be able to recognize this statement as a fact, not an opinion.

40. Answer: Answers will vary.
Explanation: The student should say what is the same in the two texts — both talk

ANSWER KEY

about caring for pets and having them eat the right food.

41. Answer: Wildlife in Kentucky
Explanation: The book is called *Wildlife in Kentucky*.

42. Answer: Seals eat both fish and meat. Walruses eat both fish and meat.
Explanation: The student should recognize that both seals and walruses eat the same thing: fish and meat.

43. Answer: Seals find their food by using their whiskers. Walruses find their food by using their whiskers, too.
Explanation: The student should recognize that both seals and walruses find their food the same way: by using their whiskers.

44. Answer: John and Jane stopped playing at first because they needed a break.
Explanation: The student should recognize that the friends stopped playing outside because they needed a break at first and not because the weather had changed.

45. Answer: John did not go inside with Jane because he had to grab his baseball glove.
Explanation: The student should recognize that John did not want his baseball glove to be ruined by the rain.

REFERENCES CITED

- *A Class of Twins*, from ReadWorks
- *A Clean Park*, from ReadWorks
- *Callie Learns to Listen*, from ReadWorks
- *Henry's Homework Folder*, from ReadWorks
- Passage adapted from "*Little Red Riding Hood*"
- Passage adapted from "*Pear Blossom*"
- Passage adapted from "*Puss in Boots*"
- Passage adapted from "*Raggedy Ann Learns a Lesson*"
- Passage adapted from "*The Little Glass Slipper*"
- Passage adapted from "*The Little Red Hen*"
- *The Beach*, from ReadWorks
- *The Crow and the Pitcher*, by Aesop
- *The Hare and the Tortoise*, by Aesop
- *The New Scooter*, from ReadWorks

Made in United States
North Haven, CT
17 February 2023

Lalique for Collectors

Katharine Morrison McClinton

CHARLES SCRIBNER'S SONS / NEW YORK

Copyright © 1975 Katharine M. McClinton

Library of Congress Cataloging in Publication Data

McClinton, Katharine Morrison.
　　Lalique for collectors.

　　Bibliography: p.
　　Includes index.
　　1. Lalique, René, 1860–　　2. Glassware, French.
3. Decoration and ornament—Art nouveau.　　4. Art deco.
I. Title.
NK5198.L44.M32　　　748.2′9′24　　74-14015
ISBN 0-684-14101-9

This book published simultaneously in the
United States of America and in Canada—
Copyright under the Berne Convention

All rights reserved. No part of this book
may be reproduced in any form without the
permission of Charles Scribner's Sons.

3 5 7 9 11 13 15 17 19　C/MD　20 18 16 14 12 10 8 6 4 2

Printed in the United States of America

*For Erma
with affection and appreciation*

ACKNOWLEDGEMENTS

My appreciation for valuable assistance in the gathering of material for this book goes to the following:

    Robert Sistrunk, Antaeus Gallery Inc.
    Richard Peters and Sheldon Barr, Sybarites Gallery Inc.
    John Jesse, London, England
    Lillian and Paul Nassau
    Minna Rosenblatt
    Barry Friedman
    Felix Marcilhac, Paris, France
    Martin Cohen
    Dennis R. Anderson, Curator of Decorative Arts,
       Chrysler Museum at Norfolk, Virginia
    Christian Rohlfing, Administrative Director,
       Cooper-Hewitt Museum of Decorative Arts and Design

I also owe a special thank you to my editor, Elinor Parker, for her careful reading and editing of the manuscript.

Contents

Introduction / 1
Jewelry and Goldsmith Work / 9
Decorative Glass Work / 33
    Glass Vases / 33
    Statuettes and Decorative Motifs / 70
    Clocks, Mirrors, and Picture Frames / 82
    Perfume Bottles / 90
    Dinner Services, Candlesticks, and Annual Plate / 104
    Radiator Caps and Paperweights / 118
    Desk Furnishings: Inkstands, Blotters, Seals, and Ashtrays / 129
    Boxes and Bonbonnières / 137
    Lamps, Lighting Fixtures, and Architectural Details / 146
Bibliography / 152

Introduction

THE ART OF RENE LALIQUE IS UNIQUE IN THAT IT COVERED two periods of decorative styles—Art Nouveau and Art Deco. Lalique's jewelry was the finest goldsmith's work produced in Art Nouveau style. He was not a follower but an innovator and his jewelry produced in the 1890s revolutionized the design and materials of the goldsmith's art. Lalique was more concerned with the decorative element and craftsmanship than he was with materials. His pieces of jewelry became valuable and highly stylized small works of art. Instead of precious expensive stones he used irregular-shaped baroque pearls, semi-precious stones, enamel, and translucent horn. He made brooches, combs, pendants, and other pieces of jewelry in his own imaginative non-traditional forms. In his jewelry Lalique combined all the forms and materials of plastic art.

After the Universal Exhibition of 1900 Lalique found himself deluged with more jewelry commissions than he could fill. Also there were many imitators who debased his style. Although Lalique continued to produce jewelry for a number of years more he lost his incentive and his interest gradually turned to glass. Lalique had already studied and experimented with glass. He had included small beads of glass and medallions and plaques of colored *pâte-de-verre* in his articles of gold and enamelled jewelry and he had made cups and small flacons of glass. Soon after 1900 his interest centered on glassmaking; he began specializing in the production of small flacons and *services de table*. In 1898 Lalique exhibited a glass and silver vase, and in the 1902 Salon he showed two *coupes*.

In about 1902 Lalique acquired a small glassworks at Clairfontaine in the forest near Rambouillet where he set up a small kiln and employed four workers. Here Lalique made experimental statuettes, unique *cire perdue* vases, and glass panels which he mounted in doors and chandeliers. About this time Lalique designed and built his sumptuous premises at 40, cours de la Reine in Paris where he installed his workshop and all his services. The doors of the house had panels of *pâte-de-verre* and he also created the furniture and interior decorations and architectural embellishments. In 1905 a shop for the sale of his artifacts was opened at Place Vendôme No. 24.

In 1907-1908 when François Coty invited Lalique to design bottles for his perfumes Lalique accepted the commission with enthusiasm and this collaboration was successful from the start. Later Lalique designed bottles for other perfume manufacturers. The bottles were made by Legras & Cie. de St. Denis, a glass manufacturer with a factory on the Seine.

In 1909 Lalique opened his own glassworks at Combs called "Verrerie de Combs-la-Ville." Here Lalique manufactured his glass vases, lamps, statuettes, and various small accessories of glass executed in molds with applied foliage, animals, and insects. The pieces were also often ornamented with engraving and enamel. These pieces were exhibited in 1912 for the first time and this date also marks the end of Lalique's production of metal jewelry.

Between 1918 and 1922 Lalique constructed a large glassworks at Wingen sur Moder in the Bas-Rhin called "Verrerie d'Alsace René Lalique & Cie."

Here Lalique produced articles of molded glass on a large commercial scale with hundreds of reproductions of each article. With his cast glass with molded ornament ("*verre moulé décoré en creux*") Lalique again became an innovator. Although Lalique's importance as a glassmaker came late in the period, the designs of his major production of glass are easily traced to Art Nouveau. Yet like the majority of the artists at this time Lalique reacted against Art Nouveau which had now become cheapened by commercialism. In his search for a new decorative idiom Lalique turned to the stylized forms of Art Deco for much of his glass. Here Lalique again showed his originality, for although the majority of the glassworkers were creating glass with designs of many colors Lalique's glass was monotone. He was interested in the natural qualities of the glass and the form of the articles as much as he was in the ornamentation.

In Lalique's career as a *verrerier* his aims were strictly commercial and he sought to sell as many reproductions of his creations as possible. The glass was mass-produced and hundreds of copies were made of each piece, but a high quality of design and originality was always present. Although the concept of the original model was by Lalique—some later by his grand-daughter—Lalique did not play any active part in the making of the glass except supervising the manufacture. Lalique had a thoroughly modern attitude toward his glass. He accepted mechanical methods of production which allowed him to sell at prices within the reach of many. His color was monotone and the shapes were simple and rational. The decoration consisted of motifs from nature, female figures, and children. His dinner services and perfume flasks made Lalique glass known to the general public and his lighting fixtures and features such as portals and fountains of Lalique design were architecturally useable. Also, since Lalique glass was unlike any glass made previously, its originality and decorative qualities made it in constant demand in France, and in England as well.

By 1925 Lalique had become the most important manufacturer of fine mass-produced glass in France and at the Exposition Internationale des Arts Décoratifs et Industriels Modernes held in Paris in that year Lalique was commissioned to design the fountains and glass portal of the exposition. Examples of Lalique glass were also to be found in the various French pavilions of the exposition. The most important Lalique exhibit apart from the fountains and screens was the dining room in Le Pavillon de la Manufacture Nationale de Sèvres with its beams of molded glass designed by Lalique and lighted from concealed panels. On the massive glass table was a setting of Sèvres porcelain and wine glasses and candlesticks of molded and engraved Lalique glass.

Architectural glass was one of Lalique's most important contributions. Lalique's churches and shrines are outstanding works of modern ecclesiastic art. He designed complete altars with crucifixes, candlesticks, and reredos of molded glass. The glass panels, windows back of the altar, and the glass altar rail in the Chapelle de la Vierge Fidèle all have the Madonna lily as a motif. Lalique also designed many figurines of the Virgin and Saints.

When the French Line ship "Normandie" was launched in 1932 she carried important examples of Lalique glass. The main dining salon, 305 feet in length, 46 feet in width, and 25 feet in height, had walls constructed of thirty-eight glass panels, and the room was lighted by two gigantic chandeliers and twelve decorative standard lights of Lalique glass.

Through the offices of Breves Galleries, London, a great deal of Lalique glass paneling and lighting fixtures was used in important decorating projects in England in the 1930s. Lalique maintained his important position during the Depresssion period and each year his repertory of stock designs was increased. He managed to keep up with the times since his style evolution followed the changes that affected design generally. However, in 1937 Lalique closed the factory at Combs-la-Ville and between 1939 and 1946 all production of Lalique glass was discontinued. The factory was partially destroyed in the war and the craftsmen scattered, and in 1945 Lalique died. Although the firm continues today the majority of the most beautiful and artistic pieces have been discontinued. In many cases the original molds were destroyed and other pieces have been found too expensive for reproduction today. This has opened the field of Lalique glass to the antiques collector. Today collecting Lalique glass has become such an active pursuit that prices have risen and Lalique glass has become an important and expensive field for only the advanced collector.

The following quotation from *The Architectural Review*, February, 1928, which was reprinted in the Breves Galleries catalogue of "Lalique Lights and Decorations" is an indication of the esteem and popularity of Lalique at the height of his career. He is described as "Artist Master Craftsman"—at once an honorable and perfect description of René Lalique.

> For he is an artist in an artist's sense of the word; his knowledge is so secure that he is able to bring elimination to a fine point; each line of his design is essential, he never strikes a false note.
>
> Lalique served a long apprenticeship; he originally began life as a goldsmith and jeweller. This helps to explain the beautiful delicacy of his work and the extraordinary detail which he introduces into his glass work, detail which, though it delights the eye, never obscures the meaning and pleasure of the whole design.
>
> The simplest forms of Nature delight him most, and in his translation of them one sees one of the most attractive facets of his genius. . . .
>
> With his human figures the chief thought which comes to one's mind is their rhythm. One knows, of course, that they are static, but the feeling of movement is so brilliantly expressed that one subconsciously carries on the movement and the figures live again.
>
> When he uses colour (always with great restraint) it is always to enhance the meaning; be it a hunting scene with archers he chooses dark ruby, be it mermaids and fishes he takes the pearly blue light over the sea at dawn.
>
> One may sum up his genius aptly in the words of Paul Fallot: 'His palette is sumptuous, but always temperate, he loves delicate harmonies, tone on tone, and in his invention of forms his fantasies obey the order of logic.'

A later estimate is not so generous. It speaks of the "increasing overelaboration of Lalique's designs." Also a gross abuse of the decorative resources of acid-engraved and sandblasted glass and of sentimentality is present in some of Lalique's designs. Lalique had found a popular repertory of design motifs and these were repeated again and again from important vases to paperweights and tiny ashtrays, and this commercialism sometimes interferes with our final estimate of his present place in the glass world.

Lalique glass contains over 24 percent lead oxide and therefore it is properly termed "lead crystal." Crystal is composed, fused, and treated in the same way as ordinary glass with the fundamental difference that it contains at least 24 percent lead oxide; glass does not. Crystal when cold will catch the light and reflect it with an unmistakable metallic sheen and brilliance. Ordinary glass with no lead has no sparkle. Lead crystal also has a lasting musical tone when tapped with the finger, while glass has a dull tone. Crystal is also heavier and softer than ordinary glass which makes it easier to cut and engrave. Lalique is especially famous for his soft satin-finish lead crystal which has an unmistakable personal character of its own.

Lalique understood the glass materials and recognized their possibilities. His glass was produced in powdered form and then cast in hot metal molds. The work of Lalique depends in most cases upon shaping by blowing or pressing in a mold and therefore does not give the impression of blown glass. (Blown wares were almost always confined to stemware and large vases, however even in these instances the stem and foot of the glass and the neck of the vase were molded.)

The light passing through the glass reflects the opal-blue tints and dramatizes the designs molded on the outside. The color of Lalique glass was obtained by metal oxides added to the glass batch; and I am indebted to the collector Robert Sistrunk for the following list of metal oxides used by Lalique to produce the colors of his glass.

> Gold oxide produced fiery and blue opalescents and ruby reds.
> Silver produced greens.
> Platinum was used for tones of gray.
> Tin gave cloudy opalescent "clam broth" effects.

Black oxide of manganese produced amethysts, purples, and black. Cobalt produced blues.

Of course the color varies according to the proportions used and the basic composition of the glass batch and to the degree of heat and the length of cooking time after the addition of the coloring agent. The color of some blown vases is altered by interior casing. When enameling was desired the powdered materials were mixed with oil thus forming paint. The decorator painted the desired design on the glass with a brush and the piece was then fired in a small furnace in order to bring about the proper fusion in the enamels and their union with the glass. Parts of the molded designs were treated with acids to produce a frosted or satin effect in contrast to the bright glistening polished effects. Iridescent effects were produced on the surface of the glass by subjecting it to gaseous fumes in a muffle furnace.

Some few pieces of Lalique glass were made by the *cire perdue* or lost wax method. These designs were first modeled in wax, then covered with a ceramic paste. After the paste hardened the paste-covered model was heated to melt out the wax model. This left a hollow ceramic mold. Into this mold the molten glass was poured. When the glass had hardened the mold was broken away leaving a perfect reproduction of the wax model in glass. This method produced a unique piece.

Although some of the original Lalique designs are still in production the marks on them have been changed and no longer bear the initial "R." Collecting interest is usually confined to the years before René Lalique's death in 1945. One way of judging the age of the glass is to look for signs of wear on the embossed surfaces.

The "Catalogue des Verreries de René Lalique" 1932 is a valuable source of information. I have given the Catalogue numbers of the articles since many pieces are marked with numbers in addition to the Lalique signature. In most cases these numbers refer to the 1932 Catalogue. However this does not mean that the piece was made at that date; in fact it indicates that it was made before 1932. The number of examples of each piece is also not exact because the Catalogue only indicates how many pieces were available, but it also is an indication of how many were actually made—whether in the hundreds or the thousands. If few pieces of a particular vase or object are listed in the Catalogue, as in the case of the vase "Méduse," it may indicate an early design which is sold out. I have given the French names of the articles since they are the key to the design but they also add romance and foreign flavor to the collecting.

Jewelry and Goldsmith Work

René Jules Lalique was born June 4, 1860, at Hay, Marne. He studied drawing at Turgot College and continued his studies at the Ecole des Arts Décoratifs in Paris during an apprenticeship to the important Paris jeweler M. Louis Aucoc. From 1878 to 1880 Lalique studied in England. When he returned to France he worked as a freelance designer for various Paris jewelers including Aucoc, Jaca, Cartier, Renn, Gariod, Hamelin, and Destape. In addition to jewelry, in the early years of his career he drew designs for fans, wallpapers, and textiles. For a short time Lalique collaborated with Charles Arfidson to furnish drawings of jewelry for the publication *Le Bijou*. In his spare time Lalique studied sculpture with the artist Lequien who was the son of his old teacher at Turgot College.

In 1883 Lalique entered a partnership with Varenne (Lalique et Varenne) which lasted two years. During this time Lalique designed many original and amusing trinkets including a balloon, a mill and a jumping jack. Lalique later took over the shop of Jules Destape where he continued to execute orders for the more important jewelers of Paris. In 1885 Lalique set up his own atelier and for the first time exhibited jewels of his own design and workmanship at the Exposition Universelle of 1889 in Paris.

In 1890 Lalique moved his atelier to larger quarters at 20, rue Thérèse, at the corner of the avenue de l'Opéra. Here he installed a complete glass workshop. He also collaborated with two sculptors and experimented in several other mediums including enameling, employing these various plastic arts in the jewelry and other artifacts which he exhibited each year in the salons.

As early as 1887 Lalique was making coffres, cups, swords, and vases. There were small flacons entwined with serpents, and a serpent's head as the stopper. Other flacons were studded with jewels. There were complete sets of *orfèvrerie de toilette* including mirrors, brushes, boxes for powder and soap, and bottles for toilet water and perfume. These articles continued to be made later when Lalique turned to commercial glassmaking. At an early date Lalique also considered making *orfèvrerie de table* including serving dishes and *couverts* of flat silver. However his jewelry was in such demand that he had no time for additional enterprises, also such articles necessitated equipping a special workshop.

In 1893 Lalique was given a prize of 500 francs for a chalice ornamented with his thistle motif. There are a group of these cups or chalices with rich ornamentation of metal, ivory, enamel, semi-precious stones, and glass that were made at about this time. The motifs used to decorate them were both figural and floral. One chalice of gold, ivory, and enamel had sculptured figures at the base of the stem and an enamel frieze of prophets around the cup. Other chalices had nude figures of ivory or *pâte-de-verre* and enameled wheat or grape motifs. A cup of clear crystal with an openwork pattern of silver pine-needles—one of a set of six or more—is in the collection of Maurice Rheims in Paris. Rheims also owns a pectoral cross of silver-gilt, enamel, and mother-of-pearl anemones set within a framework of thorns. These pieces have more decorative than religious significance but as works of art the chalices rank with antique chalices.

During this period, 1890–1893, Lalique executed several curious pieces including a small head of John the Baptist, a *cire perdue* panel representing a centaur and a centauress, and several vases of glass of various colors. Before Lalique moved to the rue Thérèse atelier he had been busy to a great extent with the execution of diamond-set pieces for the better known jewelry firms of Paris. Now with enlarged quarters and the assistance of several workmen he could develop his passion for enameling and his ability as a sculptor and a glassmaker.

Lalique's first glass objects were exhibited in the Salon of 1895. Among these pieces was an oval cameo of a nude woman combing her tresses. In 1896 Lalique executed a large brooch with colored crystallizations of landscape and snow-capped trees called "L'Hiver" for the Russian nobility. The theme of this piece was repeated at least once in a pendant in blue and white enamel on gold which is now in the Museum für Kunst und Gewerbe, Hamburg, Germany.

Lalique's imaginative novel color combinations and shapes and new techniques brought about a revolution in the design of jewelry, which together with the excellence of his design and workmanship made Lalique one of the leading figures in the field of Art Nouveau. Lalique remained faithful to tradition in his designs. Although the subject matter was drawn from nature, he drew upon strange or eerie aspects—the coils of writhing snakes, insects with the torso of a woman, a green lizard with gaping mouth twisted around a flacon, a beetle clutching a fly, or a huge bizarre cock's head with its beak grasping a large diamond. The materials too were dramatic and revolutionary. Lalique often rejected the traditional diamond, emerald, or ruby in favor of semi-precious stones—the opal, jade, coral, amethyst, crystal and chrysolite, combined with colorful enamel and *pâte-de-verre* in various colors. Color, design, and workmanship were always more important to Lalique than precious materials. In addition to gold and silver Lalique used iron, copper, aluminum, brass, ivory, enamel, and mother-of-pearl. His models inspired by nature—the animal and vegetable world including flowers, trees, peacocks, serpents, and insects—were used again and again in his original fantastic designs.

Early brooches and pendants included swans, peacocks, serpents, fish, dragonflies, butterflies, bees, birds, rooster heads, and lizards. The motifs from the botanical world included iris, pond lilies, poppies, orchids, roses, violets, fuchsias, thistles, cow parsley, grapes and grape vines, and pine cones and branches. The pine seemed to be a special favorite with Lalique. There are several pendants with women's heads of ivory or chrysolite surrounded by frames of green enamel pine cones. Pine cones also formed the motif for rings; a watch was ornamented with enamel pine cones, and when Lalique built his own house and atelier the doorway was ornamented with a sculptured pine tree and a wrought iron balcony of pine branches. Grapes, berries, and various fruits were also favorite motifs. However, the most characteristics motif of Lalique jewelry was the nude. Full length nude figures centered pendants and brooches and several nude figures were often entwined with gold, enamel, and semi-precious stones such as opals. There were strange figures of Salomés and Salammbôs of Flaubert and Gustave Moreau, nymphs and other figures from mythology and legend, as well as the modern nudes of Art Nouveau with their flowing tresses. Sculptured heads of ivory or semi-precious stones, such as agate, set in Art Nouveau swirled line designs were exhibited by Lalique in 1898. One corsage ornament has a sculptured agate head with flowing tresses of gold ornamented with flowers centered with small diamonds and a comb of ivory has a draped figure of ivory set among garlands of gold flowers accented with enamel and diamonds.

Although nature and Art Nouveau seem to dominate the designs of Lalique jewelry there were other important influences. Lalique had studied the history of ornament and knew the decorative arts of ancient as well as modern art. The Renaissance influence was important in some of the brooches made in the 1890s and this influence is illustrated in a brooch and pendant exhibited at the Paris Salon of 1895. These pieces had outlines of Renaissance bandwork and the brooch with gold, opals, and amethysts has a figure of a classic nude.

The Egyptian influence on Lalique was especially important and many of the pieces of early jewelry were of Egyptian inspiration. A page of original sketches in *Art et Décoration,* (1897), includes a *flacon* of lotus design and a diadem with borders of Egyptian winged figures and geometric motifs. Enamel borders of Egyptian motifs are also seen on pendants, combs, bracelets, and diadems. A corsage exhibited at the Exhibition of 1900 in Paris was ornamented with a band of scarabs.

Lalique was also fascinated by the groups of veiled and nude figures in Roman and Pompeiian frescoes and he used these figures in plaques of ivory and *pâte-de-verre* in his pendants and brooches. These groups of classic figures were later used on Lalique's glass pendants and on the covers of small glass boxes. Lalique's jewelry also shows the influence of Arabian, Assyrian, and Oriental art; from Merovingian sources came the use of cabochon stones.

Much of Lalique's early jewelry was concentrated on articles for the adornment of women. In addition to brooches, rings, bracelets, pendants, necklaces, belts, corsages, and collars there were diadems and even hat pins and hair pins. One of the articles that Lalique made in his early period was the comb. There are numerous examples of ivory and horn combs with top ornaments of gold, enamel, and precious and semi-precious stones. Motifs on combs included butterflies, bats, nude figures, angels, and a forest scene in enamel. One comb of horn with a large enamel pansy is called "Pensée Fanée," but the most elaborate comb designs were the figures of the Three Graces, bees and a honeycomb, and a peacock.

Between 1891 and 1894 Lalique made an important group of jewels for Sarah Bernhardt which were worn in her roles of "Iseyl," "Gismonda," and "Théodora." These included diadems, collars, and belts of large size and ornate decoration since they were to be seen at a distance. They were made of silver, semi-precious stones, brass, and even aluminum. Lalique also designed stage jewels for Mme Bartet in her role of Bérénice. One large diadem of aluminum had a border of the winged figure of Isis, lotus flowers, and five medallions with scenes of the life of courtesans sculptured in ivory bas-reliefs. These theatrical jewels were greatly admired and created good publicity for

Lalique. He also made many jewels such as collars, necklaces, and diadems for important titled women of France, Russia, Italy, Spain, and England.

In 1894 Lalique exhibited an ivory bas-relief in the Salon de la Société des Artistes Français. He also engraved several metals at this time. In the Salon of 1896 Lalique exhibited a group of jewelry, several vases, and an important coffre, "Le Triomphe de la Richesse," which had figures of men and women in bronze relief as handles. The most unique exhibit was a bracelet of horn, since it was the first time this material had been used in any except barbarian jewelry.

However, the most important exhibition of Lalique jewelry was at the Exposition Universelle of 1900 in Paris. The articles were displayed in a vitrine constructed with a grille of iron accented with female bronze figures. This grille served as a background screen in front of which the jewels were displayed on a ground of white moiré silk. Lambrequins of gray were appliquéd with velour bats. The rug and the draperies were of gray and on the wall at the back was a large painting by Georges Picard which represented small sylphs frolicking by moonlight among the trees at the border of a lake. A mirror reflected two huge bronze serpents. In this spectacular setting Lalique exhibited twenty horn combs ornamented with enamel, opals, amethysts, and chrysoprase; and a variety of collars and diadems. A dramatic corsage ornament with enamel serpents out of whose mouths cascaded ropes of baroque pearls was an important piece. There was also a brooch with nudes of ivory surrounded by enamel snakes. An ornament in the shape of a cock's head held an immense yellow diamond in its beak and a large dragonfly, with wings of translucent enamel scintillating with rose diamonds, had a bust and head of a woman. This group of oversized fantastic objects was the crowning point of Lalique's career as a goldsmith.

Looking at the jewels shown in this exhibit leaves no doubt that Lalique represented a unique and important position in the history of jewelry. His dramatic conception of subject matter that could transform a sketch from nature into a surrealistic fantasy, his breath-taking color schemes executed in transparent *plique à jour,* and his ability as a sculptor in miniature entitle Lalique to the rank of genius. This exhibition was such a sensation and the demand for Lalique jewelry became so great that Lalique was obliged to take on several collaborators. The two names that merit mention at this time according to Henri Vever were a young sculptor named Hoffmann and Chardon, a talented designer. It is also known that both Alphonse Mucha and Eugène Feuillâtre at one time worked with Lalique. Lalique himself worked in many techniques including ceramics, enamel, glass painting, *pâte-de-verre* and engraving. At one time he registered a *poinçon* and a stamp which he used in addition to the "R.LALIQUE" stamp in block letters with which he marked the majority of the pieces of his jewelry, although early pieces are often engraved "Lalique" or "R.Lalique" in script.

In Lalique's transition from jewelry to glass he included glass in many pieces of jewelry with elaborate and expensive settings. Glass plaquettes similar to those of ivory which Lalique made early in his career were at first carved by hand but later the designs were molded and mass-produced. These molded versions of various shapes with designs of nude and draped figures and garlands were so successful that they were continued long after Lalique had shifted the emphasis of his business to mass-produced glassware. In the earlier pieces the glass was often frosted or opaline and bracelets and necklaces continued to be made in both colored and colorless crystal; later glass pendants were only made in colorless glass.

There were oval, round, and heart-shaped pendants. From 150 to 200 of each oval design were made in colorless crystal. The designs included sirens, a figurine with wings, a figurine swinging on a floral rope, a figurine with a scarf over her face and a figurine with a scarf *de dos.* There was also an oval pendant with a design of molded fuchsias, lily of the valley, and mistletoe and one with clover leaves. Round pendants were made in the following designs: "2 Figurines et Fleurs," "3 Papillons" (butterflies), and "2 Perruches" (parakeets). There were also attractive heart-shaped pendants with beaded edges and molded cupid figurines with wings, figurines with flowers, and a heart-shaped pendant with molded swans. The figures on these pendants are molded into the underside of the glass, the transparent surfaces of blank purity being hollowed out by light modeling. This type of work is representative of much of Lalique's early work as a glassmaker. "R.Lalique" in block letters is engraved on the edge of these pieces. Although in the 1890s Lalique used glass for cups, vases, and bowls with mountings of metal and enamel, it was not until after 1900 that glass was increasingly used in his jewelry. Some pieces were frosted and ivory-toned in simulation of ivory.

Glass beads in the shape of leaves and flowers were attached to gold chains. These necklaces were made in both colored and colorless glass and judging from the numbers which were recorded in the 1932 Lalique catalogue they must have been very popular. Necklaces with twelve round and oval beads were made in colored glass. A necklace with beads in the form of ivy leaves was made in both colored and colorless glass. Necklaces with lily of the valley motifs were made in various lengths in colored glass. There were also short necklaces with larger glass motifs. A necklace with sixty beads of dahlia motif was manufactured in vast quantity in colored and colorless glass. The zig-zag Art Deco motif was also popular. As listed in the 1932 catalogue 900 of these necklaces were available in colorless glass and 1,000 in colored glass. A necklace composed of dahlias and roundels was also popular. Necklaces with *décors divers* were also available and there were necklaces of molded ferns and lotus flowers.

Extendable bracelets were made to match many of the necklaces. Bracelets were also made in many other designs of molded beads including cherries, palmettes, ferns, fish, cocks, tomtits, sparrows, griffons, castles, and suns. All of these bracelets were made in both colored and colorless glass and in quantities of hundreds of each design. A bracelet of roundels with enameling was available in large quantity in both colored and colorless glass.

For those collectors who cannot afford the one of a kind pieces of Lalique's early enamel and gem jewelry these later mass-produced glass necklaces, pendants, and bracelets are available and are also again in fashion.

Pendant of Renaissance design. Lalique, 1895. (Henri Vever, *La Bijouterie Française au XIXe Siècle*, III.)

Comb with bat motif and moonstones. Lalique, 1900. (Art et Décoration, 1900.)

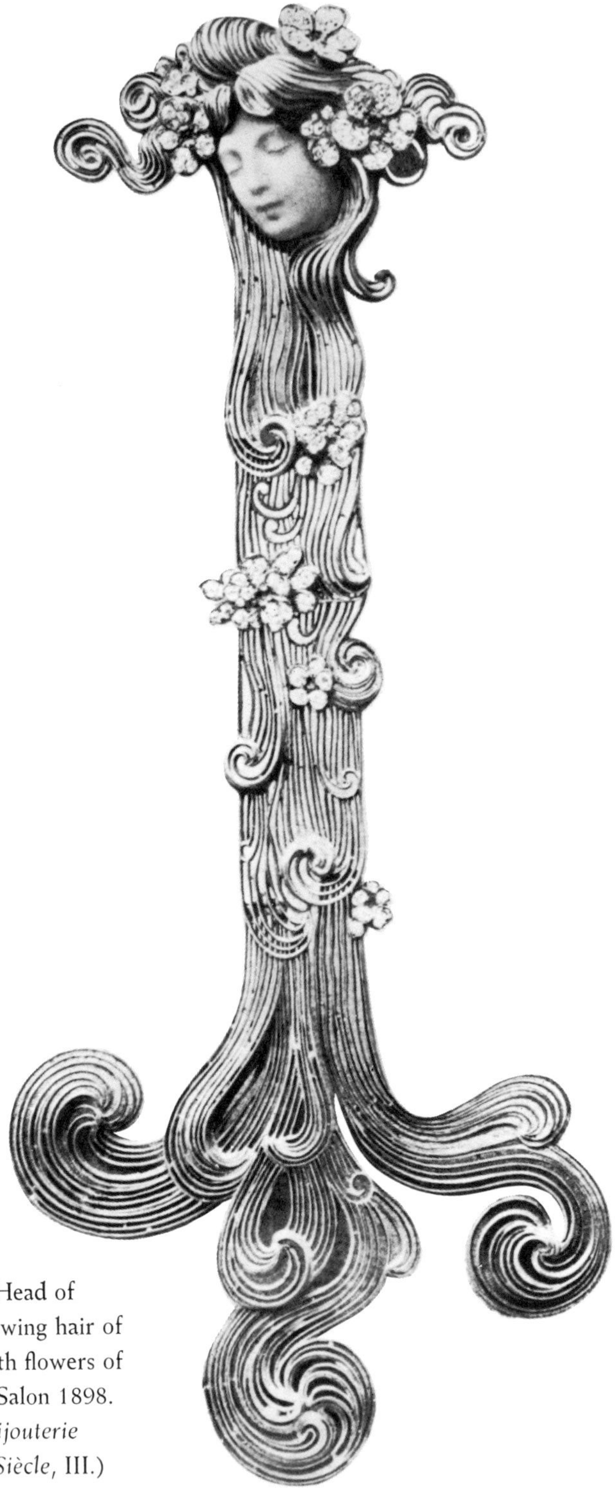

Corsage ornament. Head of sculptured agate, flowing hair of gold ornamented with flowers of diamonds. Lalique. Salon 1898. (Henri Vever, *La Bijouterie Française au XIXe Siècle*, III.)

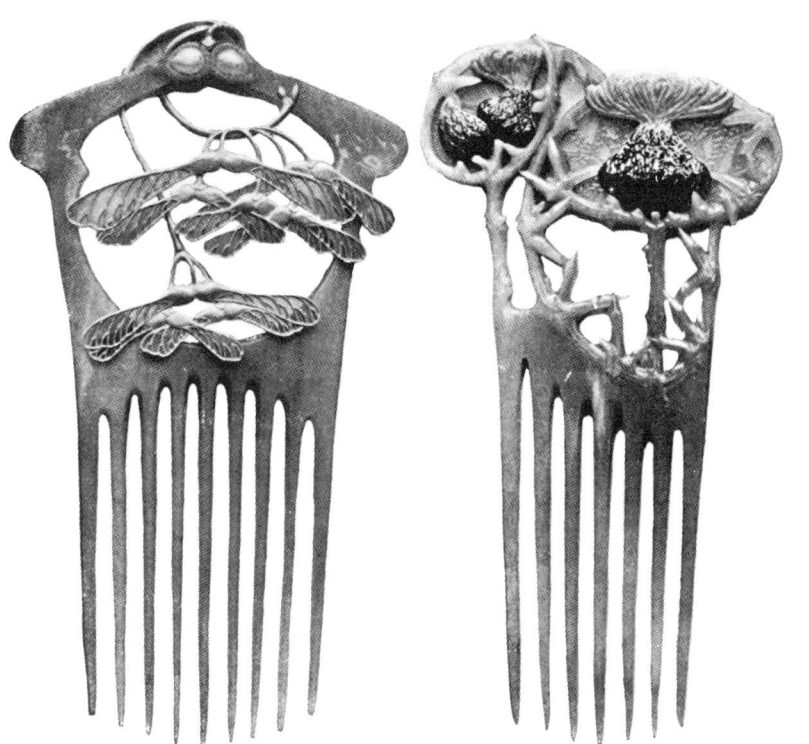

Two combs with plant and insect motifs enriched with enamel. Lalique c.1900. (Art et Décoration, 1900.)

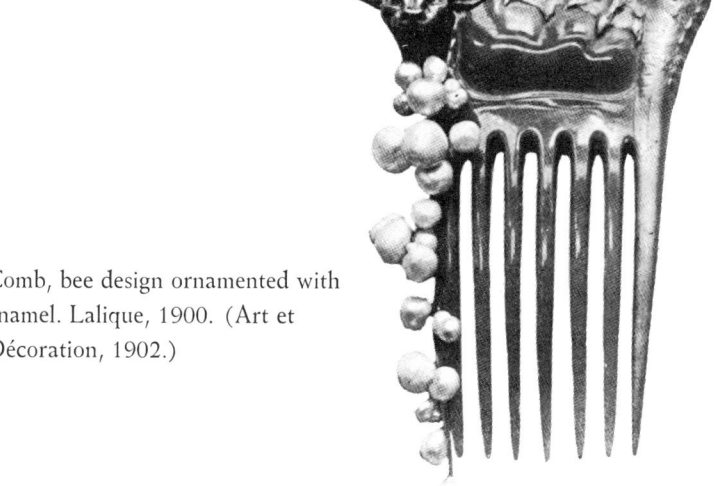

Comb, bee design ornamented with enamel. Lalique, 1900. (Art et Décoration, 1902.)

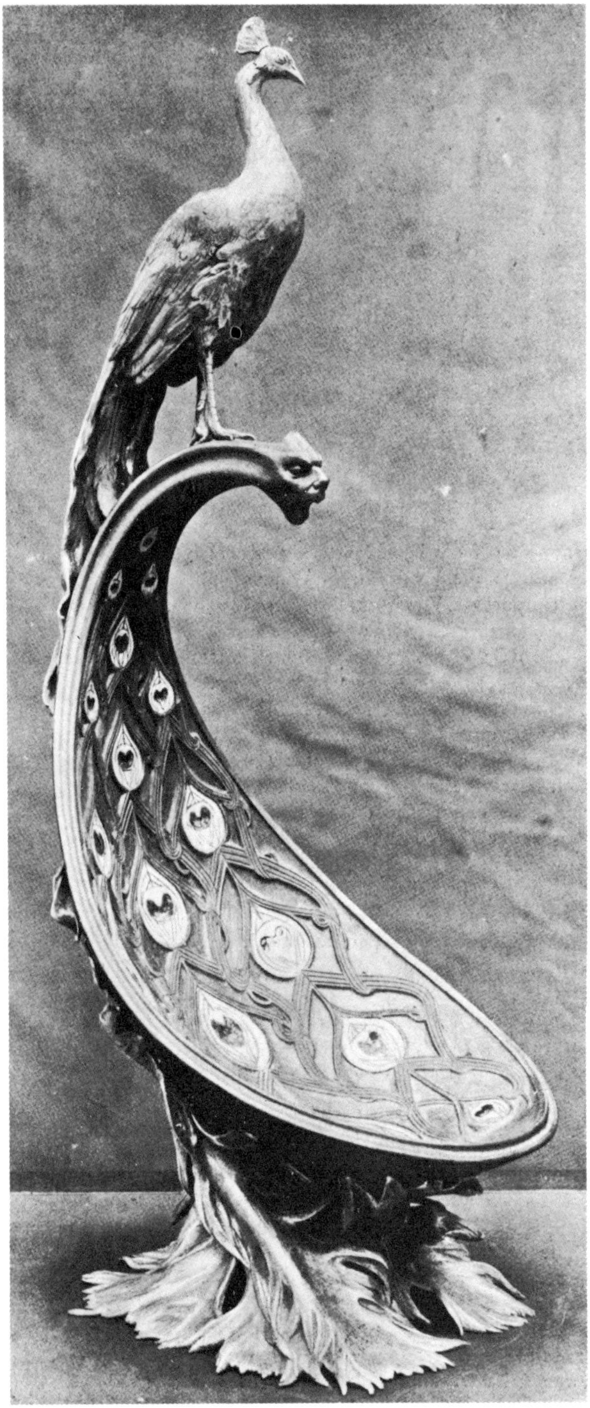

Pendant, grey, black and orange enamel and gold leaves and woman's head. Stamped "Lalique" c.1900 (The Metropolitan Museum of Art, Gift of Albert M. Kohn, 1910.)

Left, Sculptured peacock, metalwork and enamel. Lalique c.1895-1900. (Art et Décoration, 1900.)

Opposite, Gold chain with conventionalized daisy motifs decorated with colored enamel and brilliants. Engraved "R. Lalique." c.1900. (The Metropolitan Museum of Art, Edward C. Moore, Jr. Gift, 1924.)

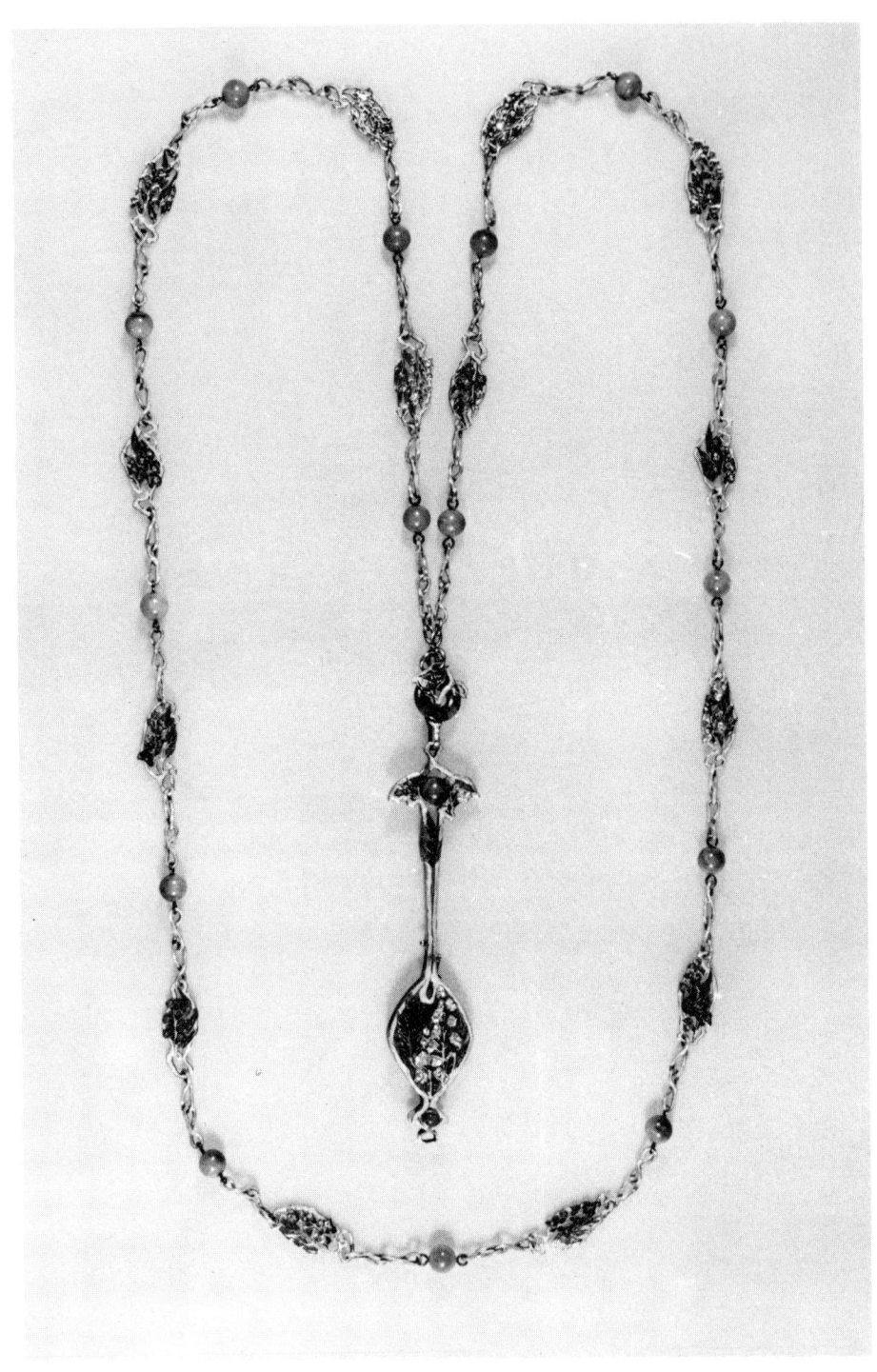

Lorgnette and chain, gold, enamel, jade, glass and diamonds. Lalique, c.1900.
(The Metropolitan Museum of Art, Gift of Mrs. J. G. Phelps Stokes, 1965.)

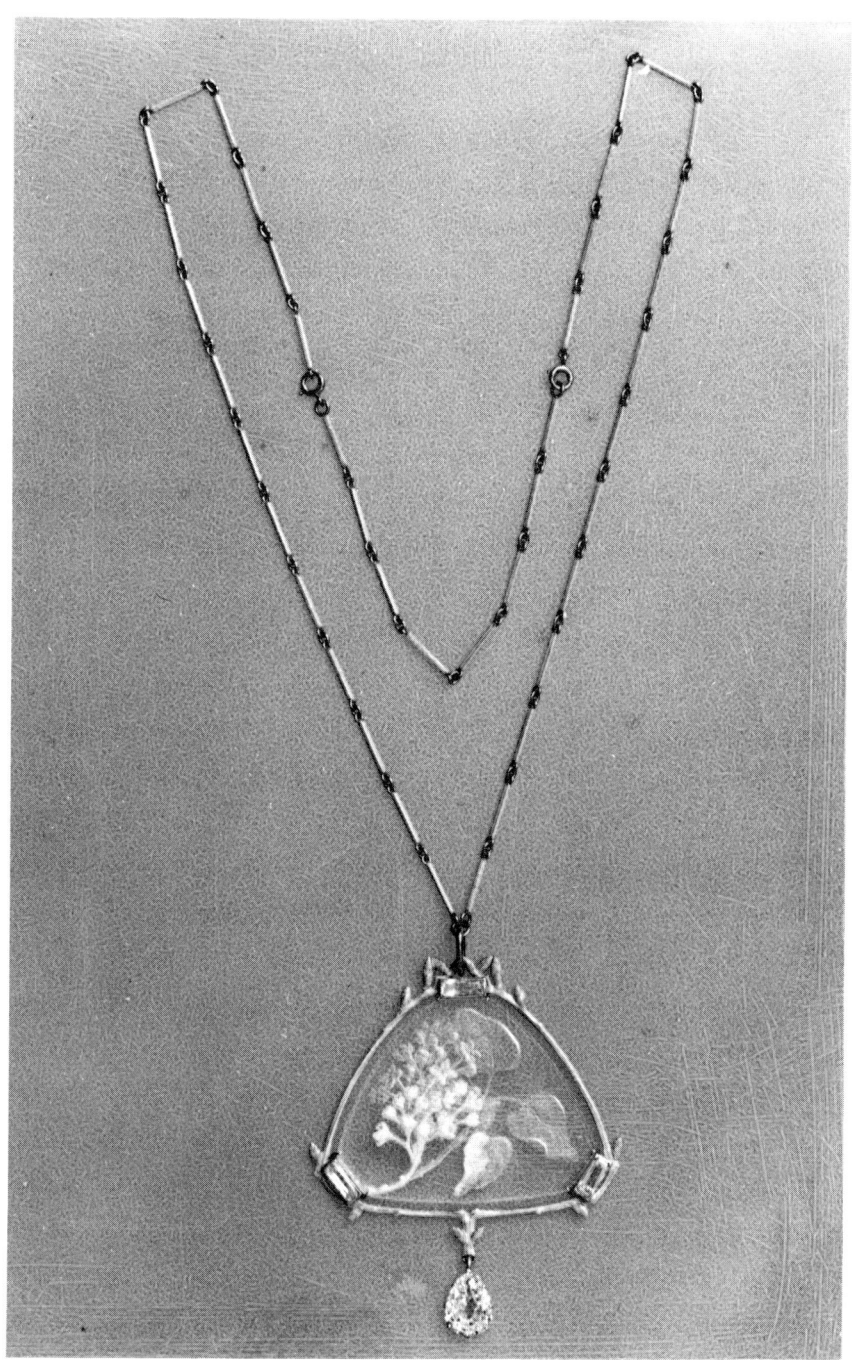

Pendant and chain, lilac motif. Gold, diamonds, enamel and intaglio on glass. Stamped "Lalique." 1905-1910. (The Metropolitan Museum of Art, Gift of Miss Mary F. Failing, 1944, offered in memory of Henrietta Ellison Failing.)

Serpent corsage ornament, blue and green enamel. Lalique, Paris Exposition, 1900. (Henri Vever, *La Bijouterie Française au XIXe Siècle*, III.)

Cock's head comb, enamel, gold and stones. Lalique, Paris Exposition, 1900. (Art et Décoration, 1900.)

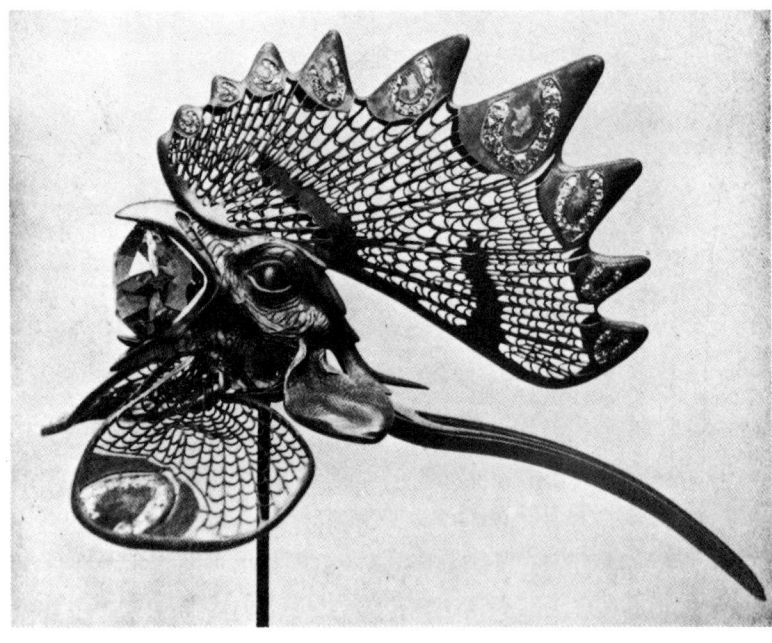

Pendant. Female head in crystal, with silver hair, poppies and suspended baroque pearl. Signed "Lalique" in block letters. Gulbenkian Collection. (*Connoisseur*, August, 1971.)

Insect-shaped pendant of crystal, sapphires, diamonds and moonstone. Signed "Lalique." Gulbenkian Collection. (*Connoisseur*, August, 1971.)

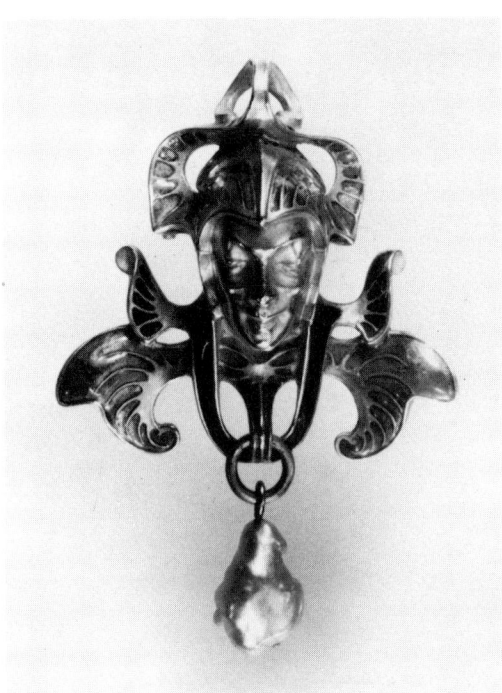

Pendant brooch modelled with a woman's head enclosed in helmet of gold leaves enamelled in pale and dark green, hung with a baroque pearl. Stamped "Lalique." c.1900. (Sotheby & Co. Sale, March 9, 1970.)

Gold brooch with blue and white glass poppies. Stems with diamonds and buds and leaves in opaque turquoise blue enamel. Hung with aquamarine. Stamped "Lalique." c.1895. (Sotheby & Co. Sale, March 9, 1970.)

Bracelet of oriental design. Silver chased with dragons enamelled in pale blue and gilt. Stamped "Lalique." c.1900. (Sotheby & Co. Sale, March 9, 1970.)

Tortoise shell comb with orchid in ivory, gilt metal, enamel and brilliants. Lalique. c.1900. (The Walters Art Gallery.)

Necklace with lion and tooth motifs in gilt metal and tortoise shell. Lalique, 1895-1898. (The Walters Art Gallery.)

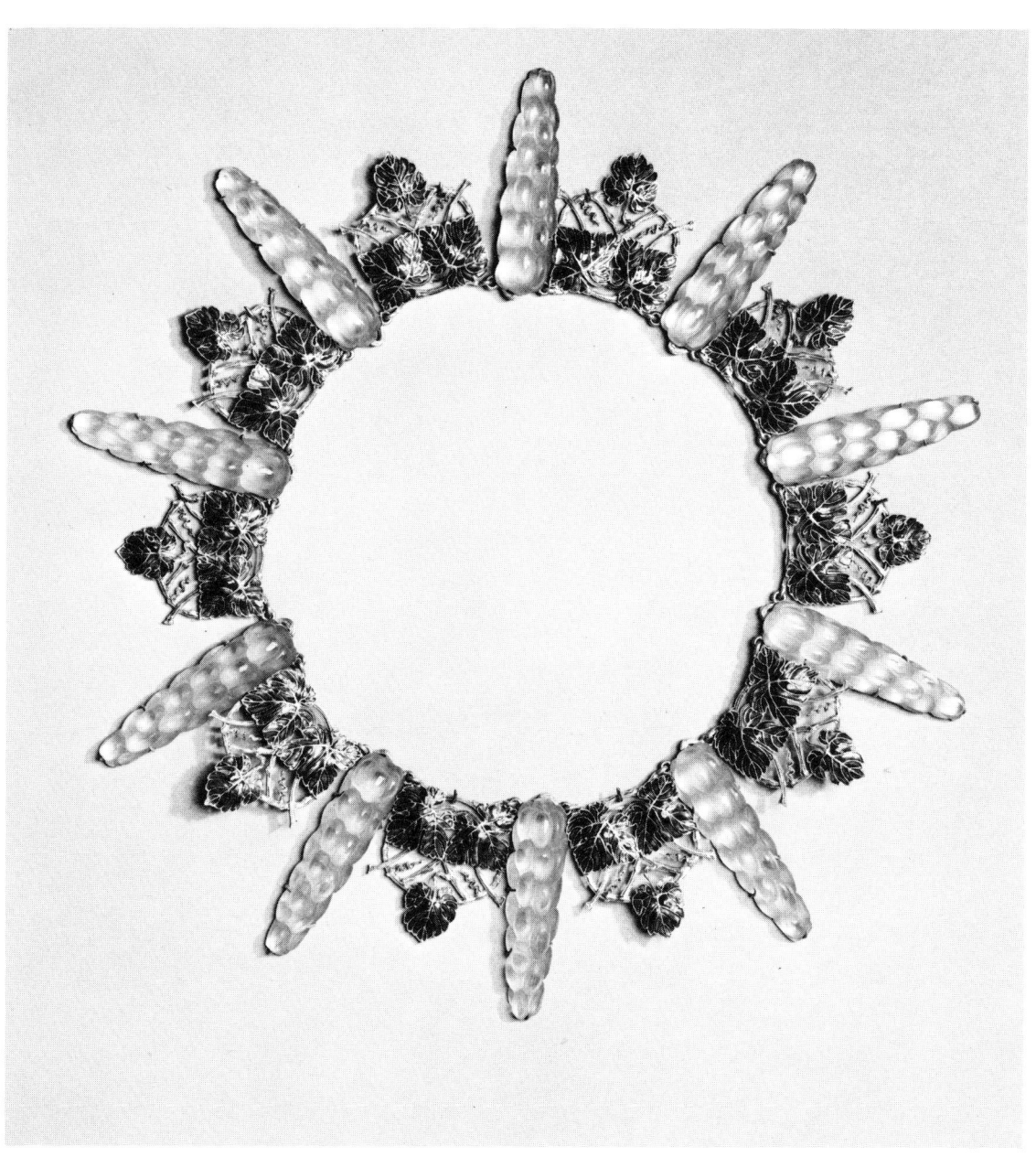

Necklace of grapes and leaves in gilt metal, green enamel and green glass. Lalique. c.1900. (The Walters Art Gallery.)

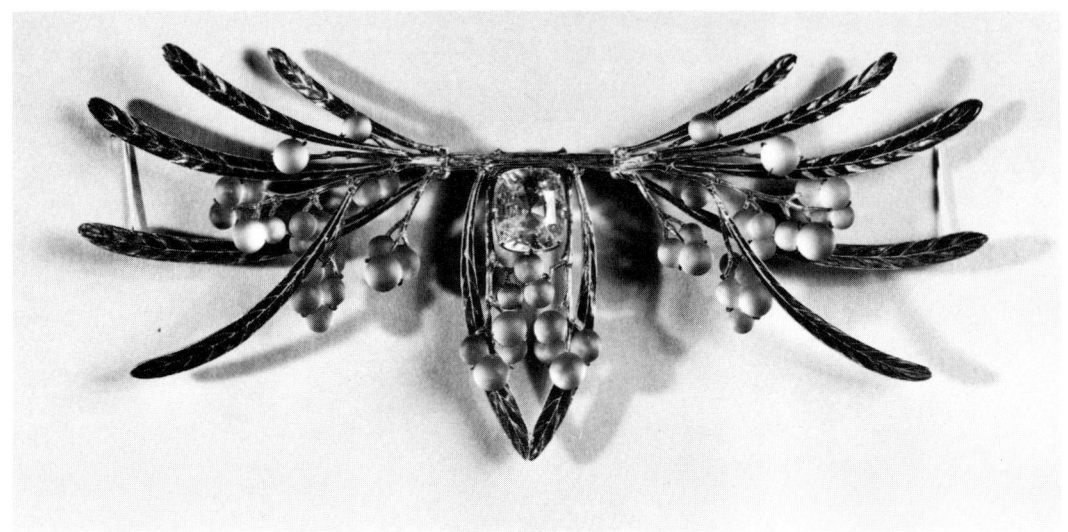

Ornament of gilt metal, glass, enamel and topaz. Lalique. c.1900. (The Walters Art Gallery.)

Pansy brooch in gilt metal, glass and enamel with sapphire in center. Lalique. c.1900. (The Walters Art Gallery.)

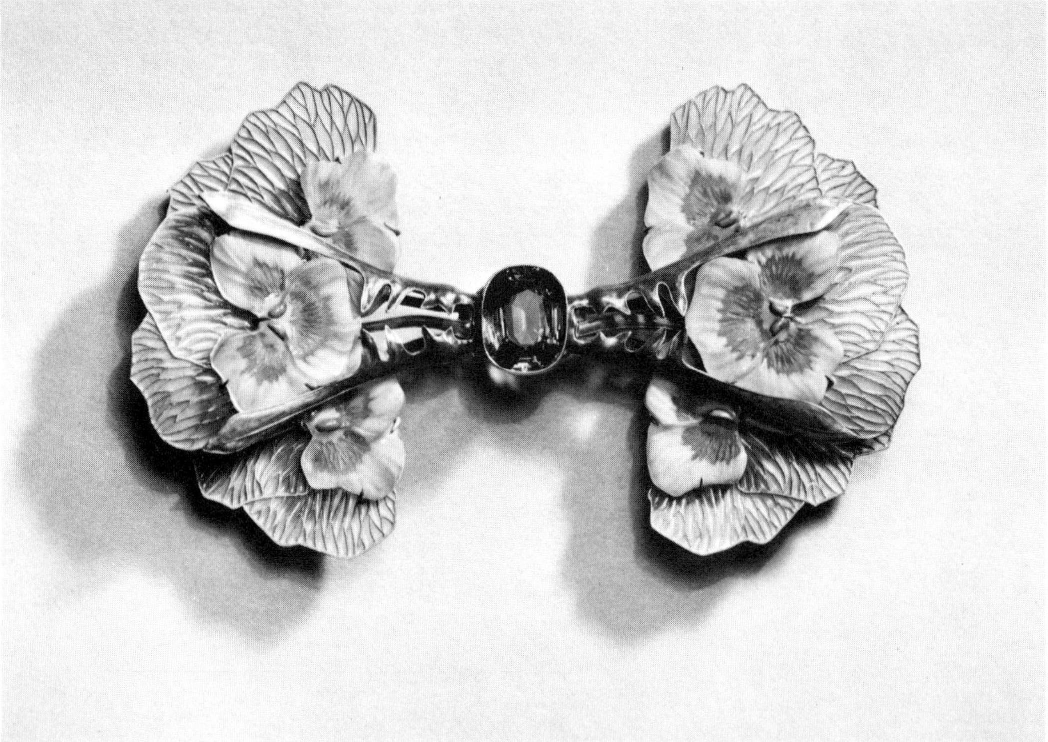

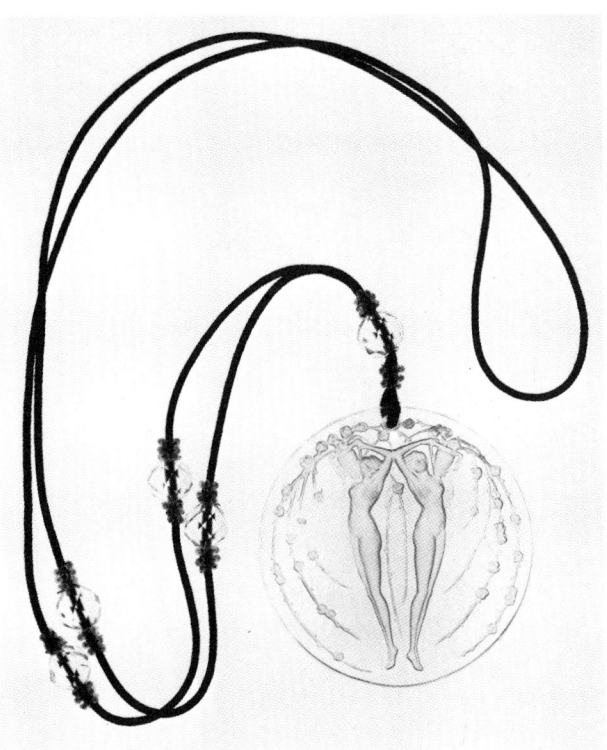

Pendant medallion on black silk cord with seed pearls. Figures of two nudes and blossoms molded on under side of glass. Mark "R. Lalique." c.1930-1935. (The Minneapolis Institute of Arts.)

Necklace with pendant in form of ivory nude standing among wisteria blossoms, of gold, enamel and topaz. Lalique. c.1902. (The Walters Art Gallery.)

Cup of alabaster, with figures of glass and bronze ornamented with grape and vine motif. (International Studio, 1905.)

Cup in ivory, enamels and gold with sculptured figures at base. Lalique. c.1900-1905. (International Studio, 1905.)

Decorative Glass Work

GLASS VASES

THE MOST IMPORTANT PIECES OF LALIQUE GLASS FOR THE collector are the vases. Between 150 and 200 different vase designs were made. The majority of the ornate large vases are no longer manufactured. For this reason and for artistic value and beauty of their designs these are the most sought after by collectors. Many of the vases are in the decorative Art Deco style, some in the later geometric patterns, but Lalique being of the older generation of designers was too established to completely change his taste and conception of design and thus he continued to favor many of the motifs of Art Nouveau. However as time went on the linear languid flowers of Art Nouveau such as the water lily, iris, and convolvulus were seen to change to formalized roses, dahlias, and sunflowers; the sinuous curves were banished in favor of stylized conventional designs. Gazelles, antelopes, birds, and sirens with flowing hair were popular motifs, and leaves, shells, fish, birds, and insects were arranged in Art Deco spirals. Vibrant colors later replaced the earlier smoky blues, ambers, and opalines and finally the designs were influenced by cubistic Art Deco designs of abstract ovals, squares, and zig-zags.

Some of the earliest Lalique vases were made by the *cire perdue* or lost wax casting process. This allowed for the reproduction of delicate and intricate detail and the results depended upon the skill of the craftsman. Such vases which are unique and few in number may have been executed by Lalique himself. They are accordingly the most valuable Lalique pieces.

Lalique *cire perdue* vases were in clear unpolished glass with tints of green, brown or other light tones. These vases were of leaf designs, nude figures with foliage, and with dragonfly and fish motifs. There is also an early unpolished Lalique vase with a band of dancing cherubs. They are marked with the engraved signature "R.Lalique," "R.Lalique France," and also with the engraved block letter signature "R.Lalique." The majority of the *cire perdue* pieces were early and were made between 1902 and 1913.

The most popular mass-produced Lalique vases were made in great numbers and should thus be available to the collector today. Here is a list of some of the most desirable vases with information about them taken from the 1932 "Catalogue des Verreries de René Lalique."

No. 875   "Antilopes émailleé" (A round vase with short neck and cabochons of clear glass against a background of engraved and enameled antelopes) c. 1925–1926. In 1932 2,000 were available in *blanc* and 2,200 in *couleur*.

No. 876   "Perruches" (Round vase with groups of paired parakeets in relief in tree branches) In 1932 there were 1,000 *blanc* and 1,200 *couleur* available.

No. 877   "Grande boule, lierre" (Spheroid shaped vase with bold pattern of ivy leaves) 2,000 *blanc* and 2,400 *couleur* listed in 1932 Lalique Catalogue.

No. 961 "Cluny" (Spheroid shaped vase blown in mold with bronze handles of masque design) 2,850 *couleur* listed in 1932 Lalique Catalogue. First made c. 1925.

No. 962 "Senalis" (Spheroid shaped vase blown in mold with bronze handles of Stylized leaves) 2,750 listed in *couleur* in 1932 Lalique Catalogue. c. 1925.

No. 1024 "Pétrarque" (Vase with heavy oval handles of molded flowers) 1,200 *blanc* and 1,500 *couleur* listed in 1932 Lalique Catalogue.

No. 1030 "Margaret" (Vase with heavy square handles of molded flowers) 900 *blanc* and 1,000 *couleur* listed in 1932 Lalique Catalogue.

No. 964 "Oranges émaillé" (Spheroid shaped vase with large oranges and enameled leaves) 1,650 *blanc* and 1,850 *couleur* listed in 1932 Lalique Catalogue.

No. 993 "Bellecour" (Vase with four frosted figures of birds at top of neck) 1,200 *blanc* and 1,400 *couleur* listed in 1932 Lalique Catalogue.

No. 997 "Bacchantes" (Straight-sided vase with figures of molded nudes) 1,500 *blanc* and 1,650 *couleur* listed in 1932 Lalique Catalogue. Vase still in production.

No. 883 "Méplat, Sirènes" (Oval vase with panels of nude figures and stopper of nude figurine) 1,250 *blanc* and 1,400 *couleur* listed in 1932 Lalique Catalogue.

No. 878 "4 Masques" (Round vase with short neck and four medallions of masques and foliage in relief) c. 1911. 1,300 *blanc* and 1,500 *couleur* listed in 1932 Lalique Catalogue.

No. 880 "Vase 2 Anneux" (A tall urn-shaped vase available with molded handles in choice of figures of scarabs, lizards, or pigeons suspended from glass loops at top of vase shoulder) 1,200 *blanc* and 1,400 *couleur* listed in 1932 Lalique Catalogue.

No. 1048   "Naïades" (Bowl with a base of molded figures of nude water nymphs) 2,000 *blanc* and 2,200 *couleur* listed in 1932 Lalique Catalogue.

No. 1054   "Nadica" (Vase with pair of molded water nymphs whose bodies extend into handles for vase) 2,800 *blanc* and 3,500 *couleur* listed in 1932 Lalique Catalogue.

No. 998   "Alicante" (Round shouldered vase with short neck and design of large parrot heads in relief) 975 *blanc* and 1,150 *couleur* listed in 1932 Lalique Catalogue.

No. 999   "Oran" (Vase with molded design of camellias) 1,000 *blanc* and 1,100 *couleur* listed in 1932 Lalique Catalogue.

No. 1015   "Salmonides" (Round vase with short neck and all-over design of molded fish) 900 *blanc* and 1,000 *couleur* listed in 1932 Lalique Catalogue.

No. 1057   "Chrysanthème" (Covered vase with stopper of wood) 1,500 *blanc* listed in 1932 Lalique Catalogue.

No. 1071   "Merles" (Vase with design of blackbirds in cut glass) 1,300 *blanc* listed in 1932 Lalique Catalogue.

In addition to the above listed vases there are others that are particularly interesting because of their subject or fine design and these are in demand with collectors today. These include the well-known

No. 893   "Archers" (An oval vase with short neck and a design in relief of nude males hunting tropical birds) Height 10 inches. It was first made c. 1923 in *blanc* and smoky colors. 750 *blanc* and 850 *couleur* were listed in the 1932 Lalique Catalogue.

No. 896   "Serpent" (A vase with molded design of a coiled snake) First made c. 1923. 500 *blanc* and 550 *couleur* were listed in the 1932 Lalique Catalogue.

No. 892 "Gros Scarabées" (Spheroid vase with short neck and an all-over design of scarabs or beetles in relief) 800 *blanc* and 900 *couleur* were listed in the 1932 Lalique Catalogue.

No. 919 "Aras" (An oval vase with a molded design of tropical birds and cherries) 550 *blanc* and 650 *couleur* listed in the 1932 Lalique Catalogue.

No. 925 "Poissons" (A large round vase with an allover design of goldfish in relief) 525 *blanc* and 625 *couleur* were listed in the 1932 Lalique Catalogue. A similar design was on a smaller vase called "Formose" No. 934.

No. 966 "Tortues" (An oval vase with short neck and an allover design of large molded turtles) First made c. 1926. 525 *blanc* and 625 *couleur* were listed in the 1932 Lalique Catalogue.

No. 977 "Sophora" (A spheroid vase with short neck and a design of a leafy vine) First made c. 1926. 375 *blanc* and 450 *couleur* were listed in the 1932 Lalique Catalogue.

There were numerous vases with leaf designs including the large spheroid vase with short neck with molded veined leaves called "Charmille" (No. 978) and "Languedoc" (No. 1021), a vase with triangular leaves and rimmed lip which was available in both colorless and colored glass. "Armorique" (No. 1000) was a vase of artichoke shape with molded artichoke leaves. This was available in both colorless and colored glass. One small vase had an allover relief pattern of palm leaves, another "Epicea" or spruce, and an important large vase, "Acanthes" (No. 902), was of oval form with small short neck and had a design of acanthus leaves in relief. It was available in both colorless and colored glass. There was a panel of molded leaves on each side of "Honfleur" (No. 994) a vase first made c. 1926-1927.

The shell was also a favorite design on Lalique vases. There was a decanter in the shape of a clam shell and a round vase, "Escargot" (No. 931), was molded in the design of a snail shell. It was made in both colorless and colored glass. "Coquilles" (No. 932), was a small upright rectangular vase with rounded shoulders and a short neck. It had a relief design of scallop shells. "Dordogne" (No. 1001) was a squat oval vase with borders of protruding molded snail shells. It was available in both colorless and colored glass.

Undoubtedly the most characteristic and most desirable of all Lalique vases are those with nude figures either molded in the design of the vase or applied as handles or stoppers. In addition to the better known vases such as "Sirènes," "Danaïdes," "Nadica," and "Bacchantes" there were vases with panels of figurines such as "6 Figurines et Masques" (No. 886) which has panels of figurines in relief alternating with panels of plain glass. This was a large vase made in both colorless and colored glass. There was also a large goblet with six panels of veiled figurines and a covered vase with panels of caryatides. "12 Figurines avec Bouchon" (No. 914) is ornamented with figures of nude women and has a nude figurine for a stopper; 600 *blanc* and 700 *couleur* were available in the 1932 Catalogue. An early funnel-shaped vase ornamented with oval medallions of nudes in relief was called "Camées"; 900 *blanc* and 1,000 *couleur* were listed in the 1932 Lalique Catalogue.

A delightful round vase with short neck and handle of nudes holding garlands of flowers is called "Ronsard" (No. 982). This vase was first made c. 1926–1927 in both colorless and colored glass. A similar vase "Bouchardon" (No. 981) was made at about the same date and both were illustrated in *Mobilier et Décoration* in 1927.

There are also attractive small vases. A bowl with a base of sculptured nude wrestlers is called "Lutteurs." It was made in both *blanc* and *couleur*. "Courges," a gourd-shaped vase in Art Nouveau style, is slightly reminiscent of the gourd vases of Gallé and Daum. It was an early vase, but 300 *blanc* and 350 *couleur* were listed in the 1932 Lalique Catalogue. "Ceylan" was a jar with pairs of parakeets in relief. It is most often seen in a pale blue opalescent color although it was made in other colors and also in colorless glass. Another small but highly desirable vase was "Lièvres" (No. 942) a round vase with short neck ornamented with leaves and a band of running hares in relief. This was available in both *blanc* and *couleur*.

Many of the designs of Lalique are influenced by Art Nouveau and there are other designs that are definitely Art Deco in style but above all else Lalique glass is unmistakably French. The flowing hair of the nude figurines and sea nymphs, the streams of water flowing from the vases held by the nudes on the vase "Danaïdes" and the stylized roses and antelope motifs are all themes of the more graceful type of Art Deco. However, there are also many designs of zig-zags, stepped shapes and geometric motifs that relate to later Art Deco and the influence of Cubism. The vase "Soleil," a flower with sun-like rays made in clear glass with enamel, and the vase "Picardie," with sunken designs of huge daisies with rayed petals, were both inspired by Art Deco. This latter vase first exhibited in 1927–1928 continued to be available in 1932 in both colorless and colored glass. Engraved spirals decorate the rare small vase "Méduse" and applied spirals of molded design are on the sides of several vases.

The vases most characteristic of Art Deco are those with molded and enameled zig-zag designs relating to Indian art. In 1925 Lalique exhibited the vase "Tourbillons," which had a large scroll design. It was made in clear glass sometimes accented with enamel. A group of small vases with allover Art Deco designs of ducks, cocks, chamois, and stylized leaves were available in colored glass in 1932.

The identification of Lalique glass is not difficult because all pieces are marked. Although glass of similar designs made by Sabino, Genet & Michon, and other glassmakers such as André Hunebelle show the signs of Lalique influence there has been no direct plagiarism of Lalique designs or marks.

Lalique glass was halfway between commercial and studio production and although it was mass-produced the high standard of quality and the distinctive touch and design were maintained for many years. Lalique glass was produced by a number of techniques including the use of fluoridic acids, polishing on the wheel, and considerable handwork.

Lalique glass for collectors dates from 1900 when the first experimental pieces were made until the death of René Lalique in 1945. In February-March, 1933, a retrospective exhibition of Lalique's work was put on at the Pavillon de Marsan of The Musée des Arts Décoratifs and the catalogue of this exhibit records the jewelry, sculpture, and glass from vases to fountains. Included was the early vase with dragonfly handles, the owl vase, and a unique vase with peacock figure stopper called "Verrier de Génie." There were also decorative lighted glass panels with horses and riders and a peacock panel. "Christ on Cross" and a Madonna were representative of Lalique's religious glass. However the catalogue of this exhibit is of little assistance in dating the vases available to the collector today since many of the pieces were one of a kind pieces.

Although there were trade catalogues put out by Lalique the only ones available for study are the lighting catalogues distributed by Breves Galleries, London, in 1928, and the large Lalique Catalogue of 1932. The latter catalogue lists and illustrates the pieces of decorative glass then available, whether the pieces were made in "blanc" or "couleur" glass and how many pieces were then in stock. This information gives little aid in dating a piece of glass for many of the articles in the Catalogue were first made earlier and also continued in production after 1932. The approximate dates of some articles can be traced in periodicals or advertisements. Any piece thus traced must have been made before the date of the publication of the article or illustration. The Lalique signature also does not definitely establish the date of a piece since various signatures were used at the same time. Also similar vases have been seen signed in script or block capitals impressed or engraved.

The signatures were "R.Lalique," engraved in script; "R.Lalique" engraved in block letters, and "R.Lalique" or "R.Lalique France" in molded block letters. A rare signature is "Lalique" in block letters molded with the base of the "L" elongated to form a base for the rest of the letters. Lalique glass is usually marked on the bottom or on the base of a piece near the bottom and it is often marked in both places and in a script as well as a block signature. The signature "Lalique" or "R.Lalique" engraved in round letters is found in the body of a vase, the beetle perfume bottle, on a paperweight, on the statuette "Moyenne Nue" (No. 830), and on a round box with a rooster. A similar rounded signature "R.Lalique" is on many vases. *Cire perdue* pieces are usually signed with engraved block letters or in engraved script which could be Lalique's own signature. When there is a number on a piece it refers to the design as recorded in the Lalique "Catalogue des Verreries de René Lalique" (1932). After 1945, the year of Lalique's death, the mark is "Lalique" without the initial "R." Today Lalique glass is marked "Lalique France" in small pointed script on the bottom or sometimes on the body of the piece. The 1932 Lalique Catalogue uses the words "blanc" and "couleur." "Blanc" however means uncolored not white and "couleur" usually means the whole range of colors from amber to deep reds, blues, and greens.

Early Lalique *cire perdue* experimental pieces are frosty but Lalique also used opalescent glass in his jewelry and there is an opaline bowl of Art Nouveau design dating from 1900. When Lalique started mass production the glass was monotone with smoky opaline tints and with contrasts of clear crystal and soft satin finished glass. The lightly tinted glass was in shades of blue, brown, and peach. The 1932 Catalogue lists the colors as "opale, bleu, vert, brun, etc." Today vases have been found in more than ten different colors including deep dark brown, red, blue, green, turquoise, purple, black, the lighter shades of yellow, amber, gray, and opaline. The darker colors tend toward the opaque. Black is especially popular with present day collectors. Many pieces were available in the whole range of colors and others were only made in clear crystal (blanc). Glass surfaces were clear, translucent, polished and matte or frosted. Enamel and engraved decoration were used in addition to molded patterns. A few pieces were also "taillé" (cut). Present day Lalique glass is generally uncolored crystal and more clinical in appearance.

Collectors are especially interested in pieces of Art Deco design and any unusual pieces. Colored pieces are more in demand than opalescent. Black is most desirable and *cire perdue* pieces in which the wax mold was broken after casting are rare one of a kind pieces. Although still much lower priced than Tiffany and Gallé and his school which preceded it in the Art Nouveau era, Lalique fits in well with the present nostalgia for the 1920's. The opaline pieces with their pale blue opal-like gleam are immediately recognizable and one soon comes to recognize the colors and designs of other pieces. Pieces with a combination of cutting and casting produce a pleasing appearance.

Left, Decanter, clear glass, stained and molded Bacchantian masques. Heart-shaped silver stopper with fruit design. Vase marked with diamond point signature "R. Lalique." Stopper marked "France, Lalique." 1911-1930. (Sotheby's Belgravia Sale, March 8, 1972.)

Below, Water nymph, *cire perdue.* Height, 3 inches. Engraved signature "R. Lalique." c.1910. (John Jesse Gallery.)

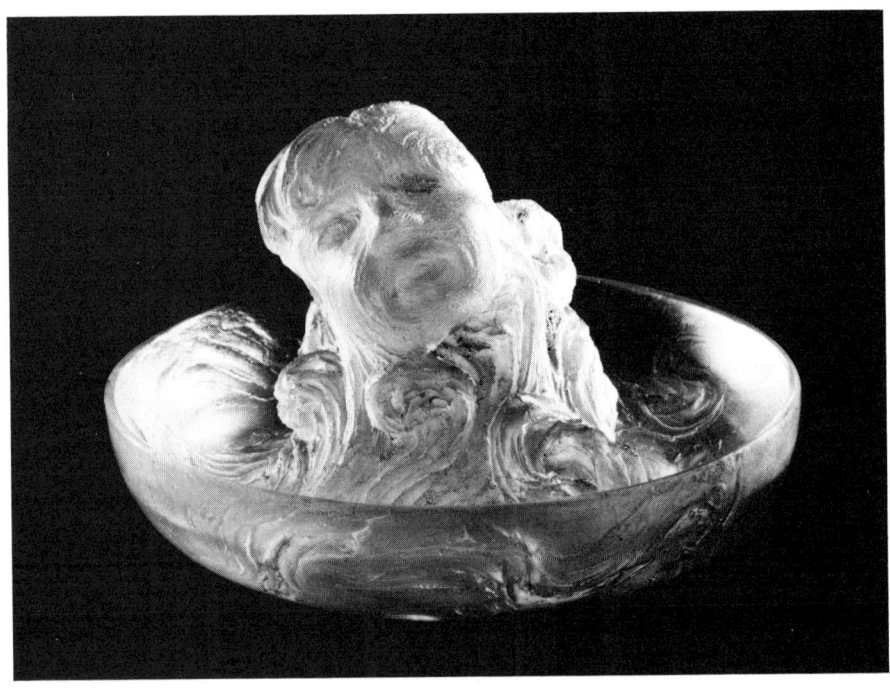

Dragonfly vase with cover, *cire perdue*. c.1910-1913. Signed "R. Lalique" in block letters engraved on lid. (The Metropolitan Museum of Art, Edward C. Moore, Jr. Gift, 1924.)

Above, Vase, fish head motif, *cire perdue.* Signed "R. Lalique France F19529." 1902-1912. (Collection Mr. and Mrs. Robert Walker.)

Opposite, Vase, brown color with female figures and foliage. Signed "R. Lalique" in block letters. c.1902-1912. (*Connoisseur,* August, 1971.)

Above, Vase with figures of children and draperies. "R. Lalique." c.1900-1910. (Musée des Arts Décoratifs.)

Left, Glass door with alternating plaques of nude male figures and greenery. c.1922. (Gallerie Felix Marcilhac.)

Right, Vase, leaf pattern in greenish-white glass, *cire perdue*. R. Lalique. 1913. (Musée des Arts Décoratifs.)

Below, "Sirens," opalescent glass dish molded with mermaids bathing in spray. Marked "R. Lalique France, No. 3003." Before 1924. (Sotheby's Belgravia Sale, March 28, 1972.)

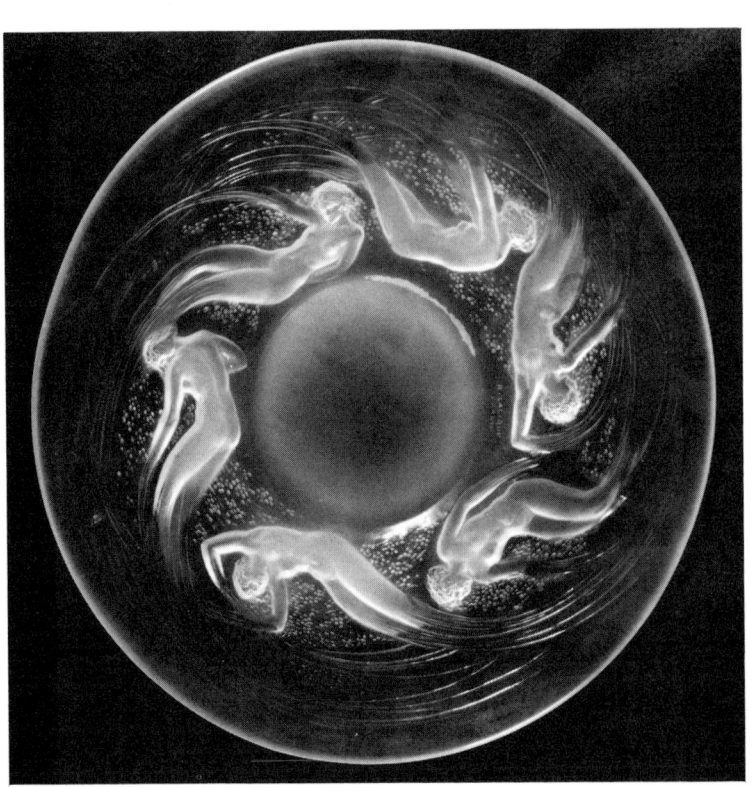

Left, Vase, brownish glass molded and engraved with leaf sprays in relief. Lalique c. 1913-1914. (The Metropolitan Museum of Art, Edward C. Moore, Jr. Gift, 1936.)

Below, Dish "Sirene" with one molded central figure of mermaid. Lalique, c.1925. (The Cooper-Hewitt Museum of Decorative Arts.)

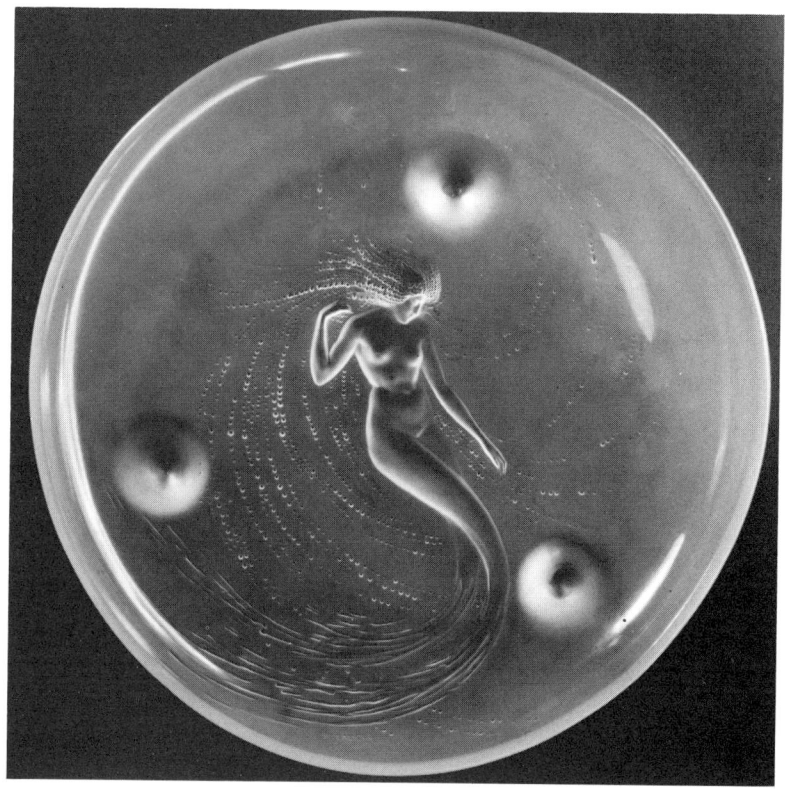

Vase of tear-drop form, trumpet neck, orange-tinted glass with stylized leaves part polished in relief against white frosted ground. Base engraved "R. Lalique France No. 1014." c.1925. (Sotheby's Belgravia Sale, June 22, 1973.)

Vase "Tourbillons," amber glass molded in high relief with motif of barbed scrolls outlined in black enamel. Base engraved "R. Lalique" incised, block letters. c.1925. (The Cooper-Hewitt Museum of Decorative Arts.)

Vase "Deux Pigeons," colorless glass with loop handles with figures of pigeons. (The Metropolitan Museum of Art, Edward C. Moore, Jr., Gift Fund, 1937.)

Vase "Perruches," bluish grey glass pressed in mold. No. 876. Also made in colorless glass. c.1925. (The Metropolitan Museum of Art, Edward C. Moore, Jr. Gift, 1933.)

Vase "Nadica." Clear colorless glass pressed in mold with design of nude sea maidens. Before 1932. Also made in color. (The Metropolitan Museum of Art, Gift of Edward C. Moore, Jr. 1936.)

Above left, Vase "Yvelines." No. 975. Made in both *blanc* and *couleur*. Before 1932. (John Jesse Gallery.)

Above right, Vase "Aigrettes," molded design in dark smoky glass. Height, 10 inches. Also made in clear colorless glass. Before 1932. (The Chrysler Museum at Norfolk.)

Left, Vase, clear colorless glass with decoration of birds in sunk relief. c.1925–1935. (The Metropolitan Museum of Art, Edward C. Moore, Jr. Gift, 1936.)

Vase "Cluny," No. 961. Smoky, transparent glass with bronze metal masque handles. Height, 10 inches. (The Chrysler Museum at Norfolk.)

Vase "Marisa." No 1022. All-over design of fish cast in mold and made in both white transparent and colored glass. Height, 9¼ inches. (The Chrysler Museum at Norfolk.)

Gold necklace with alternating plaques of gold and enamel nudes and swans, each with amethyst and opals. Made for Exposition 1900. Stamped "Lalique." (Collection Lillian Nassau.)

Left, Gold necklace with pendant of blue and white swan. Stamped "Lalique." 1898. (Collection Lillian Nassau.)

Right, Ivory brooch in frame of brown enamel oak twigs and leaves. Stamped "Lalique." c. 1899. (Collection Lillian Nassau.)

Left, Pine cone pendant, gold and enamel. Lalique. c. 1900. (Collection Galerie Felix Marcilhac.)

Left, Necklace of scarabs, gold, enamel, and cabochon stones. (Anonymous Collection.)

Below, Group of Lalique perfume flagons. Left to right: "Amphytrite," shell design, green; "Amphytrite," shell design, blanc; "Serpent," crystal with etched design of serpent and serpent stopper; "Cigales," tall crystal flagon with enamel accents; turquoise bottle with design of tropical birds in relief. Roger et Gallet "Le Jade." Marked "R. L." in moulded letters. (Collection Robert Sistrunk.)

Left, Vase "Serpent," brown-amber. Mark, "R Lalique" in block letters impressed in mould. (Antaeus Gallery Inc.)

Below left, Vase "Druids." Cased emerald green. Mark, rounded script "R Lalique France #937." (Antaeus Gallery Inc.)

Below, Vase "Poissons." Clear orange. Mark, script signature "R Lalique #925." (Antaeus Gallery Inc.)

Above, "Penthièvre." #1011. Art Deco design of fish. Mark, "R Lalique France" in script. (Antaeus Gallery Inc.)

Above right, Vase "Monnaie du Pape." Colorless glass with surface patination. Stamped "R Lalique" in block letters. (Antaeus Gallery Inc.)

Right, Vase "Courges." Rare design of pumpkins, pale amethyst glass. Mark, stamped "Lalique" with elongated "L," also engraved "Lalique" in small pointed script. (Antaeus Gallery Inc.)

Vase "Formosa." Design of gold fish in cased yellow glass. Mark, "R Lalique" in block letters. Same vase in red marked "R Lalique France" in script. (Antaeus Gallery Inc.)

Vase "Bacchantes." Opalescent design of nudes cast in mould. Mark, engraved signature "R Lalique" in script. (Antaeus Gallery Inc.)

Vase "Pigeons." Pale sapphire blue with white enamel. Mark, engraved signature "R Lalique" in script. (Antaeus Gallery Inc.)

Two vases. *Left,* "Méduse." Green. Design of spirals. Mark, "R Lalique France" in script. *Right,* red vase with small neck, design of brambles. Mark, "R Lalique" in block letters impressed in mould. (Antaeus Gallery Inc.)

Vase "Lagamar." Art Deco design in black enamel and white frosting. Mark, "R Lalique" engraved in block letters. (Antaeus Gallery Inc.)

Vase "Bouchardon." Frosted platinum grey blown in mould. Mark, "R Lalique" pressed in mould and "R Lalique France" in script. (Antaeus Gallery Inc.)

Vase "Pierrefonds" with open scroll design in handles. No. 990. Made in both colorless and color. Lalique. c.1927-8. (The Corning Museum of Glass.)

Jardinière "Saint Hubert." Handles with antelopes. Height 5¼ inches. Made in white clear glass before 1927. (The Chrysler Museum at Norfolk.)

Vase "Bacchantes." Design of nude figures made in mold. Before 1932. Still being made. (John Jesse Gallery.)

Vase "Poivre" (pepper berries), dark grey transparent glass. Mark, "R. Lalique" in block letters. (Sybarites Gallery Inc.)

Vase "Gros Scarabées." No. 892. Deep red-orange. Before 1932. Mark "R. Lalique France" in rounded script. (The Columbus Gallery of Fine Arts.)

139 VASE LAUREL LEAVES.
142 BOWL SIRENS.
141 PAPER WEIGHT SIREN
140 CLOCK LOVEBIRDS.
143 VASE LOVEBIRDS.

Page from Lalique catalogue printed in England before 1932. (John Jesse Gallery.)

Vase, grasshopper and grass design. Pressed acid finish and polish glass. Height, 11 inches. Mark, "R. Lalique" in block letters. 1920-1925. (The Toledo Museum of Art.)

Opposite, above: Vase "Dordogne" molded design of shells. Opaque white glass stamped "R. Lalique" in block letters and "R. Lalique" in rounded script. (Sybarites Gallery Inc.)

Opposite, below: Vase with base of two molded cupids. Height 10¾ inches. Mark, etched on bottom, "R. Lalique France." Before 1932. (The Toledo Museum of Art.)

Left, Vase of opalescent glass with decorative border in satin finish relief pattern of flowers. Height, 5⅝ inches. (The Toledo Museum of Art.)

Right, Vase "Camargue." Frosted and clear glass with four carved plaques with figures of horses. Height, 11⅜ inches. R. Lalique, 1940-1945. (The Toledo Museum of Art.)

Handleless amphora-shaped vase with molded design of alligators against background of pineapple branches. Black glass. Height, 13¼ inches. Signed "R. Lalique" on bottom edge. c.1920. (William Rockhill Nelson Gallery of Art.)

Vase, blue glass blown in mold; fern leaf pattern. Height, 7 inches. Mark, "R. Lalique." c.1930. (The Toledo Museum of Art.)

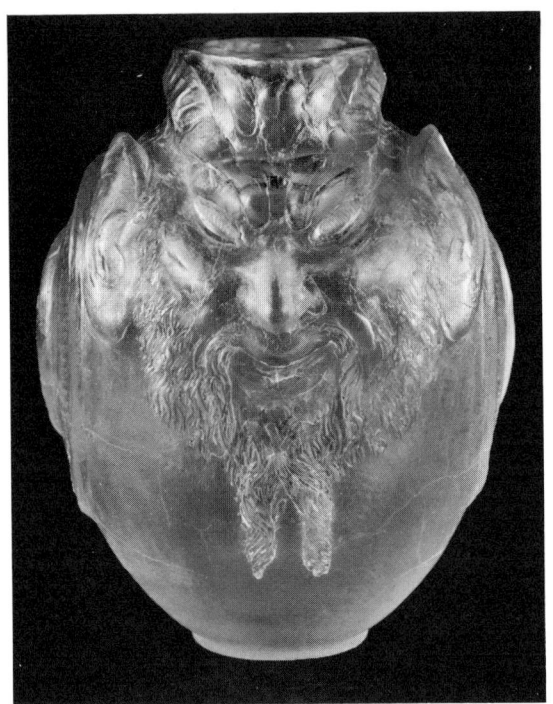

Above, left, Vase in *cire perdue* with molded face of satyr. R. Lalique, c.1922. (Sybarites.)

Above right, Vase in *cire perdue* with molded design of grapes and leaves and head of Bacchus. R. Lalique, c.1922. (Sybarites.)

Left, Vase "Escargot." No. 931. Blue-green glass. Mark, "Lalique," in rounded script. "R. Lalique," in block letters. Before 1932. (Martin Cohen.)

Vase, *cire perdue*. Colorless, pitted unpolished glass. Lalique, 1900-1910. Mark "R. Lalique" carved in block letters. (Martin Cohen.)

"The Archers" vase. Relief design of men with bows and arrows hunting birds. Colored glass. R. Lalique, c.1925. (Editions Graphiques Ltd.)

Vase "Danaïdes." Relief of nudes with water jars. R. Lalique, c.1927. No. 972 in 1932 Catalogue. (Editions Graphiques Ltd.)

STATUETTES AND DECORATIVE MOTIFS

Lalique had studied sculpture early in his career and became an accomplished sculptor. Throughout the years he continued his interest in the plastic arts. Small ivory and *pâte-de-verre* glass nude figures were often used in his jewelry designs and he continued to use sculpture on his glass vases and other articles. From time to time Lalique was associated with several well-known French sculptors. For a short while he worked in collaboration with the sculptor Gaston Lachaise and created a number of designs incorporating the human figure in molded lightly tinted glass. There were many statuettes of nudes and veiled figures. These figures were very popular and twenty-nine different figures of veiled or nude subjcts were listed in the 1932 Catalogue. The figures were made in several sizes and in different poses. Some were on metal or wooden bases with concealed lighting. The figures included such titles as "Sirènes," Naïade," and a straining figure called "Vitesse" or speed, which was also available as a radiator cap. One of the favorite figures was "Suzanne," a nude holding drapery over her outstretched arms. This figure is now known as "Suzanne au Bain." It is 8¾ inches in height and was made in both colorless and opalescent glass. It has a molded signature "R.Lalique" and the base is engraved "R.Lalique France No. 833." The figure was mounted for electricity. A figure (No. 834) in similar posture but clothed in a sheath was called "Thaïs." It represents a girl in the Art Deco style of the 1920's.

The following statuettes were listed in the 1932 Lalique Catalogue together with the number available in both *blanc* and *couleur* (colorless and colored):

No. 826 "Statuette joueuse de flûte" (flute player) 1,250 *blanc*: "Statuettes of Four Seasons" Figures of women with appropriate symbols. Motif figures of two birds on a molded arch.

No. 827 "Statuette tête penchée" (inclined head) 1,250 *blanc*, 1,500 *couleur*: Figure enclosed in oval of glass with floral decoration in relief.

No. 828 "Statuette voilée, mains jointes" (veiled nude with hands clasped at neck) *blanc* 750, *couleur* 850.

No. 829 "Statuette moyenne, voilée" (medium sized statuette 350 *blanc*, 400 *couleur*.

No. 830 "Statuette moyenne, nue" (statuette, medium sized, nude) *Blanc* 350, *couleur* 400.

No. 831 "Statuette Sirène (small nude on circular base) *Blanc* 250, *couleur* 275.

No. 832 "Statuette Naïade" (small nude on circular base) *Blanc* 300, *couleur* 350.

No. 833 "Statuette Suzanne" (nude with drapery hanging from outstretched arms) *Blanc* 550, *couleur* 625.

No. 833 "Statuette Suzanne" (on bronze base mounted for electricity) *Blanc* 1,100, *couleur* 1,175.

No. 834 "Statuette Thaïs" *Blanc* 550, *couleur* 625.

No. 834 "Statuette Thaïs" (on bronze base mounted for electricity) *Blanc* 1,100, *couleur* 1,175.

No. 835 "Statuette, grande nue, bras levés" (large standing nude with arms raised over head) *Blanc* 1,350.

No. 835 "Statuette, grande nue" (on base of wood mounted for electricity) *Blanc* 1,750.

"Statuette grande nue, longs cheveux" (large standing nude with flowing hair) On base with molded ivy and wooden stand. *Blanc* 1,900, *couleur* 2,350.

No. 837 "Statuette, Source de la Fontaine" (three different oriental figurines) made in 13 different sizes on wooden base *Blanc* 1,350–1,900.

No. 1160   "Statuette Vitesse" (nude in straining position with hands clasped back of head) *Blanc* 285, *couleur* 325.
No. 1183   "Statuette Chrysis" (nude) *Blanc* 325, *couleur* 350.

Lalique also invented decorative motifs composed of circular or semicircular pieces of glass about an inch in thickness. These had a design on their back deeply etched in acid. They were mounted on a bronze or wooden base with a concealed electric bulb and the light shone through the glass illuminating the incised design. These decorative pieces are some of the most dramatic and striking pieces made by Lalique. One of the most interesting and characteristic pieces was "Surtout 2 Cavaliers." This etched and frosted intaglio design of two plumed knights on web-footed horses tilting at each other was on an arched form panel of crystal. It was set on a bronze base with a pattern of cobwebs and stems which concealed the light fittings. The piece is 36 inches in length and the glass is engraved "R. Lalique." A piece of similar size was etched with a design of three peacocks. "Oiseau de Feu" (firebird) was another dramatic design. Inspired by the ballet of that name, first performed in Paris in 1917 and repeated through 1917, the plaque was probably designed and first produced during those years. The design is of an exotic feathered bird with the nude torso of a woman. It is set on a bronze base which conceals an electric globe. The glass is engraved "R.Lalique" in block letters.

There were more than thirty different designs of decorative motifs listed in the 1932 Lalique Catalogue. They are as follows:

No. 1100   "Gros Poisson Vagues" (large fish with mouth closed) *Blanc* 2,200, *couleur* 2,450. This was also available mounted on a bronze stand wired for electricity. *Blanc* 2,750, *couleur* 3,000.
No. 1101   "Gros Poisson Algues" (large fish with mouth closed, seaweed decoration) *Blanc* 2,000, *couleur* 2,250. Mounted on bronze base decorated with seaweed and wired for electricity. *Blanc* 2,725, *couleur* 2,975.

Statuettes and Decorative Motifs · 73

No. 1106   "Motif Hirondelles" (Group of three swallows mounted on glass base) *Blanc* 900. Also on bronze base. No. 1,107. *Blanc* 350.

No. 1108   "4 Danseuses" (group of nude dancers mounted on bronze base) *Blanc* 1,200. Also on bronze base mounted for electricity. *Blanc* 1,300.

No. 1109   "Surtout 2 Cavaliers" (centerpiece).Two cavaliers joisting on web-footed horses mounted on bronze base wired for electricity. *Blanc* 8,000.

No. 1110   "3 Paons (three peacocks) Mounted on bronze base wired for electricity. *Blanc* 8,000.

No. 1111   "Oiseau de Feu" (Firebird with exotic feathers and torso of woman) *Blanc* 1,900. Also wired for electricity. *Blanc* 2,450.

Nos. 1149 –1151   "Moineau Fier" Moineau Hardi" "Moineau Timide" (three figures of sparrows in different moods, proud, bold, and timid) *Blanc* 125 each. Satin finished.

Nos. 1154 –1156   "Moineau sur socle ailes croisées, ailes ouvertes, ailes fermées" (sparrow on base with wings crossed, with wings open, with wings closed) On square glass bases. *Blanc* 250 each. Satin finished.

Nos. 1165 –1167   "Moineau coquet" "Moineau sournois" "Moineau moqueur" (three figures of sparrows, coquette, cunning, and jeering) *Blanc* 125 each.

No. 1169   "Surtout Caravelle" (large half circle of glass engraved with galleon with sails unfurled) *Blanc* 10,000. Satin finished.

No. 1175   "Surtout Amours" (centerpiece with figures of lovers) *Blanc* 15,000.

No. 1170   "Surtout Yéso" (large centerpiece with tropical fish swimming among bubbles) *Blanc* 3,000.

No. 1171 –1173   "Surtout Fauvettes, A, B, C" (eight warblers sitting on tree branches. Three different arrangements of birds) On rectangular glass panels. *Blanc* 2,800 each.

No. 1174   "Surtout Nid d'Oiseaux" (small circular panel engraved with scene of two birds feeding small birds in nest) *Blanc* 15,000.

No. 1177   "Surtout Tulipes" (large circular centerpiece engraved with bouquet of tulips) *Blanc* 12,000.

No. 1178   "Vase 2 Anémones" (small round vase with stopper of two anemones) *Blanc* frosted 200. Still being made.

Nos. 1179 –1180   "Anémone ouverte" "Anémone fermée" (single blossoms of flowers in satin finish) *Blanc* 60 each. Still being made.

Nos. 1199 –1200   "Pigeon Liège" "Pigeon Namur" (Figures of pigeons) *Blanc* 450 each.

There were also large frosted figures of quail and after 1932 numerous figures of other birds including owls and animals such as elephants, bison, fox, dogs, and a sitting and crouching cat. The early figures were sculptured in stylized planes. Some figures were engraved showing the animals' fur but later figures show only the form of the animal in frosted glass. Animal figures were made in several sizes in both clear and satin finish glass. They do not seem to have been made in colored glass. Animal figures proved so successful that they were continued for many years and some of the original figures are still being produced while new figures are also being introduced.

Lalique designed a number of religious plaques including several different interpretations of Christ on the Cross, the Virgin and Child, and one of St. Thérèse. There was also a "Medaille Jeanne d'Arc." Religious subjects also included a scene of The Last Supper which was enclosed in a border of symbolic wheat and grapes and a Madonna and Child with a frame of satin finish angels in relief. Lalique exhibited a glass chapel at a Paris Salon in the autumn of 1930 and these subjects probably date around that time; indeed one crucifix was made for that chapel. In 1933 Lalique exhibited a larger chapel.

Opposite, Statuette "Suzanne." Molded nude with drapery. "R. Lalique," molded signature. Engraved signature on base "R. Lalique France" No. 833. c.1930. (Sotheby's Belgravia Sale. August 3, 1971.)

Surtout or centerpiece, "Deux Cavaliers." Molded panel with frosted intaglio of two horsemen on web-footed horses, joisting. Bronze base with pattern of cobwebs and stems, mounted for electricity. Glass engraved "R. Lalique." c.1930. (Sotheby's Belgravia Sale, March 28, 1973.)

Statuette "Grande Nue." Molded nude with base of ivy design on stand of carved wood. Glass engraved "Lalique." Before 1932. (John Jesse Gallery.)

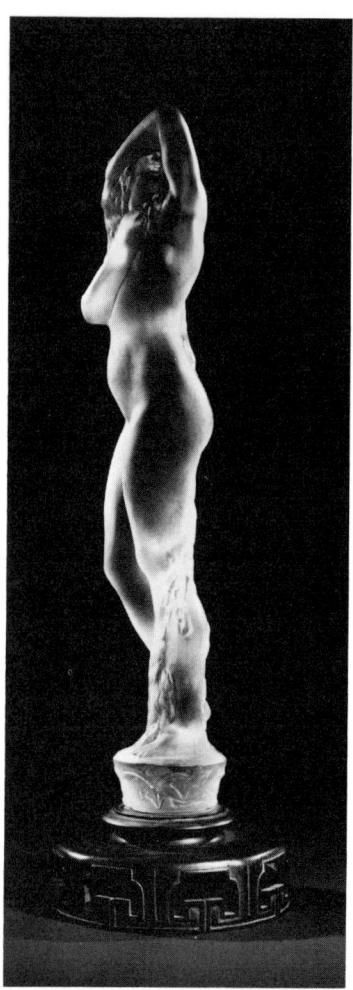

Decorative motif, two swallows on glass base. Clear pressed glass. Height, 14¼ inches. "R. Lalique" in block letters. c.1926-1932. (The Toledo Museum of Art.)

Crucifix. Frosted glass; figure in relief against black cross. Height with base 13 inches, width 6½ inches. Lalique, c.1930. (The Toledo Museum of Art.)

Sitting cat, 8¼ inches high. Two sparrows, c.4¼ inches long. Luminous satin finish. Lalique, c.1930 to present.

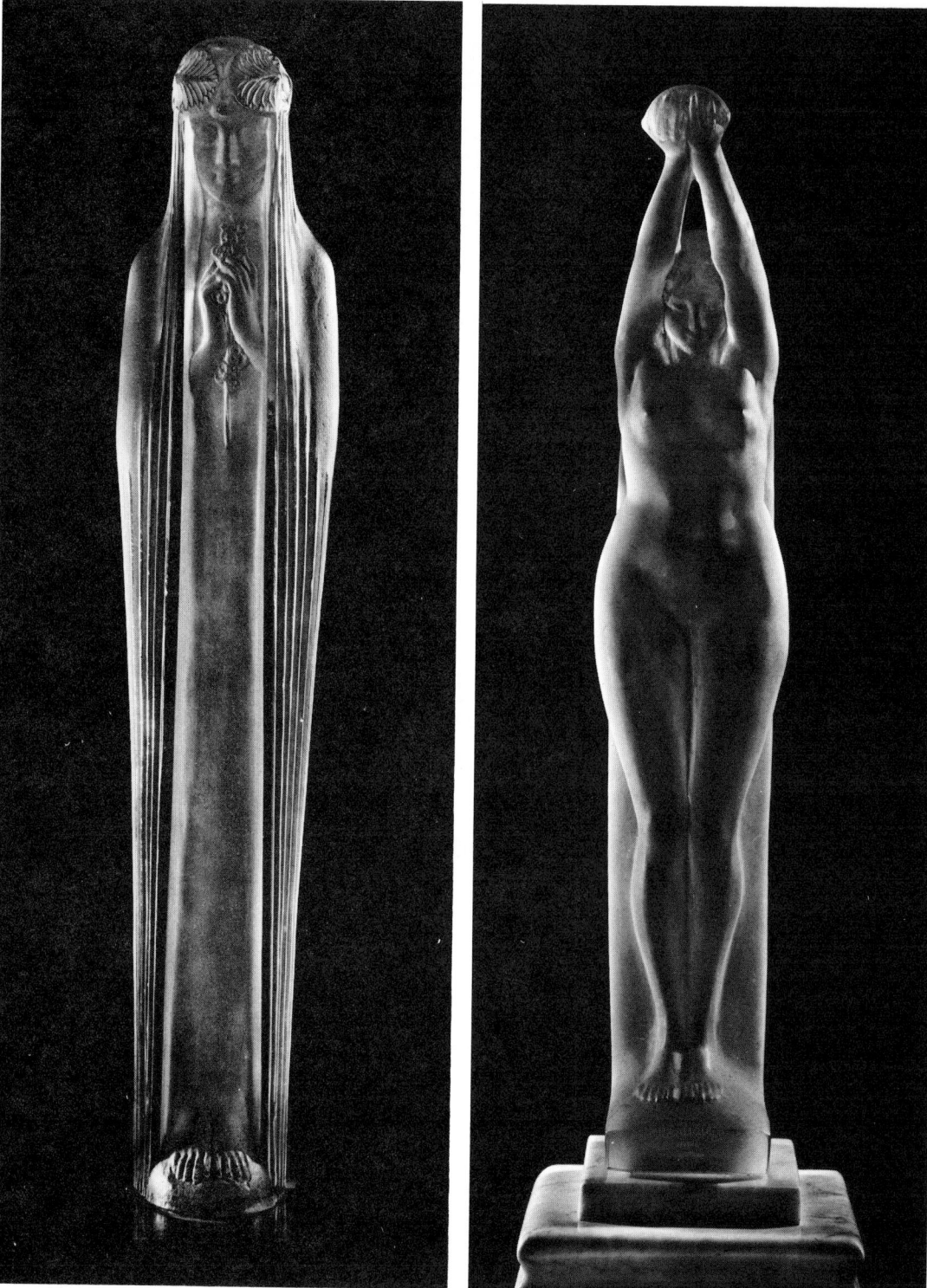

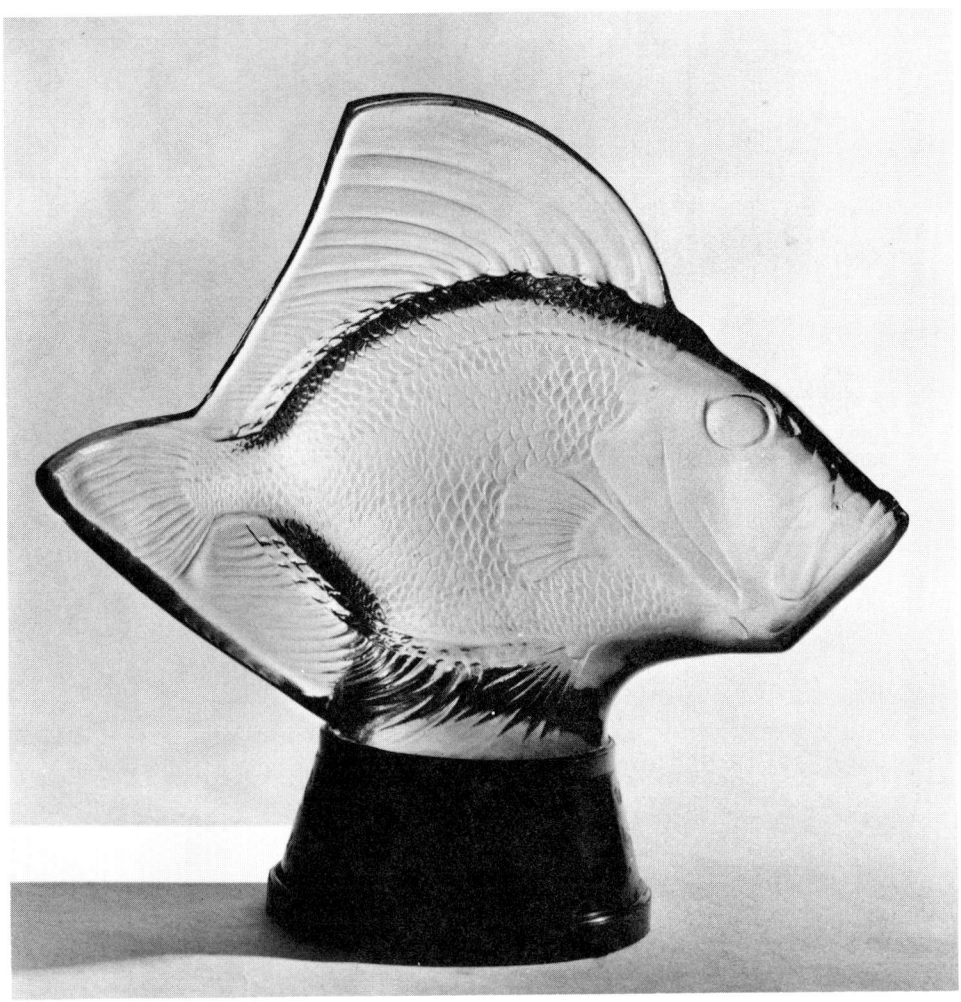

Gros Poisson Vagues, No. 1100. Light on bronze stand mounted for electricity. Colorless glass. "R. Lalique." (Sybarites Gallery Inc.)

Opposite, left: Statuette, "Source de la Fontaine," No. 837. Colorless glass on wooden stand. Figure with flower in hands. No. 700. "R. Lalique." Before 1932. (Sybarites Gallery Inc.)

Opposite, right: Statuette "Grand Nue," arms raised. No. 835. Frosted colorless glass. Mark, "R. Lalique France" in block letters. (Sybarites Gallery Inc.)

"Grand Nue" with long hair on base with ivy relief set on carved wooden stand. R. Lalique before 1932. (Editions Graphiques Ltd.)

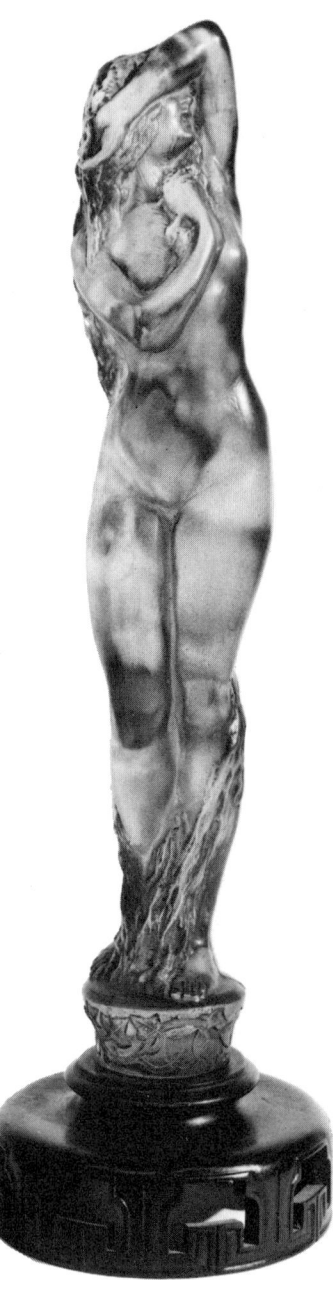

Figure experimental, *cire perdue*. "R. Lalique" in scratched block letters.

"Tête Penchée." Veiled figure in relief on oval with border of blossoms. Made in both clear crystal and color. Height, c.15 inches. Signed "R. Lalique." Before 1932. (Courtesy Fred Silberman, Antiques Center of America.)

CLOCKS, MIRRORS, AND PICTURE FRAMES

Clocks have been an important decorative accessory since their invention. Although a timepiece of some sort dates back many centuries, the clock as we know it did not come into existence until the Middle Ages. French clocks of the periods of Louis XV and Louis XVI were works of art combining marquetry of precious woods, bronze and gilt mountings, and valuable jewels. In conjunction with other decorative accessories the clock was harmonious with the design and color of the furniture and other articles in a room.

The clocks of Lalique were no exception to the rule. In line, form, color, and motifs of design Lalique clocks were in harmony with the decorative surroundings of the 1920s and 1930s. Birds, butterflies, flowers, and nudes or veiled figures conform to the graceful designs of the period rather than to the later modernistic Cubist trends.

Lalique invented lighting fixtures and clocks made of sheets of glass about an inch in thickness with a design deeply etched by acid on the back of the glass. These clocks were mounted on a base which held a concealed electric bulb and the light from the bulb shone up through the thickness of the glass illuminating the incised design. This technique was used in a circular clock with two nude figures of a man and a woman surrounding the clock face. The male figure was cut in intaglio, the female in cameo and the different treatment gave a contrast of dark and light when the light in the bronze base was switched on. This important clock was called "Le Jour et la Nuit." It was first made in the 1920s. There were 3,500 copies of this clock available in *blanc* crystal in 1932. "2 Figurines" was the name of a clock with arched top with a molded figure of a woman in Grecian costume on either side of the dial which was wreathed in flowers. This clock was also first made in the 1920s. Another popular clock was called "2 Colombes." There were two figures of doves sitting in the arched space above the clock dial; 1,350 were available in *blanc* and 1,500 in *couleur* in 1932. "Sirènes" was a square clock with molded figures of nudes and ropes of pearls; 2,200 were available in *blanc* and 2,500 in *couleur* in 1932. Another large clock "Feuilles" had a design of molded leaves about the circular clock case. There were 950 of this model available in *blanc* and 1,100 in *couleur* in 1932.

All of these above mentioned clocks were wired for electricity and were probably the most important clocks made by Lalique.

There was also a group of small eight-day clocks made in *blanc* crystal with molded designs on the clock case. These, as listed in the 1932 Lalique Catalogue, were:

No. 731   "Roitelets" (wrens) *Blanc* 1,125.

No. 732   "Papillons" (a round glass case engraved with butterflies) *Blanc* 1,175.

No. 733   "Muguet" (a round glass case engraved with a wheel-like border of lily of the valley) *Blanc* 1,175.

No. 734   "Marly" (a small circular clock case with sprays of lily of the valley accented with enamel, *Blanc* 1,075.

No. 735   "Rossignols" (a round glass clock case on a glass base with each hour on the clock face marked with a figure of a nightingale) *Blanc* 1,100.

No. 736   "Hélène" (a rectangular clock case ornamented with flower garlands and three nude figures on the pediment) *Blanc* 1,000.

There was also a group of small eight-day clocks listed as "Pendulettes" with square or rectangular cases. These included:

No. 760   "4 Perruches" (four parakeets on blossoming branches on either side of the clock face) *Blanc* 700.

No. 761   "5 Hirondelles" (five flying swallows grouped about the face of a small upright rectangular clock) *Blanc* 700.

No. 763   "6 Hirondelles" (a design of six swallows sitting on tree branches about the face of an upright rectangular clock) *Blanc* 700.

No. 762   "Marguerites" (a clock decorated with a molded pattern of marguerites about the rectangular clock case) *Blanc* 700.

No. 764   "Naïades" (a small square clock case decorated with figures of nude water nymphs with flowing pearly hair) 550 in pale opalescent color.

No. 765   "Inséparables" (a small square clock with birds grouped on branches on either side of the clock face) 550 in pale opalescent glass.

No. 766   "Pierrots" (a tiny round clock with frosted figures of two birds at the top center) *Blanc* 500.

No. 767   "Antoinette" (a small round clock with frosted figures of two birds at top center) *Blanc* 850.

Hand mirrors were among some of the early articles made by Lalique at the end of the 1890s when he was still designing jewelry. There was a mirror with a frame of serpent design and a mirror with a plaquette containing a figure of Narcissus and a border ornamentation of narcissus blossoms. It was called "Narcisse Couché." This mirror was made for many years and was included in the 1932 Catalogue which lists 800 in clear and frosted glass. There were also small oval mirrors made to hang on cords or chains and probably to carry in a purse. The backs of these little mirrors had relief designs of the following: "Psyché," a nude figure with wings; a figure of Narcissus standing; an Art Deco design of a locust; a design called "Tête." All of these designs were made in *blanc* or colorless glass.

A group of larger round mirrors were made with handles or decorative silk tassels. The designs included: "Oiseaux" (birds); "Chèvres" (goats); "Muguets" (lily of the valley); "3 Paons" (peacocks). All were made in large quantities in *blanc* or colorless glass. The 1932 Catalogue also illustrates two large round mirrors, "Rond Grand Eglantine," a design of wild roses and "Rond Grand Epines," a design of hawthorn. Each design is divided into panels and separated by bands of cords or ribbon all executed in relief on colorless glass. These were made in quantities of thousands, so there should be some available to the collector. A large mirror was also made with a frame of serpents.

Lalique also put many of his popular designs on picture frames. There were square, rectangular, and round picture frames with relief decoration made in several sizes and in both color and colorless glass. The designs included the "Inséparables" (parakeets on blossoming branches) which was available in both colored and colorless glass. A small square frame was ornamented with a design of "Muguets" (lily of the valley) and the well-known design "Naïades" (nudes with long pearly tresses) was on another small picture frame. "Guirlandes" was the name of a design of daisies and *bergeronettes* or wag-tail birds nested in the foliage of the engraved design of that name on another frame. Other patterns included: "Hirondelles" (swallows); "Etoiles," a design of stars; "Lys" (lilies); "Bleuets," an allover pattern of these flowers; "2 Figurines et Fleurs," a small round frame with a design of nudes and flowers and an oval center mirror. A large frame "Laurea Grand Modèle" was an Art Deco design of interlacing borders engraved with zig-zag patterns. All of these frames were made in both *blanc* and *couleur*.

The collector may not want to concentrate on mirrors and picture frames, in fact there are not too many available, but the designs include several that are not found on other articles of Lalique glass. Mirrors and *cadres*, or picture frames, listed in the 1932 Catalogue are as follows:

MIRRORS

No.	675	Miroir "Narcisse couché" (hand mirror) *Blanc* 800.
No.	677	Miroir rond "2 Oiseaux" *Blanc* 500.
No.	678	Miroir rond "2 Chèvres" *Blanc* 500.
No.	679	Miroir rond "3 Paons" gland (tassel de soie) *Blanc* 650.
No.	680	Miroir ovale "Sauterelles" (grasshopper) *Blanc* 250.
No.	681	Miroir ovale "Psyché" *Blanc* 250.

No. 682   Miroir ovale "Tête" Blanc 250.
No. 683   Miroir ovale "Narcisse debout" (standing) Blanc 250.
No. 684   Miroir rond "Muguets" gland de soie. Blanc 550.
No. 685   Miroir rond grand "Eglantines" Blanc 2,800.
No. 686   Miroir rond grand "Epines" Blanc 2,800.

All round mirrors are large, 160 mm. Oval mirrors are small, 70 mm., and "rond grand" mirrors are 430 mm. Mirrors were made in *blanc* or clear glass.

CADRES OR PICTURE FRAMES

No. 250   Cadre "2 Figurines et fleurs" Blanc 600.
No. 253   Cadre "Muguets" (lily of the valley) Blanc 225, couleur 250.
No. 254   Cadre "Bleuets" Blanc 600.
No. 255   Cadre "Laurea" (pattern of interlacing lines) Blanc 650.
No. 256   Cadre "Bergeronnettes" (birds and fruit) Blanc 375, couleur 425.
No. 257   Cadre "Hirondelles" (swallows with spread wings) Blanc 275, couleur 325.
No. 258   Cadre "Inséparables" (pairs of love birds in branches) Blanc 250, couleur 300.
No. 259   Cadre "Etoiles" (pattern of stars) Blanc 450, couleur 550.
No. 260   Cadre "Lys" (pattern of lilies in relief) Blanc 600, couleur 725.
No. 263   Cadre "Guirlandes" (pattern of flower garlands) Blanc 225, couleur 250.
No. 264   Cadres "Naïades" (nudes with flowing pearly hair) Blanc 300.

Opposite:
Above, Clock of clear opaline glass with figures of love-birds in relief and painting of same birds on clock dial. "Inséparables." No. 765. Signed "R. Lalique" in glass. (Christie sale, December, 1973.)

Below, Clock "Le Jour et la Nuit." Intaglio and cameo technique on glass stand. No. 728. *Couleur*, 3500. Before 1932.

Silver hand mirrors. *Left:* Leaf and vine design. *Right:* Art Nouveau design of figures and leaf scrolls. R. Lalique, c. 1917. (Editions Graphiques Ltd.)

Opposite:
Above left, Clock "Two Figurines," molded glass ornamentation. No. 726. Lalique c.1926. 3500 available in *couleur* in 1932.

Above right, Small 8 day clock. No. 761. Lalique. 700 available in "blanc" in 1962.

Below, Mirror, molded colorless glass. Lalique. c. 1930-1940. (Martin Cohen.)

PERFUME BOTTLES

Perfumes and essences were known in ancient Egypt and early Greece. The first perfume containers were terra cotta with grotesque head stoppers. There were also bottles of carved onyx and alabaster. The eighteenth century was the real beginning of the perfume industry. In France, Revillon, Houbigant, and Lubin were all established as perfumers at this time. The French perfume containers were flacons with straight sides and molded designs in the style of Louis XV or enameled with flowers or Watteau figures. This was the period when exquisite articles *de toilette* came into use. There were flacons of cut crystal, Sèvres, and Meissen porcelain, and of painted enamel with mountings of engraved gold or ornamented with wood marquetry. There were also bottles of Battersea enamel and Chelsea bottles in the form of animals, Chinamen, and dancing figurines. Bottles of opaline glass were decorated with flowers and butterflies. In England, Apsley Pellat (c. 1820) made cut glass bottles with cameo portrait medallions of Royalty and other famous people. Tiny blown glass Nailsea perfume bottles with fluted necks, dates, and inscriptions were sold at fairs for almost nothing but they have become valuable collectors' items today.

By the nineteenth century the fine perfumers realized the need of special packaging for their perfumes and for the collector of glass perfume bottles this is the important period. The manufactory of Baccarat was founded in 1764. In the mid-nineteenth century the square or round cut glass flacons with decorative designs and hermetically sealed stoppers made by Baccarat were an elegancy of supreme distinction in the Second Empire. Other glass houses besides Baccarat that were making perfume bottles at this time were Cristalleries de Nancy, Cristalleries de Saint Louis, Verreries d'Argenteuil, Viard, and Viollet-le-Duc. In the 1880s cut glass bottles were made in contrasting colors heavily engraved at Stourbridge in England.

At the end of the nineteenth century the genius glassmaker Emile Gallé often created flacons of cameo glass. However the flacons of Gallé were never made for commercial distribution but created as unique pieces to be placed in a vitrine for display.

Lalique too had been experimenting with glass since the 1890s and some of his earliest pieces were small perfume flacons. There was one in Egyptian design and another with a serpent motif. In 1902 Lalique employed four workmen in a glass studio at Clairfontaine, but it was not until 1907 that he exhibited perfume flacons in the vitrines of his shop in the Place Vendôme. M. François Coty had been packaging his perfume in bottles made by Baccarat but when he saw the Lalique flacons Coty approached Lalique with the project of designing for Coty perfumes. The bottles which were made in mass production were manufactured by Legras & Cie. de St. Denis. The flacons were of artistic and harmonious design adapted to the particular essence. Some of the bottles were in Art Nouveau design. This collaboration revolutionized the perfume industry and from this time on all perfumers used decorative bottles for packaging their perfumes.

Although the Coty records are not too clear as to which was the first bottle made by Lalique for Coty, one of the earliest bottles was made for the scent "Ambre Antique" in 1910. Under the heading "Lalique Series" the Coty catalogue of 1928 lists the perfums "Le Cyclamen," "Ambre Antique," and "Styx" with illustrations of the bottles designed by Lalique. In the 1937 Coty catalogue the "Ambre Antique" and "Styx" Lalique bottles are illustrated. The bottle which Lalique designed for "Ambre Antique" followed the Mediterranean concept and was a graceful slender shape of amber glass ornament with figures of women in Grecian costume. The bottle was stamped "R.Lalique" in block letters. A tall slender bottle etched with nude figures and a rounded flat stopper marked "Cyclamen" was designed for "Le Cyclamen" perfume. The perfume "Styx" was also presented in 1910. The bottle was of cut crystal with a molded stopper. There are several sizes and styles of paneled bottles with decorative stoppers that were made for "Styx." The Lalique bottle for "L'Effleurt" depicts a nude dancing figure in a panel among flowers of Art Nouveau style and the stopper is a geometric design enameled in black. It is marked "Lalique L'Effleurt De Coty." A squat circular bottle is marked "Au Coeur des Calices Coty." It has a stopper with a decorative pressed design and is illustrated in a Lalique catalogue. There were other interesting bottles made for Coty perfumes but the records do not tell whether they were made by Lalique or not. The perfume "Jacée" in a square cut crystal bottle with carved stopper packaged in a box of Chinese design is illustrated in the 1937 Coty catalogue. The bottle for "Heliotrope" has a decorative molded stopper and the bottle for "Paris" (1922) is of pale blue glass in a flattened circular form with molded floral stopper and a case decorated with a view of Paris on a blue ground. The bottle for "A Suma" (1929) was round with a molded floral pattern. It was boxed in a lacquer-red box decorated with Oriental motifs. Both this box and the autumn leaf box which was used for "Jacée," "L'Ambre Antique," "L'Emeraude," and "L'Origan" may have been designed by Lalique because we do know that he designed the well-known powder box for "L'Origan" which is still in use. The perfume "Le Vertige" (1936), probably the last fragrance created by M. Coty before his death, was packaged in a bottle with molded design but the records do not indicate if it was of Lalique glass.

Two interesting perfume bottles were illustrated in a Lalique catalogue: No. 528 "Flacon Satyre" has a molded satyr head in the bottle extending from the end of the stopper; No. 528 "Jeunesse" has a molded figure of a nude cherub at the end of the stopper which extends down into the bottle. Both of these flacons are rare.

Lalique also designed bottles for other French perfume manufacturers including D'Orsay, Roger et Gallet, Arys, Rigaud, Forvil, Vigny, and Worth between 1910 and 1925. For Forvil he designed the bottle for "Perle Noire" and for Worth Lalique designed the bottle for "Je Reviens," "L'Ambre" for Vigny and "Les Deux Colombes" for D'Orsay. These included tall mushroom-stoppered bottles, round bottles decorated with mollusks of contrasting colors, and engraved bottles of mushroom or sea urchin shape made for Worth. The bottles were of clear crystal with moldings, sunken panels, and decorative stoppers. If color was used it was pale mauve, blue, green, antique ivory, amber or topaz to harmonize with the amber, topaz and emerald of the essences. There were a variety of forms—flat, round, cylindrical, cubic, oval, and stirrup-cup shapes. Some bottles had long silk tassels attached to their neck. The designs drew inspiration from the Orient, from classic Greece and Rome, and from French historic styles, as well as from new motifs of Art Deco. There were bottles with dancing nudes and garlands of flowers on a diadem stopper for "Leurs Ames D'Orsay." A bottle for D'Orsay perfume, c. 1912, has tall figures of Grecian women set in panels. Another bottle for D'Orsay perfume was of oval form molded with an allover pattern of lines and had a tall Grecian figure for a stopper. Bottles for Arys were of plain oval or round shapes with decorative stoppers. The bottles for La Parfumerie Rigaud were ornamented with molded designs and had large decorative stoppers. Several strikingly designed bottles were made for Roger et Gallet perfumes. One oval bottle had a sunburst flower design and the bottle for "Paquert" had an elaborate circular stopper with engraved daisies which enclosed the top of the bottle in a grand floral diadem similar to those of Lalique lights. The green bottle for Roger et Gallet "La Jade" has a design of tropical birds in relief. Within ten years Lalique is known to have manufactured from 250 to 500 million perfume bottles for various French perfumers.

In about 1909 Lalique opened Verrerie de Combs-la-Ville where he manufactured his own glass on a commercial scale. This glass included vases, statuettes, perfume flacons, and many other articles with molded, engraved, and enameled designs.

The perfume bottle had been such a success that Lalique continued to include flacons, *brûle-parfums*, and *garniture de toilette* in many different designs in his commercial output of glass from about 1909 until the present day. The 1932 Lalique Catalogue lists between 90 and 100 different designs of perfume bottles with three plates illustrating the designs. Many of the flacons illustrated were first made as early as 1912; some are made in clear crystal, others are also made in color, and still others are decorated with

94 · Lalique for Collectors

enamel. There are a few flacons with decorative tiara stoppers that are especially valuable collector's items. As listed in 1932 Catalogue they include:

No. 493   "Bouchon Fleurs de Pommier" (bottle with an allover design of scallops and tiara-type bouchon or stopper of engraved apple blossoms) 500 were available in clear transparent glass.

No. 494   "Bouchon Cassis" (plain paneled bottle with a tiara stopper of grapes) 225 were listed in clear glass, 250 in color.

No. 495   "Bouchon Mûres" (rectangular paneled bottle with a tiara stopper of mulberries) 225 were listed in clear glass, 250 in color.

No. 496   "Bouchon 3 Hirondelles" (plain bottle with a tiara stopper of three flying swallows) 250 were available in clear transparent glass.

No. 507   "Bouchon Eucalyptus" (slender bottle with a tiara stopper of eucalyptus pods and leaves) 130 were available in clear glass, 165 in color in 1932.

No. 525   "Muguet" (small flacon with a bunch of lily of the valley as a stopper) 125 were available in clear glass.

No. 526   "Clairfontaine" (small round bottle with a spray of lily of the valley on the stopper) 150 available in clear glass. Still being produced.

Other especially interesting perfume flacons are:

No. 514   "Amphridite" (engraved and molded bottle in the shape of a snail shell with the kneeling figure of a nude as a stopper) 115 were listed in clear glass, 140 in color in 1932.

No. 524   "Tantôt" (tall oval bottle with a molded design of fan-like leaves and a molded stopper of the same design) The bottle was first made in 1924. In the 1932 catalogue 80 are listed in clear glass, 100 in color.

No. 502   "Serpent" (An oval flacon molded in a pattern of a serpent's skin with a stopper in the form of a molded serpent) In 1932 only 50 were available in clear glass. This bottle is also found with an engraved serpent.

No. 508   "Telline" (small bottle in the shape of a clam shell molded with a pattern of the shell and with a stopper in the form of a shell) It was available in small quantity: 65 in clear glass, 80 in color.

No. 475   "4 Cigales" (tall rectangular bottle with four molded cicada) First made c. 1912. In the 1932 Catalogue 185 were listed in clear glass, 200 in color.

No. 477   "A Côtes Bouchon Papillon" (rounded squat bottle with molded butterflies on the stopper) 100 were available in clear glass in 1932.

No. 490   "Méplat, 2 Figurines" (flattened rectangular bottle with an oval panel of two nude figurines and a stopper with molded figurines) 450 were listed in clear glass.

No. 489   "Fougères" (tiny rectangular bottle with a molded pattern of ferns and an oval medallion of the bust of a woman with a mirror) There were 350 listed in clear glass.

No. 488   "Rosace Figurines" (round bottle with a design of nude figurines and fan-like molded stopper) First made in the 1920s. 250 were listed in clear glass in 1932.

No. 476   "Pavot" (small rounded bottle molded with a design of the petals of a poppy) It has a decorative molded stopper. First made in the 1920 s. In 1932, 150 were available in clear glass.

No. 522   "Hélène" or "Lotus" (a small squat bottle molded with a pattern of lotus leaves and seed pods) In 1932, 70 were available in clear glass and 80 in color.

Nos. 511–512   "2 Danseuses" "6 Danseuses" (two flattened round bottles with designs of nude dancers) There were 350 of each bottle available in clear glass.

No. 487   "Panier de Roses"—one of the loveliest bottles—a tall column with a pattern of trellis work over the bottle engraved with roses. A molded border of roses at the top of the vase and a stopper of molded roses. Only available in clear glass.

No. 484   "Capricorne"—also an interesting bottle—has an engraved and enameled design of scarabs on the bottle and on the flattened round stopper.

No. 504   "Pan" (bottle with a masque of the god Pan and garlands of leafy ornament) Made in clear glass. Only 80 were listed in 1932.

There were several bottles with molded handles and stoppers and some of the leaf patterns that were used on large vases were also to be found on the bottles. No. 519, "Cactus," a frosted bottle with enameled pattern of all-over dots is still being made.

The 1932 Catalogue also illustrates several larger bottles for brûle-parfums. The molded designs on these bottles are particularly interesting. "Sirènes" is a bottle with molded figures of nudes. "Papillons" has a molded pattern of butterflies. "Faune" is a cylinder-shaped bottle with a pattern of fluting and circles and a stopper in the shape of a nude figure. Brûle parfum "Carrousel" is a round bottle with frosted figures of birds. These are all desirable bottles.

Flacons were also included in the *garniture de toilette* sets for a lady's dressing table. The "Enfants" pattern had a band of molded nude infants. This set included a round box and a vaporizor and was made in both clear and colored glass. Another pattern of garniture de toilette was "Perles," a design of ropes of pearls which included bottles of three sizes, covered boxes, and trays and was made in both polished and satin glass. "Epines," a pattern of molded hawthorn included bottles of four sizes, boxes of three sizes, and trays for hairpins, combs, and soap. It was made in both clear and enameled

Opposite: left, Perfume flacon "Capricorne." Engraved and lacquered design of beetle on clear crystal. Marked, "R. Lalique" in rounded script. Before 1932.

Right, Perfume flacon "Panier de Roses." Molded and engraved design on clear crystal. Lalique, before 1932. (both, John Jesse Gallery.)

glass. The pattern "Fleurettes" had a narrow molded floral border at the edges and on the stoppers of bottles and boxes and on the rims of trays. There were three sizes of bottles, two covered powder boxes, three rectangular trays, and one oval bowl. The pattern was available in both transparent and satin glass. The pattern "Myosotis" was decorated with narrow borders of floral design and had a figurine stopper. There were three sizes of bottles and a round covered box. A garniture de toilette called "Duncan" had a center panel of molded nudes with molded line borders. There were three sizes of square bottles and two small vertical rectangular bottles, one a vaporizer. There was also a covered square box and a square tray, both with figure panels and two undecorated rectangular trays and a transparent undecorated round bowl. The attractive "Dahlia" pattern had a large molded flower on the sides of the bottles and vaporizers and the tops of two covered boxes. This pattern is still in production. In about 1950 Lalique made an apple-shaped bottle for the Nina Ricci "Fille d'Eve" perfume. Also today there are several Lalique bottles made for Nina Ricci perfumes. These include the heart-shaped bottle with molded floral design made for "Coeur-Joie" and the bottle and dusting powder box with stoppers of a gracefully sculptured single or double dove which is made for "L'Air du Temps." These bottles are collectors' items and the empty bottles often sell for more than the bottles when they were filled with perfume.

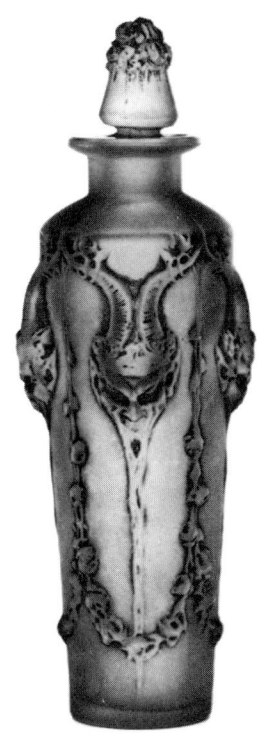

Above left, Perfume flacon, "Pan," with design of head of Pan and garlands in relief. Clear crystal. Lalique before 1932. (John Jesse Gallery.)

Above right, Perfume flacon "Serpent." Molded pattern of snake skin with serpent stopper. Clear crystal before 1932. (John Jesse Gallery.)

Left, Perfume flacon "Carré Hirondelles" with relief design of flying swallows. Clear crystal, Lalique, before 1932. (John Jesse Gallery.)

Above, Group of Lalique perfume flacons. Eagle seal at far right. (Sotheby Belgravia Sale, June 22, 1972.)

Right, Dusting powder box of frosted crystal with molded figure of dove. (Nina Ricci Parfums.)

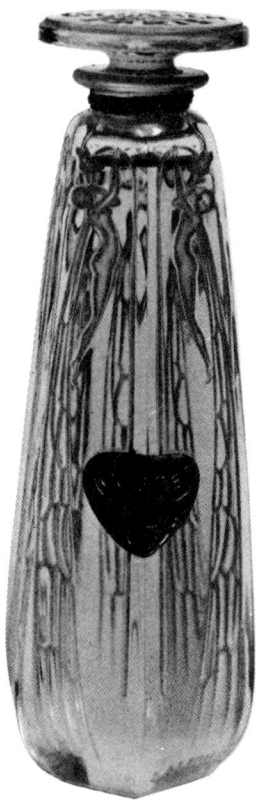

Above left, Perfume bottle for "L'Effleurt de Coty." Relief panel of nude and molded stopper of Egyptian design tinted with black. Marked "R. Lalique." (Coty International.)

Above right, Perfume bottle for "Ambre Antique" with engraved classic figures and molded stopper. Marked "R. Lalique." c.1910. (Coty International.)

Right, Perfume bottle for "Cyclamen." Engraved with design of nudes. Lalique before 1928. (Coty International.)

Flacon with three groups of two nude dancers each in relief and figure of sitting nude as stopper. R. Lalique, c.1925.

Group of perfume bottles. *Left,* Lalique with molded butterfly stopper. *Rear center,* Lalique with blossoms in relief and flower stopper. *Front right,* Lalique bottle with molded design of artichoke leaves called "Marquita." All before 1932. (Barry Friedman.)

Bottle with relief designs of nudes and blossoms. (John Jesse Gallery.)

Brûle Parfum with Art Nouveau design of nude sirens. R. Lalique, c.1920-1925. (Editions Graphiques Ltd.)

～～ DINNER SERVICES, CANDLESTICKS, AND ANNUAL PLATE

Lalique acquired his glassworks Verrerie d'Alsace René Lalique & Cie. at Wingen sur Moder in the Bas-Rhin, the historic glass making center of France, in 1920. At this time he enlarged his production of glass to include not only such articles as vases and statuettes, but also all sorts of useful pieces such as complete sets of services for the dining table. These table services included almost every article used on the dining table from hors d'oeuvre services to finger bowls. There were semicircular shaped side dishes, plates of several sizes, bowls, and sauce dishes, water glasses, goblets and glasses for different wines, champagne glasses, and champagne stirrers, ice buckets, saucers and cups with butterfly and flower handles, cheese dishes, sardine dishes with sardines in relief on their covers, knife rests, menus and holders for place cards. Carafes had matching glasses and services for port wine had matching trays and portable liquor cabinets consisted of a stand holding three liquor flacons. The service for orangeade consisted of a pitcher and matching glasses. There were also flower vases, figurines, plateaux for the center of the table—including the engraved "Cygnes" (swans)—candlesticks and candelabra. These articles were made in great quatities, the number varying with the popularity of the design. The patterns included Lalique's repertory of popular designs and the majority of the articles were made in both clear and colored glass.

Coupes and assiettes comprised the largest group and these were made in fifty different designs. The most popular design was "Coupe Sirènes" and in 1932 there were 2,200 bowls of this pattern available in colorless glass (*blanc*) and 2,500 in colored glass. "Martigues," a design of ten goldfish arranged on a bowl, was another favorite pattern. There were 900 available in *blanc* and 1,100 in colored glass. "Cyprins" was another plate with a fish design; 900 were available in colorless glass in 1932. The bowl "Phalènes" had a border of butteflies. This pattern was available in colored glass. "Flora Bella" a sunflower design; "Anvers," a pattern of seedpods, and "Anges," a stylized design of vase forms and leaves were also available in colored glass. There were 1,200 crystal bowls with figures of two mocking birds, "2 Moineaux Moqueurs," of frosted glass sitting on the rim of the bowl. Two unusual designs were "Madagascar," a bowl with heads of monkeys in relief and "Eléphants" a bowl with a wide flange and a band of elephants in frosted relief on the base of the bowl. Other attractive bowls included "Gazelles," a bowl with leaves and figures of gazelles, "Saint Vincent," a pattern of grapes and grape vines, and "Filix," a pattern of fern fronds. This last was available in color and colorless glass and also with the pattern outlined in enamel. It was made in both bowl and plate form. There were several patterns of allover designs of flowers and the bowl "Nemours" with a design of daisies in relief with enamel centers was made before 1932 and is still being produced. The bowl "Gui" (mistletoe) was made in several sizes. It sits on tripod glass feet and was made in *blanc, couleur,* and enameled glass.

Other attractive designs of bowls included "Coquilles," shells, made in both *blanc* and *couleur* and "Nonnettes," a pattern of birds available in color only. "Bol Fleur" was a small bowl in clear crystal accented with enamel. There were also bowls and plates in the "Ondines" pattern of nude sea maidens. Both bowls and plates were made in the popular "Calypso" design with figures of five watery nudes in relief. These were available in both colored and colorless glass. The plates were marked in their centers "R. Lalique" in block letters. There was also a small plate with a figurine and flowers. The plate was available in colorless glass. The pattern "Chasse Chiens" with a rim border of hounds chasing was made in clear crystal with accents of enamel. Other typical Lalique designs included "Véronique," "Volubilis," "Vernon" (daisy), "Chicorée," and "Eglantine." One of the most desirable bowls for the collector is "Armentières" which has a molded border of stylized roses around its rim. There were also several bowls with Art Deco designs.

The carafe was one of the most attractive pieces of Lalique tableware. Carafes were early in Lalique's glassmaking career at Verrerie de Combs-la-Ville. They were decorated with designs in relief and engraved and enameled designs. An interesting carafe is called "6 Figurines." It has alternating vertical panels of nudes in relief and clear glass. There was a goblet in matching design. This carafe is similar to the rare carafe in *verre blanc* which was exhibited in the Art Décoratif Salon in 1911. In addition to the panels of nudes the neck of the carafe is ornamented with "tears" of applied glass which terminate in frogs' heads. The carafe has a tall pointed stopper. This design relates to the earlier work of Lalique before he began mass production. The carafe is now in the Musée des Arts Décoratifs. It is marked "R.Lalique" in block letters at the base of a plain panel. The "Masque" carafe was also first made c. 1911. In the 1932 Lalique Catalogue it is listed as being available in color or enamel. The stopper was of molded glass but it was also available with a silver stopper. A vase of similar design with a masque medallion was also made. There is also a carafe with figures of two veiled dancing nudes. Another especially desirable design is "Carafe Coquilles." Its shape is that of a clam shell and it is pressed with the shell design and has a molded stopper of shell pattern. This carafe was made in both colored and colorless glass. An attractive design is a carafe with a thorny relief pattern and there is one with a hawthorn pattern in relief. Another desirable carafe is the one with molded square repeats ornamented with a zig-zag pattern. There is a carafe with a grape design and a slender carafe with tall pointed stopper with a design of marguerites. This has a goblet to match. A pyramid shaped carafe is also interesting.

Caves à liqueurs holding three flacons were made in large quantities of over 3,000 sets in colorless crystal. One set included a center flacon engraved with a figure of Pan and two side flacons with figures of Bacchantes. The "Cave Enfants" had stoppers of molded figures of infants. The bottles and rounded stoppers of "Cave Vigne" were decorated with an engraved design of vines. Another set of flacons had beaded borders and a stopper in the beaded pattern in relief.

Glasses and goblets were produced in a variety of shapes and designs. There were slender stemmed funnel-shaped glasses engraved with patterns of vines and convolvulus. There were also goblets with a frieze of molded personages, goblets with molded frogs at their bases, and others had a molded band of dogs, cocks, or lizards; still others had scenes of hunting dogs. These goblets were all available in color or enamel decoration. There were also goblets with engraved designs of spirals, a lotus, and poppy. *Services à porto* included a pitcher, tray, and matching glasses. The pitcher usually was ornamented with a molded design at its base and the glasses also had similar designs at their bases. The trays were ornamented with molded designs at their rims. "Bamboo" was an effective design of stepped borders of molded vertical bamboo stalks. There were also pitchers, glasses, and trays for services of orangeade and ice cream services consisting of a bowl and six dishes. These were made in a variety of designs in both colored and colorless glass. Round trays or *plateaux* were available in more than a dozen different patterns in both clear and colored glass.

There were vases especially made to hold flowers including vases of crystal with frosted molded figures of pigeons or crickets at the handles. A group of funnel-shaped vases had molded figures at their bases. These included figures of birds, cocks, flowers, or squirrels in frosted glass while the vase itself was in clear crystal with vertical fluting. The vase "Faune" had a base design of a faun's face in cut glass. Candlesticks were also made in designs to match these vases. The vase and candlestick "Mésanges" (tomtit) are still being made. There were many different designs of single candlesticks including birds, leaves, flowers, and geometric patterns. Two or three candlesticks were joined together to form candelabra. Especially effective was the design called "Volutes" which was of similar design to the vase made c. 1932. Another attractive candelabra had angled branches with sockets for four candles and was ornamented with a relief pattern of mountain ash leaves and berries. A *garniture de cheminée* consisted of a pair of three branched candelabra with frosted figures of flying wrens. There was a round clock with a frame of figures of the same birds and a funnel-shaped vase with wrens at the base also matched.

Dining tables of glass were also made by Lalique. These tables consisted of a sheet of transparent glass with an equally transparent base and had framework supports of chromium plated metal. The glass of these tables was ornamented with designs that were acid etched or made by sandblasting. The thick glass of the table top had an arrangement for lighting the central panel from underneath. The supports and glass plinth were cast. These tables were made in limited quantities. They were advertised by Breves Galleries, London, in *The Studio Yearbook* for 1931.

The following are lists taken from the 1932 Lalique Catalogue.

COUPES ET ASSIETTES (BOWLS AND PLATES)

- No. 375   Coupe "Sirènes" (bowl with border of nudes) *Blanc* 2,200, *couleur* 2,500.
- No. 376   Coupe trépied "Sirène" *Blanc* 800, *couleur* 925.
- No. 377   Coupe "Martigues" (design of goldfish) *Blanc* 900, *couleur* 1,100.
- No. 378   Coupe "Cyprins," plate (goldfish) *Couleur* 900.
- No. 379   Coupe "Cyprins" refermée (bowl) *Couleur* 900.
- No. 380   Coupe "Ondines" ouverte (nude) *Blanc* 185, *couleur* 200.
- No. 381   Coupe "Ondines" fermée *Blanc* 185, *couleur* 200.
- No. 382   Coupe "Lys" satiné tripod *Blanc* 160, *couleur* 200.
- No. 383   Coupe "Volubilis" (design of leaves) *Blanc* 80, *couleur* 100.
- No. 385   Coupe "Coquilles" (shells) *Blanc* 165, *couleur* 235.
- No. 387   Coupe sur pied "Clairvaux" émail (bowl on stem with sculptured knob) *Blanc* 250, *couleur* 275.
- No. 388   Coupe sur pied "Saint Denis" émail (bowl on stem with sculptured knob) *Blanc* 250, *couleur* 275.
- No. 389   Coupe "Filix" (fern pattern) *Blanc* 160, *couleur* 250. Also with enamel)
- No. 390   Coupe "Gazelles" (deer) *Blanc* 275, *couleur* 335.
- No. 391   Coupe "Saint Vincent" (pattern of grapes and vines) *Blanc* 325, *couleur* 450.

Dinner Services, Candlesticks, Annual Plate · 109

No. 392 Coupe "Cernuschi" (deep bowl with rim of relief design) *Blanc* 325, *couleur* 375.

No. 393 Coupe "Armentières" (bowl with rim border of roses) *Blanc* 375, *couleur* 425.

No. 395 Coupe "Vernon" (three large flowers) *Couleur* 65.

No. 396 Coupe "Mont Doré" (wreath) *Couleur* 100.

No. 397 Coupe "Véronique" (three veronica blossoms) *Couleur* 90.

No. 398 Coupe "Nonnettes" (three groups of birds with spread wings) *Couleur* 70.

No. 399 Coupe "Montigny" (geometric design of lines) *Blanc* 300, *couleur* 400.

No. 400 Coupe "Crémieu" (geometric ropes and bubbles) *Blanc* 250, *couleur* 350.

No. 401 Coupe "Tournon" (flower heads) *Blanc* 250, *couleur*, 300.

No. 402 Coupe "Villeneuve" (star design in bowl) *Blanc* 300, *couleur* 375.

No. 403 Coupe "Madagascar" (border of monkey heads) *Blanc* 375, *couleur* 500.

No. 404 Coupe "Nemours" émail (allover pattern of flower heads with enamel centers) *Blanc* 200, *couleur* 225. (Still being made)

No. 405 Coupe "Fleurville" (consecutive borders of flower heads) *Blanc* 160, *couleur* 225.

No. 406 Coupe "Phalènes" (border of butterflies) *couleur* 900.

No. 407 Coupe "Flora Bella" (bursting blossoms) *Couleur* 900.

No. 408 Coupe "Anvers" (border and center of stems and seed pods) *Couleur* 900.

No. 409 Coupe "Rosace" (geometric pattern of borders of triangles) *Couleur* 200.

No. 410 Coupe "Anges" (pattern of angels and vases of flowers) *Couleur* 900.

No. 411 Coupe "Eléphants" (border of elephants in relief in base) *Blanc* 800.

No. 412	Coupe cristal "2 Moineaux Moqueurs" (mocking birds) *Blanc* 1,200.
No. 413	Coupe "Calypso" (nude sea maidens) *Blanc* 350, *couleur* 350.
No. 414	Assiette "Calypso" *Blanc* 400, *couleur* 400.
No. 414	Assiette "Eglantine" (crystal plate with group of flowers in relief in center) *Blanc* 210, *couleur* 210.
No. 3001	Assiette "Chasse Chiens" émail (plate with border of chasing hounds) *Blanc* 330.
No. 3002	Assiette "1 Figurine et fleurs" (nude figurine and flowers) *Blanc* 175.
No. 3003	Assiette "Ondines" (nudes) *Blanc* 225, *couleur* 260.
No. 3023	Assiette "Filix" (ferns) *Blanc* 350, *couleur* 375.
No. 3100	Coupe "Bol Fleur" émail (small bowl with large flower in relief) *Blanc* 140.

CAVES A LIQUEURS

No. 1184	Cave à liqueurs "Pan et Bacchantes" (carafes with figures of Pan and Bacchantes) *Blanc* 2,700.
No. 1185	Flacon seul "Pan." *Blanc* 300.
No. 1186	Flacon seul "Bacchantes." *Blanc* 300.
No. 1187	Cave à liqueurs "Enfant" (stoppers have pressed figures of infants) *Blanc* 2,250.
No. 1188	Flacon seul. *Blanc* 250.
No. 1189	Cave à liqueurs "Vigne" (design of vines) *Blanc* 2,250.
No. 1190	Flacon seul. *Blanc* 250.
No. 1201	Cave à liqueurs "Glasgow" (bottles with molded stoppers and edges) *Blanc* 2,250.
No. 1202	Flacon seul. *Blanc* 250.

BROCS ET CARAFES (PITCHERS AND CARAFES)

No. 3152	Carafe pyramidale (clear glass pyramid form) *Blanc* 150.

No. 3153 Carafe plate, "2 Danseuses" (carafe with center medallion of two dancers and garlands) Blanc 700.
No. 3155 Carafe "Reine Marguerite" (flowers) Enamel or *couleur* 450. Same vase with glass stopper, enamel or *couleur* 525.
No. 3156 Carafe "Masque" Enamel or *couleur* 450. Same carafe with glass stopper 525, with silver stopper 625.
No. 3157 Carafe "Aubépine" (hawthorn design) Blanc 525, *couleur* 600.
No. 3158 Carafe "6 Figurines" Enamel or *couleur*, 600. Goblet to match.
No. 3161 Carafe "Marguerites" bouchon pointu (marguerites with pointed stopper and goblet to match) Blanc 275, *couleur* 325.
No. 3163 Carafe "Coquilles" (clam shell design) Blanc 250, *couleur* 300.
No. 3164 Carafe "Vrilles de Vigne" (round form with design of vine tendrils) Blanc 200.
No. 3165 Carafe "Raisins" (grape design with glasses and tray to match) Blanc 225, *couleur* 275.
No. 3166 Carafe plate "Epines" (thorn design) Blanc 190, enamel or *couleur* 225.
No. 3169 Carafe "Dundee" (molded design or repeat squares with triangles) Blanc 175, enamel or *couleur* 200.
No. 3170 Carafe bantam. Blanc 100.

Today a new phase of collecting is centered on annual limited editions. This includes annual plates and other articles such as mugs, sculptures, paperweights, and commemorative medals of glass, porcelain, silver, or other metals which are sold as "limited editions." A limited edition is any object produced in multiples of a certain number after which the original mold or pattern is destroyed and production ceases.

Good antiques are getting more and more difficult to find and are now priced beyond the purse of the average collector. But the interest in collecting continues and limited editions provide a new field at a reasonable price and a continuing increase. In most cases prices have soared from year to year.

In 1965 René Lalique & Cie. of France decided to make an annual plate.

These plates are designed by Marie-Claude Lalique and grand-daughter of René Lalique. The subjects of the plates are drawn from nature but the motifs are stylized in a modern manner. The technique is a combination of transparent clear glass and satin etched surfaces. The first plate was issued in September 1965; 2,000 were made. This plate was a design of stylized flowers and branches and in the center of the plate are two decorative birds with necks entwined. The title of the plate is "Deux Oiseaux," two birds. The plates are $8\frac{1}{2}$ inches in diameter. Each plate is dated and signed "Lalique France" in small script. This first plate was issued at $25 but now sells for about $2,000. The second Lalique plate was issued in May 1966. It is a design of a large single rose and is entitled "Dreamrose." A larger quantity (c. 3,000) of this plate was made. This plate now sells for about $500. The 1967 plate is a design of swirling seaweed and five fish. Issued at $25, the plate now sells for $400. The 1968 plate is a stylized deer with long curled horns; it now sells for $200. The 1969 plate is a modern design of a butterfly, star-like flowers, and stems; its present price is $150. A peacock was the inspiration for the 1970 plate. The peacock body is in the plate center and it is surrounded by conventionalized peacock feathers. The 1971 Lalique owl plate is the most dramatic design. Since owls are favorites with collectors the price should mount. In 1973 it was priced at $100. The 1972 Lalique plate has a large stylized shell. This plate which came out at $40 was priced at $75 in 1973. The 1973 Lalique plate is a large realistic eagle head; the eagle has long been a favorite Lalique motif. Between 8,000 and 10,000 plates are now made.

In collecting Lalique annual plates one should know how many plates there are in the edition. The name of the designer and the mark as well as the esthetic value are important. If you have lost out on the first plate pay a premium and buy it, as a complete collection has more value than single plates. The chance to collect an object that not everyone can have and the hope that it will increase at least to double or triple price not only as a collectable but as an investment is what lures the collector into the field.

Carafe with figures of nude maidens. Applied glass ending in frogs' heads on neck of carafe. Mark "R. Lalique" in block letters near base. Before 1911. (Musée des Arts Décoratifs.)

Glass bowl with design of whirling fish and bubbles. Lalique before 1932. (The Minneapolis Institute of Arts.)

LALIQUE GLASS for the CONNOISSEUR

Glass Table with design of fruit and leaves – one of the many exclusive exhibits at Breves' Lalique Galleries.

Among the works of René Lalique there are certain "collectors' pieces" of such beauty and rarity that they are seldom to be obtained outside Paris. The only exhibition in England which includes these desirable acquisitions is at Breves' Lalique Galleries. Not merely a small selection, but the whole range of Lalique's creations is here presented, and the prices are as varied as the glass itself. Two books of interest to every connoisseur of glass – "The Art of René Lalique" and "Lalique Lights" – will be sent post free for 1s. 6d.

Every genuine example of Lalique Glass bears one of the artist's marks reproduced here.

BREVES' LALIQUE GALLERIES
2 BASIL ST., SLOANE STREET, LONDON, S.W.3
Lift to Galleries.
(Close to Knightsbridge Underground)   *Telephone:* Kensington 1928-7471

Advertisement of Breves' Lalique Galleries showing glass table and Lalique marks. (Studio Yearbook, 1931.)

Right, Pair of candlesticks. Clear and frosted glass with molded leaf pattern partially polished. Height, 7⅞ inches. Mark "R. Lalique France" in block letters on base. (The Toledo Museum of Art.)

Below, Round platter, sculptured fern design radiating from the center. Diameter, 17½ inches. Signed "R. Lalique France" in block letters. (The Chrysler Museum at Norfolk.)

Lalique Annual Plate, 1968. (Jacques Jugeat Inc.)

Below, Round plate, clear glass with sculptured dandelion leaf design radiating from center. Diameter 12 inches. Signed "R. Lalique France." (The Chrysler Museum at Norfolk.)

Lalique Annual Plate, 1969.
(Jacques Jugeat Inc.)

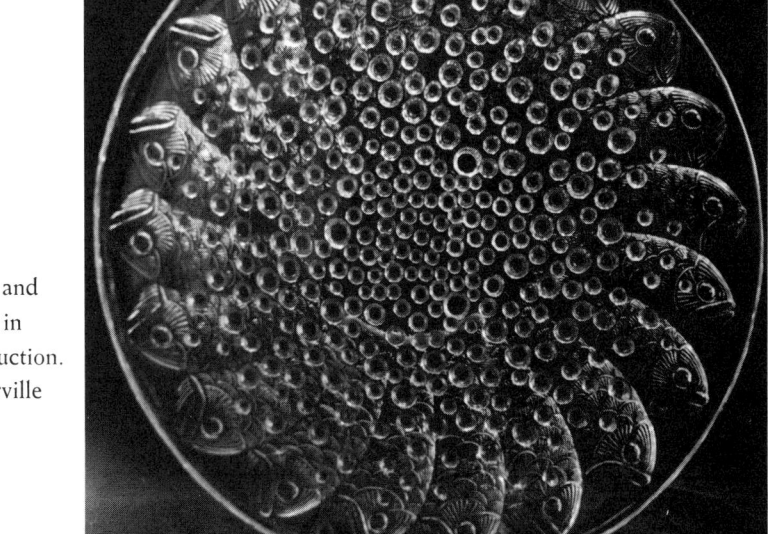

Shallow bowl fish pattern and bubbles. Signed "Lalique" in small script. Current production. (Maler's Gift Gallery.) Orville Voight, photo.

~~ RADIATOR CAPS AND PAPERWEIGHTS

The first Lalique radiator caps were made in the middle or late 1920s. The "Archer," a design of a kneeling male nude with bow and arrow molded in intaglio was illustrated in *Mobilier et Décoration* in 1927; an article on Lalique radiator caps appeared in *The Studio* in 1931, and *The Studio Yearbook* for 1931 carried an illustration of the elongated racing greyhound that Lalique designed for H.R.H. Prince George. A similar design was later included in the 1932 Lalique Catalogue. These decorative *bouchons de radiateur* became so popular that forty-six designs were listed and illustrated in the 1932 Lalique Catalogue. The majority of the radiator caps were available in clear crystal (*blanc*) but some could also be had in *couleur*. Lalique's realistically modeled head of an eagle with molded feathers, part polished and part frosted, was used by officers of Hitler's Reich. This figure was 4½ inches in height and was marked "R.Lalique France" in block letters. According to the 1932 Lalique Catalogue there were 400 of these eagle heads available. The "Libellule" or dragonfly design was one of the most popular. It was made in two sizes: "Libellule Petite" with block letter signature and "Libellule Grande" which was 8½ inches in height and had an engraved and molded signature "R.Lalique France" in script. The dragonfly was fastened on a bronze base beneath which was attached a multicolored lighted disc connected to the dynamo of the car so that the disc revolved and cast rainbow shades of light through the insect which changed with the speed of the car. "Vitesse" a figure of a kneeling nude was also a popular model. It was available in both *blanc* and *couleur*. This figure was also made as a paperweight. A similar figure called "Danseuse" is now being manufactured. "Chrysis" was also a nude figure. Models of this figure were made in *blanc* and *couleur*.

A large figure of a cock, "Coq Houdan," was also a favorite radiator cap. It was available in both clear crystal and in color and was marked "R.Lalique France" in block letters. Other figures of cocks included "Coq Nain," a small figure in crystal and in color. A figure of five horses galloping in Greek style is 8½ inches in height. It was made in clear crystal and marked "R.Lalique" in block letters. "Epsom" and "Longchamps" were figures of horses' heads made in clear crystal. A woman's head "Victoire" or "Spirit of the Wind" with hair flying back in Art Deco style was first made before 1930. It was marked "R.Lalique France" and was listed as being made in clear crystal in the 1932 Lalique Catalogue. There was also a star in Art Deco style.

The complete list of radiator caps—Bouchons de Radiateur—as listed in the 1932 Catalogue is as follows:

BOUCHONS DE RADIATEUR

No. 1122	"5 Chevaux" (horses) *Blanc* 280.
No. 1123	"Comète (comet) *Blanc* 275.
No. 1124	"Faucon" (hawk) *Blanc* 285.
No. 1126	"Archer" (figure of nude archer engraved on circle of glass) *Blanc* 285.
No. 1135	"Coq Nain" (figure of small cock in clear and frosted glass) *Blanc* 400, *couleur* 435.
No. 1136	"Tête de Bélier" (head of ram) Marked "R.Lalique" in block letters. *Blanc* 285.
No. 1137	"Tête de Coq" (head of cock) *Blanc* 420.
No. 1138	"Tête d'Aigle" (head of eagle) *Blanc* 400.
No. 1139	"Tête d'Epervier" (head of hawk) *Blanc* 245, *couleur* 275.
No. 1140	"Tête de Paon" (head of peacock) *Blanc* 320, *couleur* 350.
No. 1141	"Lévrier" (greyhound) *Blanc* 285.
No. 1142	"Saint Christophe" (intaglio design of saint against a rayed figure of child on circle of clear glass) Marked "R.Lalique France" in block letters. *Blanc* 285.
No. 1143	"Hirondelle" (figure of swallow with spread tail) *Blanc* 285.
No. 1144	"Petite Libellule" (small figure of dragonfly) *Blanc* 275.
No. 1145	"Grande Libellule" (large figure of dragonfly) *Blanc* 385.

No. 1146   "Grenouille" (small figure of frog) *Blanc* 245, *couleur* 275.
No. 1147   "Victoire" or "Spirit of Wind" (head of woman with stylized hair flowing out behind) *Blanc* 450, c. 1930.
No. 1152   "Longchamps" (head of horse) *Blanc* 350.
No. 1153   "Epsom" (straining head of horse) *Blanc* 350.
No. 1157   "Sanglier" (small figure of boar) *Blanc* 245, *couleur* 275.
No. 1158   "Perche" (figure of fish) *Blanc* 295, *couleur* 320.
No. 1160   "Vitesse" (speed, figure of kneeling nude with arms behind head) *Blanc* 420, *couleur* 460.
No. 1161   "Coq Houdan" (tall standing figure of cock) *Blanc* 370, *couleur* 400.
No. 1164   "Pintade" (figure of guinea fowl) *Blanc* 295.
No. 1181   "Hibou" (figure of owl) *Blanc* 385.
No. 1182   "Renard" (figure of running fox) *Blanc* 635.
No. 1183   "Chrysis" (figure of kneeling nude with arms stretched out back of head) *Blanc* 460, *couleur* 485.

Paperweights are also an interesting and less expensive item for the collector. Lalique made as many as fifty of these little figures. Some were the same designs as the radiator caps but there were also other figures such as the cat, the elephant, the rhinoceros, the bison, the horse, the moose, two turtle doves, and a double marguerite that were not made as radiator caps. However, according to the Catalogue any of the figures could be mounted as bouchons de radiateur at an extra cost of 135 francs. The majority of the paperweights are much smaller than the radiator caps.

The list of paperweights as given in the 1932 Lalique Catalogue is as follows:

PRESSE-PAPIERS (PAPERWEIGHTS)

No. 801   "2 Aigles" (two eagle heads) made in both *blanc* 250, *couleur* 300.

No. 802   "Double Marguerite" (sunburst design of marguerite) made in both *blanc* 225, and *couleur* 250.

Nos. 803–04   "2 Sardines" and "3 Sardines" (small fish) available in *blanc*, 150 each.

No. 1126   "Archer" (figure of archer engraved on round disc of glass) 150 available in *blanc*.

No. 1128   "2 Tourterelles" (figures of two turtle doves with bills together) made in both *blanc* 400, and *couleur* 500, figures of doves frosted, floral base.

No. 1135   "Coq Nain" (small figure of cock) available in both *blanc* 265, and *couleur* 300.

No. 1136   "Tête de Bélier" (head of ram) signed "R. Lalique" in block letters. *Blanc* 150.

No. 1137   "Tête de Coq" (head of cock) *Blanc* 285.

No. 1138   "Tête d'Aigle" (eagle head) in clear and frosted glass.

No. 1139   "Tête d'Epervier" (head of sparrow hawk) in *blanc* 110 and *couleur* 140.

No. 1140   "Tête de Paon" (head of peacock with tall crest) *Blanc* 185 and *couleur* 215. Marked "R.Lalique" in block letters.

No. 1141   "Lévrier" (figure of greyhound engraved on plaque of glass) *Blanc* 150. Marked "R.Lalique" in block letters.

No. 1142   "Saint Christophe" (figure of St. Christopher against rayed background engraved on circular plaque of glass) Marked "R.Lalique France". *Blanc* 150.

No. 1143   "Hirondelle" (figure of swallow with spread tail) *Blanc*. Marked in block letters "R.Lalique France." *Blanc* 150.

No. 1145   "Libellule grande" (large figure of dragonfly) *Blanc* 250. Marked in script.

No. 1146   "Grenouille" (small figure of frog) *Blanc* 110 and *couleur* 140.

No. 1148   "Antilope" (small standing figure of antelope) *Blanc* 100 and *couleur* 125.

Nos. 1149 "Moineau Fier, Hardi, et Timide" (frosted figures of sparrows proud, bold, and timid) *Blanc* 125 each.
-1151

No. 1152 "Longchamps" (heads of horses) *Blanc* 215.

No. 1154 "Moineau sur socle, ailes croisées" (sparrow with wings crossed) *Blanc* 250.

No. 1155 "Moineau sur socle, ailes ouvertes" (sparrow on base with wings open) *Blanc* 250.

No. 1156 "Moineau sur socle, ailes fermées" (sparrow on base with wings closed) *Blanc* 250.

No. 1157 "Sanglier" (wild boar, frosted figure on stand) *Blanc* 110 and *couleur* 140. Still made in white frosted glass.

No. 1158 "Perche" (frosted and clear figure of perch) *Blanc* 160 and *couleur* 185.

No. 1159 "Cheval" (small figure of horse with arched neck) *Blanc* 100 and *couleur* 125.

No. 1161 "Coq Houdan" (large figure of standing cock) *Blanc* 235 and *couleur* 265.

No. 1162 "Chat" (reclining figure of cat on stand) *Blanc* 150 and *couleur* 175.

No. 1164 "Pintade" (figure of guinea fowl on stand) *Blanc* 160.

No. 1168 "Daim" (small figure of deer on stand) *Blanc* 110 and *couleur* 140. Still made.

No. 1176 "Barbillon" (small figure of barbel fish on base) *Blanc* frosted 135.

No. 1181 "Hibou" (figure of owl on round base) *Blanc* frosted 250.

No. 1182 "Renard" (large figure of fox standing on circular base) *Blanc* and frosted 500.

No. 1183 "Chrysis" (kneeling figure of nude with arms back of head) *Blanc* 325 and *couleur* 350.

No. 1191 "Eléphant" (elephant on rectangular stand with trunk thrown back) *Blanc* 600.

No. 1192 "Toby" (small figure of elephant standing on circular base) *Blanc* 125.

No. 1193 "Chouette" (small figure of barn owl) in satin finish. *Blanc* 100. Still made.

No. 1194 "Taureau" (satin finish bull on clear crystal base) Height 3½ inches. Signed in block letters on base "R.Lalique." *Blanc* 100. Still being made.

No. 1195 "Rhinocéros" (standing figure of rhinoceros) On rectangular clear crystal base. *Blanc* 150.

No. 1196 "Bison" (figure of bison with head down) On clear crystal rectangular base. *Blanc* 250.

No. 1197 "Renne" (small figure of moose standing on small rectangular crystal base.) *Blanc* 125.

Many of these paperweights are still being made. They are marked "Lalique" in block letters. The ones made in 1932 and before are marked "R.Lalique" in block letters.

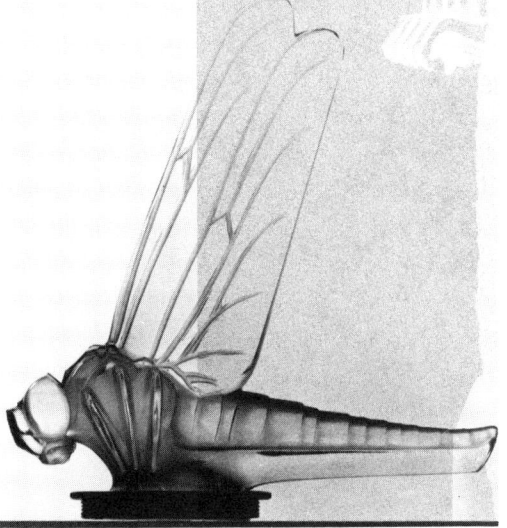

Radiator cap, dragonfly. Height, 8½ inches. Engraved signature in script on side of body "R. Lalique France." 1925-1931. (Christie, photo A. C. Cooper.)

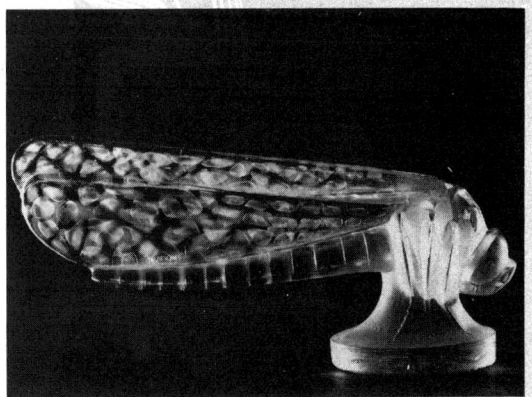

Radiator cap, "Petite Libellule," clear crystal. Signed on wing "R. Lalique France" in block letters. 1925-1931. (John Jesse Gallery)

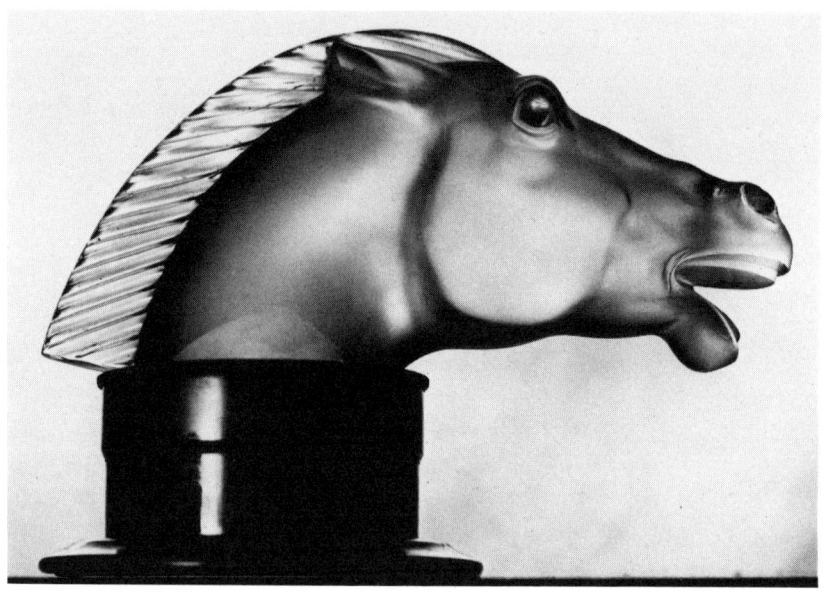

Radiator cap, horse's head "Epsom." c.1931. (John Jesse Gallery.)

Radiator cap, 5 horses. 8½ inches height. Marked "R. Lalique France" in block letters. 1925-1931. (John Jesse Gallery.)

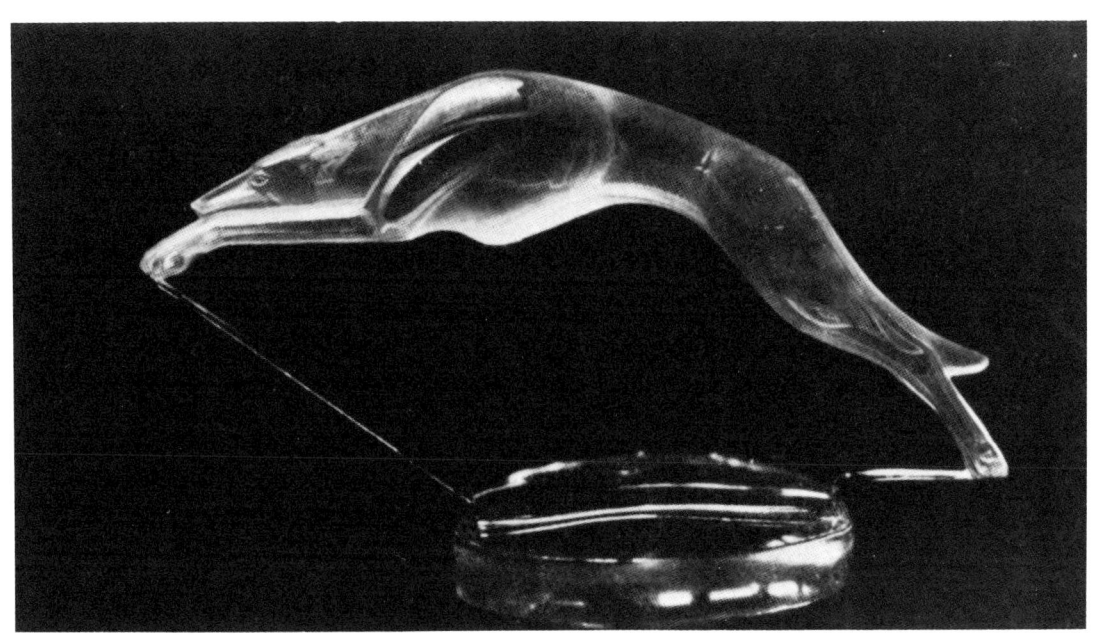

Above, Motor mascot designed for H.R.H. Prince George. c.1931. (Studio Yearbook, 1931.)

Left, Radiator cap "Hirondelle" (swallow) c.1931. (John Jesse Gallery.)

Right, Radiator cap, cock. Clear and frosted glass. Height, 7⅝ inches. Marked "R. Lalique France" in block letters. c.1930 (The Toledo Museum of Art.)

Below, Radiator cap, Fish. Clear and frosted glass. Height, 3⅞ inches. Marked "R. Lalique France" in block letters. c.1930.

Radiator cap, Archer. Intaglio on clear glass, figure frosted. Height, 5 inches. Marked "R. Lalique France." c.1930. (The Toledo Museum of Art.)

Radiator cap, Greyhound. Intaglio frosted figure in relief on clear glass. Height, 3½ inches. Length, 7¼ inches. Marked "R. Lalique France" in block letters. c.1930. (The Toledo Museum of Art.)

~~ DESK FURNISHINGS: INKSTANDS, BLOTTERS, SEALS, AND ASHTRAYS

Between 1918 and 1922 Lalique had constructed a large factory at Wingen sur Moder in the Bas-Rhin especially planned for the mass production of objects in monotone pressed glass. The manufactory was called "Verrerie d'Alsace René Lalique & Cie." In addition to vases, lamps, statuettes, and other decorative objects that had been manufactured at Lalique's glassworks Verrerie de Combs-la-Ville since 1909 this new factory also manufactured many small household articles. The pieces included a large selection of useful and decorative articles such as complete sets of glass for a lady's dressing table; dining table services including plate, bowls, water and wine glasses, pitchers and carafes; furnishings for the writing desk. The first exhibition of this new collection of decorative accessories was in 1923. Among the quantities of small articles shown were fittings for the writing desk, including inkstands, seals, blotter covers, and ashtrays. These articles were manufactured in great numbers in a wide variety of designs and are evidence of the extensive commercialism that Lalique entered into in the 1920s and 1930s.

Inkstands were made in square and round shapes and in long rectangular forms which held two containers for ink and a trough for pens. There was also a rectangular glass tray or plateau that could be had with a figure of an eagle, pigeons, or mice. Small round ink bottles were made in the designs "Nénuphar" (water lily) in both *blanc* and *couleur*. A small round bottle called "3 Papillons" (butterflies) was a favorite, made in both *blanc* and *couleur*. Designs of other round bottles made in both *blanc* and *couleur* were "Mûres" (mulberries); "Serpents"; "Escargots" (snails); "Cernay," a leaf design; and "4 Sirènes," nude sea maidens, one of the most characteristic Lalique designs. The square bottle "Biches" was an Art Deco design of deer and greenery. It was an early bottle made in both *blanc* and *couleur* but continued to be made at least until 1932. The long rectangular inkstand called "Mirabeau" had a design of birds, fruit, and foliage. It was made with a sliding lid. "Sully" was a rectangular stand with a pattern of zig-zag borders and the long inkstand "Colbert" had a center container pressed with a design of leaves and berries.

Buvards or blotters were made in a group of interesting and characteristic Lalique designs. The designs included: "Grosses Feuilles" (large leaves); "Escargots" (snails); "Cerises" (cherries); "Faune et Nymphe" (deer and nude); "2 Sirènes enlacées, assises" (two sirens sitting in each other's arms); "Feuilles d'Artichauds" (artichoke leaves); "Mûres" (mulberries); and "2 Sirènes face à face couchées" (two sirens lying face to face). All of these blotter designs were in Art Nouveau style. Although one or two might not seem important a group could be framed or put under glass in a coffee table.

The small cachets or seals with decorative engraved or molded designs offer an inexpensive item for the collector of Lalique glass. There were about fifty different designs of Lalique seals. The majority of the seals were made in clear or frosted colorless crystal but some were also available in colored glass. Seals can be divided into two groups. There is one group of standing figures of animals and humans. The majority of the figures are animals including figures of dogs, rabbits, a fox, squirrels, mice, goats, and birds including the turkey, duck, pelican, eagle, pigeon, and sparrow; there were also designs of locusts and flies. Human figures included a group of four figures: a figure of a veiled nude, a figurine with clasped hands, and a small figure of "Victoire." The other group of seals included those of round or oval pieces of glass with engraved intaglio designs. The designs on these included swallows, flying storks, and the favorite "Perruches" or parakeets. There were also several designs of butterflies, coiled lizards, and one with the arms of England in relief. Flower designs included "Bleuets," "Fuchsias," "Double Marguerite," and "Vase Fleurs." There were three circles of glass with nude figures and flowers, and three ovals with the same designs that were used on jewelry pendants. These were a nude swinging on a flower garland, a winged nude, and "Sirènes." There were also round seals engraved with figures of a "Faune," a goat, and one of a chamois. One rectangular piece of glass has a relief design of athletes, and two figures of birds sit at the top of another rectangle of glass. An engraving of a ship, "Caravelle," is on another seal and the favorite "Naïade," a nude sea maiden with pearly tresses, decorated a rectangular piece of glass with curved top.

Seals could be engraved with a monogram of one, two, or three letters at a small extra cost; thus it is possible to find seals with various monograms as well as the Lalique mark. The new seals—like other pieces of new Lalique glass—are marked "Lalique France" in script.

Many of the seal designs were also used as center figures of ashtrays. These included the pelican, duck, two doves, sparrow, finch, turkey, dog, rabbit, squirrel, mouse, fox, and a standing figure called "Statuette de la Fontaine." Forty-four different designs are listed and illustrated in the 1932 Lalique Catalogue. The dish ashtrays were made of clear crystal with a sculptured figure of satin finish glass in the center. Others have a round, rectangular, or semicircular piece of glass with an engraved design in their centers. These panels were engraved with the following well-known Lalique motifs: "Naïade," a nude with flowing pearly tresses; "Caravelle," a galleon ship; "Faune," a figure of a man with cloven feet; "Bélier," a figure of a goat; "Athlètes," an upright rectangular panel with a band of athletes in relief; and "Chamois," a figure of a chamois engraved on a circular piece of crystal. The majority of these ashtrays were made in colored glass as well as clear crystal.

Round, oval, square, and star-shaped ashtrays were made with molded borders of floral, leaf, and nude designs. There is also a round ashtray with a border of beetles in relief and another with a border of birds in relief. A rare ashtray is molded with a dahlia design and has a figure of a butterfly sitting on its rim.

A group of small ashtrays with frosted figures in their centers that are the same designs as those made in 1932 and before are still available today. These are "Naïade," a figure of a sea maiden; "Caravelle," the engraved ship; "2 Colombes," two doves, the squirrel, the pelican, the mouse, the sparrow, and the finch. These are now marked "Lalique France" in script instead of the old mark "R.Lalique" engraved in block letters. There are two new attractive ashtray figures—a dolphin and two swans. The large masque that was made in bronze for the handles of the large spheroid vase "Masque" is now made in colored glass on a crystal ashtray.

Lalique used many of his popular figures as subjects for bookends. These included "Pintade" or guinea fowl, "Coq Houdan," "Coq Nain," and the horse's head, "Epsom." There were also bookends with the "Tête de Bélier" or ram's head and with figures of nude children. These were usually signed "R.Lalique France" in block letters.

The following is a complete list of seals made in 1932 and listed in the Catalogue of that year:

No. 175   Cachet "Tête d'Aigle" (head of eagle) *Blanc* 165, *couleur* 185.
No. 176   Cachet "4 Figurines" face (front) *Blanc* 100, angle (side) 100.
No. 178   Cachet rond "Bleuets"(round, kingfishers) *Blanc* 100, *couleur* 120.
No. 179   Cachet "Anneau, Lézards" (coiled lizards) *Blanc* 100.
No. 180   Cachet "Mouche" (fly) *Blanc* 175.
No. 181   Cachet "Statuette Drapée" (draped statuette) *Blanc* 175, *couleur* 190.
No. 182   Cachet "Poisson" (fish) *Blanc* 125, *couleur* 150.
No. 183   Cachet "Sauterelle" (grasshopper) *Blanc* 95, *couleur* 110.
No. 184   Cachet "Motif Aigle" (eagle stopper for inkwell) *Blanc* 325.
No. 185   Cachet "Motif Souris" (mouse stopper for inkwell) *Blanc* 325.
No. 186   Cachet "Motif Pigeons" (stopper for inkwell) *Blanc* 325.
No. 187   Cachet "Perruches" (parakeets) *Blanc* 185.
No. 188   Cachet "Hirondelles" (swallows) *Blanc* 185.
No. 189   Cachet "Vase de Fleurs" (vase of flowers) *Blanc* 185.
No. 190   Cachet "Papillon, ailes fermées" (butterfly, wings closed) *Blanc* 175.
No. 192   Cachet "Papillon, ailes ouvertes" (butterfly, wings open) *Blanc* 175.

Desk Furnishings • 133

No.	193	Cachet rond "Figurine dans les Fleurs" (figurine in flowers) *Blanc* 150.
No.	194	Cachet rond "2 Danseuses" (2 dancers) *Blanc* 150.
No.	195	Cachet "Armes d'Angleterre" (English coat of arms) *Blanc* 200.
No.	196	Cachet "Double Marguerite" *Blanc* 185, *couleur* 200.
No.	197	Cachet rond "3 Papillons" (3 butterflies) *Blanc* 150.
No.	198	Cachet rond "2 Perruches et Fleurs" (2 parakeets and flowers) *Blanc* 150.
No.	200	Cachet rond "2 Figurines et Fleurs" *Blanc* 200.
No.	201	Cachet ovale "Figurine Ailée" (figurine with wings) *Blanc* 200.
No.	202	Cachet ovale "Figurine" (balancing) *Blanc* 200.
No.	209	Cachet "Figurine, mains jointes" (figurine, hands joined) *Blanc* 175, *couleur* 190.
No.	210	Cachet "Victoire" (figure etched on glass) *Blanc* 65, *couleur* 75
No.	211	Cachet ovale "Sirènes" (nude female figures) *Blanc* 150.
No.	212	Cachet ovale "Fuchsias" (fuchsias) *Blanc* 150.
No.	213	Cachet rond "Cigognes" (storks) *Blanc* 150.
No.	214	Cachet "Lapin" (rabbit) *Blanc* 45, *couleur* 50.
No.	215	Cachet "Dindon" (turkey) *Blanc* 45, *couleur* 50.
No.	216	Cachet "Chien" (dog) *Blanc* 45, *couleur* 50.
No.	217	Cachet "Renard" (fox) *Blanc* 45, *couleur* 50.
No.	218	Cachet "Souris" (bat) *Blanc* 45, *couleur* 50.
No.	219	Cachet "Canard" (duck) *Blanc* 45, *couleur* 50.
No.	220	Cachet "Moineau" (sparrow) *Blanc* 45, *couleur* 50.
No.	221	Cachet "Naïade" (nude with flowing hair etched on glass plaque) *Blanc* 70, *couleur* 70.
No.	222	Cachet "Pélican" *Blanc* 45, *couleur* 45.
No.	223	Cachet "Pinson" (finch) *Blanc* 50, *couleur* 50.
No.	224	Cachet "Caravelle" (ship) *Blanc* 50, *couleur* 50.
No.	225	Cachet "Bélier" (goat) *Blanc* 50.

No. 226 Cachet "Chamois" *Blanc* 45.
No. 227 Cachet "Ecureuil" (squirrel) *Blanc* 80, *couleur* 80.
No. 228 Cachet "Faune" (faun) *Blanc* 60.
No. 229 Cachet "Athlètes" (moulded band of athletes on rectangular piece of glass) *Blanc* 550.
No. 230 Cachet "2 Colombes" (doves) *Blanc* 60, *couleur* 60.
No. 231 Cachet "Nice" (figures of two doves at top of rectangular piece of glass) *Blanc* 125.

Inkstand "Biches" with relief pattern of foliage and deer. Made in both clear and colored glass. c.1910. (Musée des Arts Décoratifs.)

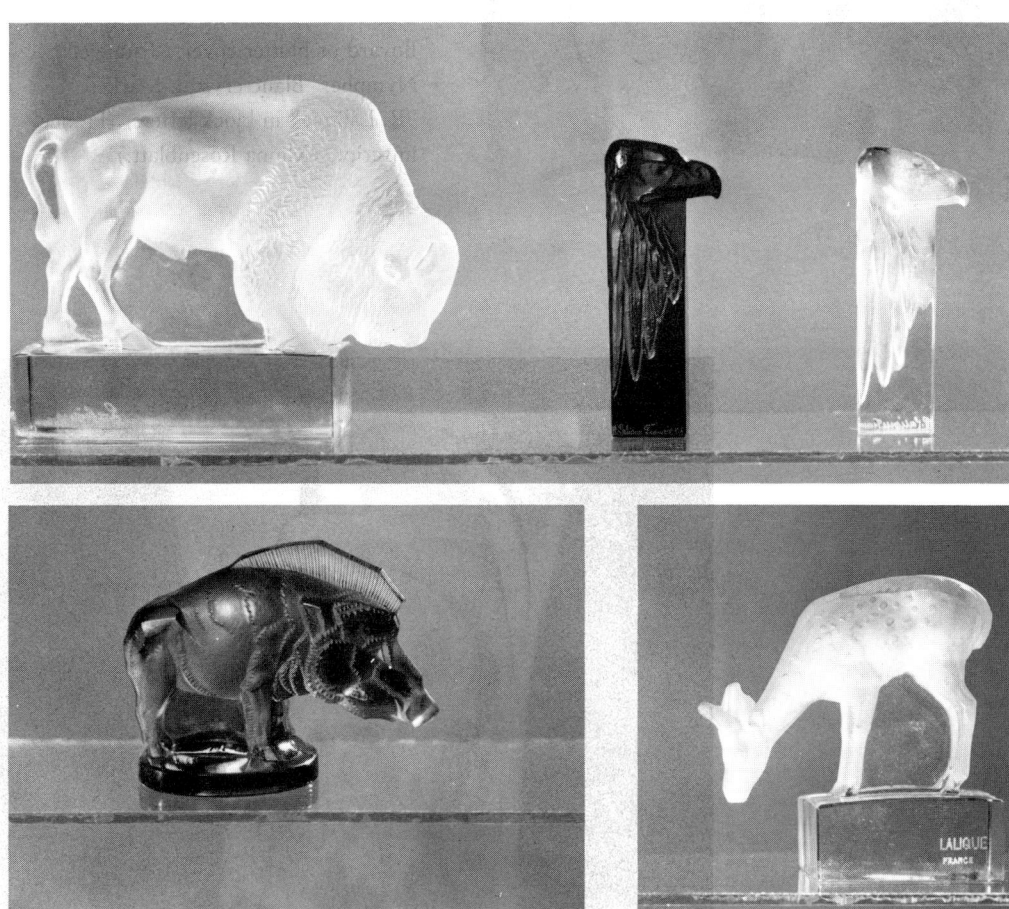

Seals. *Left to right*: Buffalo in frosted glass on clear base. Height, 3 13/16 inches. c.1932-1940. Seal Hawk's head, black glass. Height, 3 3/16 inches. Signed in script, "R. Lalique France." Same seal in clear and frosted glass. (The Toledo Museum of Art.)

Bottom. Figure of boar, dark grey glass frosted and clear. Height, 2 9/16 inches. c.1945. (The Toledo Museum of Art.) Seal, figure of deer. Frosted glass on clear base. Height, 3 3/16 inches. Marked "Lalique France." After 1945. (The Toledo Museum of Art.)

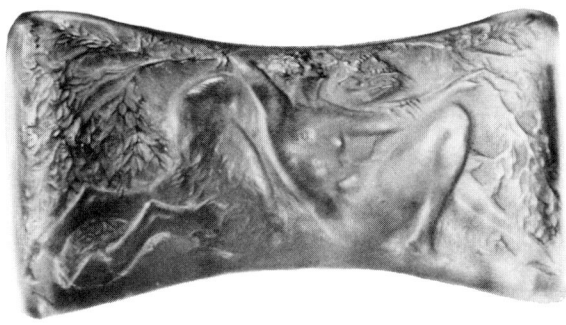

Buvard or blotter cover. "Faune et Nymphe." Blanc crystal. Marked "R. Lalique" in block letters, "France" in script. (Minna Rosenblatt.)

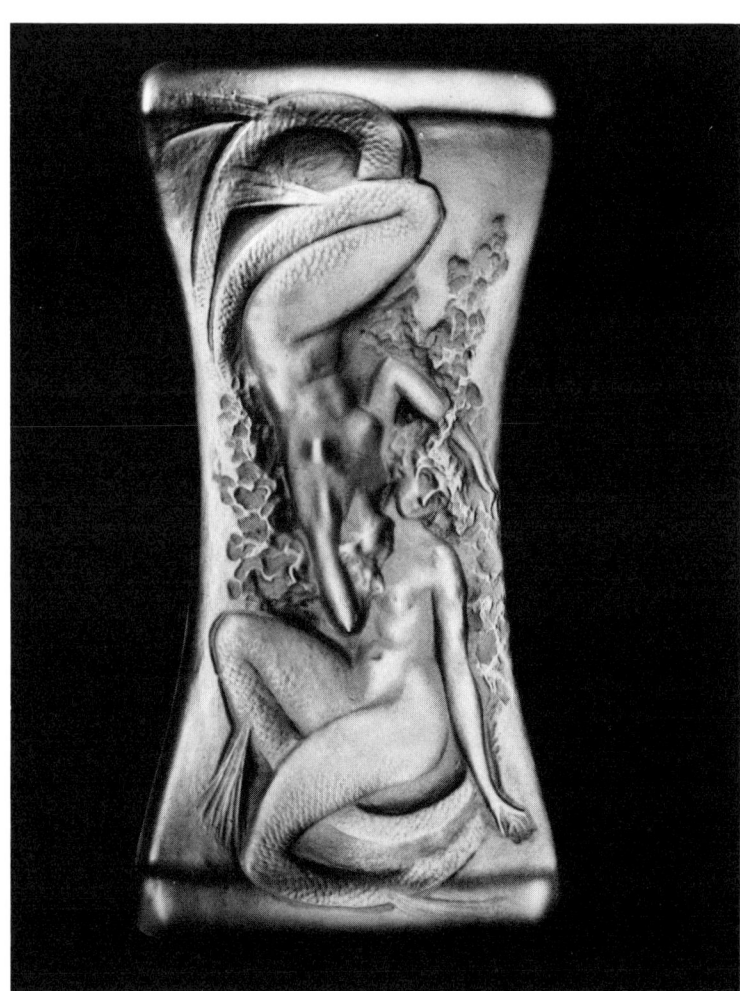

Buvard or blotter cover, Relief design of two nude sirens. Lalique. Before 1932. (Editions Graphiques Ltd.)

∻ BOXES AND BONBONNIERES

Lalique made a great quantity of covered boxes. There were square and rectangular boxes for cigars and cigarettes and round sweetmeat boxes of various sizes, as well as several egg-shaped boxes. The box covers were molded with characteristic Lalique bird, flower, insect, and nude figure designs. The favorite peacock, dragonfly, cicada, sparrow, and wren designs seen on vases, clocks, and decorative motifs were also adapted to the tops of boxes. According to the number of boxes recorded in the 1932 Lalique Catalogue there should be many boxes available to the present day collector. However, while there are quantities of vases in the antique shops there seem to be few boxes. The "Houppes" or powder puff box design first made for Coty powder in 1913 was also available in glass of pale colors and opalescent glass. A box called "Roger" had a design of crystal cabochon circles on a background of birds and grapevines. It was made in both color and colorless glass with enamel.

There was a group of boxes with knobs and finials of flowers or nude figures. The box "Primevères" has a molded design of flowers and a flower knob. It was made in both *blanc* and *couleur*. The box "Sultane," made for cigars, has an allover line design and a knob of a nude figure sitting with folded legs and arms folded behind the head. The box was made in both *blanc* and *couleur*. Other boxes with figure knobs included "Vallauris" with a molded design of leaves and flower knob and "Amour Assis"—a charming and most desirable box. It has a figure of cupid sitting on its cover and it was made in both *blanc* and *couleur*. There were several other small boxes with molded figures on their covers.

Another group of boxes had designs of birds. Two molded birds are on the cigar box called "Saint Marc"; this box was available in color. There were two boxes with designs of molded peacocks. One box has a peacock with a large spreading tail, the other box has a design of three peacocks. Both boxes were available in colorless crystal (*blanc*). There was a box with two pigeons sitting among blossoming branches, a similar box with two birds, another box with tropical birds with long feathered tails, and a box with two swans. A rectangular cigarette box has an allover design of flying swallows, and another box has a swirling design of flying tomtits. The majority of these boxes were made in *blanc*.

Of special interest are the egg-shaped boxes. There were just two of these, one with a design of periwinkle flowers in relief and the other with a pressed design of chicks in ovals. These boxes were available in both colored and colorless crystal.

Deer and foliage decorated the panels of a box in Art Deco style called "Chantilly" and "Victoire" was another Art Deco of a winged figure with a sword. Both of these boxes were available in colorless crystal. There were many boxes with designs of flowers including roses, zinnias, dahlias, cherry blossoms, and lily of the valley. Particularly decorative are "Roses en Relief," a box with ropes of naturalistic roses, and "Panier de Roses," a box with a basket of roses that matched the flacon of the same design. These boxes were all made in colorless glass. A group of dancing nudes with garlands of flowers are especially interesting. There is also a figure of a veiled nude holding a vase from which falls a decorative stream of water, and another box with two figures wearing ballet tutus. An important box has a design of two nude sirens with pearly tresses. Attractive box designs with insects include one with three dragonflies, one with beetles and garlands of leaves, and one called "Cigales" which is divided into six triangular panels and decorated with a design of cicadas in relief.

Any boxes with designs of nudes are good collectors' items and the box with small cupids called "Amours," the box with two angels' heads, "Anges," "Victoire," and the egg-shaped boxes, are also rare boxes. These boxes were made in both *blanc* and *couleur* in large quantities and none of these original designs are now being made. The current production of Lalique boxes includes a design called "Cactus," "Dahlia," and another floral pattern, and a box with a metal mounting and a molded design of two nudes on the cover. All of these patterns except "Cactus" were first made after 1932 and possibly as late as 1950. A square box with an engraved cat's head was made c. 1950.

Boxes and Bonbonnières · 139

A group of coffrets or jewel cases were decorated with the following designs in plaques: "Monnaie du Pape" (a pattern of honesty leaves), "Papillons" (butterflies), "Chrysanthèmes," and "Figurines." These were all available in quantities of thousands in 1932.

Boxes are not inexpensive. No Lalique glass is inexpensive but if your purse does not allow you to collect large vases, boxes offer an interesting alternative; so far they are not in demand and thus not overpriced. There are over seventy different designs and they include Lalique's repertory of important designs. All boxes are signed, usually with the molded block letter mark "R.Lalique." The majority of the boxes were made in both *blanc* and *couleur*.

Boxes and Bonbonnières listed in the 1932 Lalique Catalogue include the following:

No. 1 Boîte ronde "Paon" (peacock) 450 *blanc* or clear glass.
No. 2 Boîte ronde "Coq" (cock) 300 *blanc*, 325 *couleur*.
No. 3 Boîte ronde "Amour assis" (with figure of cupid on cover) 375 *blanc*, 425 *couleur*.
No. 4 Boîte ovale "Roses en relief" 450 *blanc*. 500 *couleur*.
No. 5 Boîte ronde "Louveciennes" (two veiled dancing figures) 300 *blanc*.
No. 6 Boîte ronde "Ermenonville" (veiled dancing figure with urn) 250 *blanc*.
No. 7 Boîte ronde "Fontenay" (two dancing nudes with garlands of flowers) 165 *blanc*.
No. 9 Boîte ronde "1 Figurine et Raisins" (Nude figurine with grapes) 200 *blanc*.
No. 10 Boîte ronde "1 Figurine et Bouquets" (figurine with flowers) 200 *blanc*.
No. 11 Boîte ronde "2 Figurines et Branches" (two figurines with garlands of leaves) 200 *blanc*.
No. 14 Boîte ronde "4 Papillons" (four butterflies on cover) 100 *blanc*, 185 *couleur*.

No. 14 Boîte ronde "4 Scarabées" (four scarabs on cover) 165 *blanc*, 185 *couleur*.
No. 20 Boîte ovale "Amours" (dancing children on cover) 200 *blanc*.
No. 21 Boîte ovale "Panier de Roses" (basket of roses on cover) 200 *blanc*.
No. 22 Boîte ovale "Gabrielle" (powder puffs on cover) 200 *blanc*.
No. 23 Boîte ovale "Cygnes" (swans on cover) 200 *blanc*.
No. 24 Boîte ovale "2 Danseuses" (two dancers in ballet skirts on cover) 200 *blanc*.
No. 26 Boîte ronde "Pommier du Japan" (cherry blossoms on cover) 150 *blanc*, 175 *couleur*.
No. 28 Boîte ronde "Guirlande de Graines" (cover with design of grain) 100 *blanc*.
No. 29 Boîte ronde "Houppes" (powder puff design) 250 *couleur*.
No. 30 Boîte ronde "3 Paons" (cover with three peacocks) 125 *blanc*.
No. 31 Boîte ronde "Victoire" (cover with winged man with sword) 125 *blanc*.
No. 32 Boîte ronde "2 Figurines" (cover with two nudes and flowers) 125 *blanc*.
No. 33 Boîte ronde "1 Grand vase" (cover design of large vase with stopper of flowers) 125 *blanc*.
No. 34 Boîte ronde "2 Pigeons" (cover with design of two pigeons) 125 *blanc*.
No. 35 Boîte ronde "2 Oiseaux" (cover with two birds and flowers) 125 *blanc*.
No. 37 Boîte ronde "3 Vases" (vases and flowers) 125 *blanc*.
No. 39 Boîte ronde "Anges" (design of angel heads) 125 *blanc*.
No. 41 Boîte ronde grande "Muguets" (cover with design of lily of the valley) 425 *couleur*.
No. 42 Boîte ronde grande "Cyprins" (cover with design of goldfish) 450 *couleur*.

No. 43　　Boîte ronde grande "2 Sirènes" (cover design with two dancing nudes and bubbles) 42 *couleur*.

No. 44　　Boîte ronde grande "Cigales" (cover divided into six sections each with figure of cicada) 375 *couleur*.

No. 45　　Boîte ronde moyenne "Georgette" (cover design of three dragonflies) 350 *couleur*.

No. 46　　Boîte ronde moyenne "3 Dahlias" (large dahlias) 300 *couleur*.

No. 47　　Boîte ronde moyenne "6 Dahlias" (six small dahlias) 325 *couleur*.

No. 49　　Boîte ronde petite "Cléones" (cover design of insects and leaves) 175 *couleur*.

No. 50　　Boîte ronde petite "Tokio" (cover of bursting blossom) 165 *couleur*.

No. 51　　Boîte ronde petite "Libellules" (cover dragonfly design) 160 *couleur*.

No. 52　　Boîte ronde petite "Mésanges" (cover with six tomtits with spread wings) 150 *couleur*.

No. 53　　Boîte à cigarettes "Hirondelles" (rectangular box with design of swallows) 125 *blanc*.

No. 54　　Boîte à cigarettes "Zinnias" (rectangular box with cover design of zinnias) 125 *blanc*.

No. 57　　Boîte ronde "Geneviève" (cover design of stylized feathers and figures of two birds in center triangle) 135 *blanc*.

No. 58　　Boîte ronde "Compiègne" (design of tropical birds and foliage) 95 *blanc*.

No. 59　　Boîte ronde "Fontainebleau" (cover design of animals) 95 *blanc*.

No. 61　　Boîte ronde "Meudon" (flowers and foliage) 95 *blanc*.

No. 62　　Boîte ronde "Chantilly" (design of deer and foliage divided into six sections) 95 *blanc*.

No. 63　　Boîte ronde "Cheveux de Vénus" (small box with center finial on cover) 100 *blanc*.

No. 64   Boîte ronde "Isabelle" (floral design) 70 *blanc*.

No. 65   Boîte ronde "Gui" (cover design of mistletoe) 70 *blanc*, 80 *couleur*.

No. 66   Boîte ronde "Degas" (figure in center of cover) 75 *blanc*.

No. 67   Boîte ronde "Lucie" (cover design of forget-me-nots) 65 *blanc*.

No. 68   Boîte ronde "Vaucluse" (cover design of leaves) 65 *blanc*.

No. 69   Boîte ronde "Marguerites" (allover design of marguerites) 50 *blanc*.

No. 70   Boîte ronde "Emiliane" (allover flower design) 55 *blanc*.

No. 71   Boîte ronde "Coquilles" (shell design in eight sections) 45 *blanc*, 55 *couleur*.

No. 75   Boîte ronde "Roger" (clear glass cabochons and enameled background of birds and foliage) 200 *couleur*, 200 *émaillé*.

No. 76   Boîte hexagonale "Sainte-Nectaire" (stylized swirl design of leaves) 40 *blanc*.

No. 77   Boîte ronde moyenne "Primevères" (design of flowers in relief) 200 *blanc*, 225 *couleur*.

No. 78   Boîte ovale "Dinard" (relief design of roses) 175 *blanc*.

No. 79   Boîte à cigares "Roméo" (fluted design with sliding cover) 550 *blanc*.

No. 80   Boîte à cigares "Corona" (allover design of stylized leaves) 600 *blanc*.

No. 81   Boîte ronde "Saint-Marc" (two birds in relief on cover) 450 *couleur*.

No. 82   Boîte oeuf "Pervenches" (egg-shaped box with pressed design of periwinkle flowers) 90 *blanc*, 100 *couleur*.

No. 83   Boîte carrée "Sultane" (box of allover rope design in relief and seated figure of nude with legs crossed and arms folded back head on cover of box) 350 *blanc*, 450 *couleur*.

No. 84   Boîte ronde "Vallauris" (cover design of leaves in relief and finial of berries) 150 *blanc*, 185 *couleur*.

No. 85 Boîte oeuf "Poussins" (egg-shaped box with medallions of chicks in relief) 110 *blanc*.
No. 86 Boîte ronde grande "Primevères" (box with design of flowers in relief) 275 *blanc*, 325 *couleur*.
No. 87 Boîte carrée "Palmettes" (design of palm fronds in relief) 240 *blanc*.

There were also coffrets with plaques of butterflies, chrysanthemums, figurines, and monnaie du pape leaves in relief. These small boxes were made in quantities of thousands in both *blanc* and colored glass.

"Houppes," round box with design of powder puffs. Made for Coty L'Origan powder. c.1913. (John Jesse Gallery.)

"4 Scarabées" round box with relief designs of beetles. No. 15. R. Lalique before 1912. (John Jesse Gallery.)

"Roger," round box of clear and frosted glass with designs of birds, grape vines and grapes in black enamel. No. 75. R. Lalique, before 1932. (John Jesse Gallery.)

Covered Box with relief Art Nouveau design of two draped figures. R. Lalique before 1932. (Editions Graphiques Ltd.)

Above left, "Amour Assis," round box with floral decoration and figure of cupid sitting on cover of box. No. 3. Made in c.1910. (Catalogue des Verreries de René Lalique. 1932.)

Below, Box, dark green glass with design of intertwined thistle branches; silver hinges and clasp in form of scarabs. Length, 17.8 cm.; height, 7.7 cm. Lalique c.1910-1920. (The Corning Museum of Glass.)

LAMPS, LIGHTING FIXTURES, AND ARCHITECTURAL DETAILS

From the beginning of his career as a glassmaker Lalique made use of the effects of light and glass. He designed decorative plaques of glass with engraved designs which were illuminated by indirect lighting in their bases. Many of these plaques were later provided with shades and thus made into lamps. There is a lamp with three nude figures, another with butterflies engraved in its shaft, one of a centaur, a circular lamp engraved with a goat, and one with a design of three fish. These lamps are all marked "R.Lalique" together with the catalogue number in block letters. The shades are of glass with engraved line designs. A lamp with base and design of stylized petals called "Tears" was first made in c. 1927. There was also a lamp with figures of caryatides on the shaft and an engraved shade with lines of stylized leaves. Another lamp is upheld by two figures of nude infants at its base, and one called "Feuillage" (foliage) has a vase-shaped base ornamented with a wide band of leaves; the glass shade is engraved with a spiral leaf design. An iron-mounted glass lamp has a hemispherical shade of gray glass deep molded with an Art Deco pattern of curves. The shade is engraved on the rim in handscript "R.Lalique." These lamps were made 1925–1930. They were not included in the 1932 Catalogue but must have been in a separate catalogue of Lalique lamps.

A catalogue—"Lalique Lights and Decorations"—distributed by Breves Galleries, London, in 1928 illustrates a group of Lalique flacon-type lights with frosted vertically ribbed molded glass flacon bases and tiara-like or fan-shaped plaques engraved with decorative designs. These designs included "Cupids" (16 inches), "Apple Blossoms" (16 inches), "Pigeons" (16 inches), and "Love Birds" (17 inches). There was also a group of smaller lights including "Dandelion" (6½ inches), "Roses" (7 inches), "Carnation" (7 inches), "Almond Blossom" (7 inches), "Swallows" (7½ inches), "Cupids" (8¼ inches), and "Apple Blossom" (8 inches). These lights with engraved nosegay stoppers were similar to some Lalique flacons made for Roger et Gallet perfume. These are some of the most decorative pieces made by Lalique. Because of the delicacy of the stoppers they are hard to find in perfect condition.

Lalique also made large ceiling lights and wall fixtures. These included large crystal lusters or chandeliers of traditional shaped branches as well as modern star-shaped designs with molded leaf patterns. Lighting bowls were made in various sizes from 17 inches to 20 inches in diameter. They were made in white, smoky gray, or brown glass in contrasts of clear and frosted glass. There were also some in opalescent glass. The designs included Lalique's repertory of motifs—shells, leaves, flowers, fruit, birds, and butterflies. There was also an Art Deco design of bold curves and one called "Soleil" (sun) and a strange design of stalactites made in "ice color." A lighting bowl of the siren design was made in opaline glass. A design with borders of roses was in frosted glass with the molded design of roses in brown or white. Another bowl had an Art Deco design of curves or *rinceau*. It was available in white or amber and the same design was made in a table lamp. Many of these lighting bowls were both molded and engraved.

There were also hanging balls with allover designs such as mistletoe which was made in brown frosted glass with the berries in relief. Other hanging balls were in sunflower, dahlia, leaf, and Art Deco triangular designs. A Lalique hanging shade of hemispherical form molded in opalescent glass with raised bosses set in intaglio sunbursts, complete with hanging chains and hook, was sold at Sotheby's, Belgravia, on March 28, 1973. It had the engraved mark "R.Lalique France" and brought about £25.

Torchères and lanterns were made in traditional shapes with panels of molded glass and there were also lanterns with designs of modern spirals and squares in Art Deco style.

Wall plaques and corner lights consisted of a frosted bowl for light globes and a panel of glass engraved with designs such as tulips, dahlias, ivy leaves, beech leaves, shells, berries, and birds. The mistletoe wall light was made in frosted glass in brown with berries in relief and the dahlia corner light was available in brown, green, or white. A shell wall plaque was made in opalescent glass. According to the Breves Galleries catalogue only a certain number of each design was made and then the molds were destroyed. The pieces were marked "R.Lalique France," usually engraved. Arrangements could be made for installation. Lalique also designed complete decorations for rooms or for a complete house including glass doors, wall panels, and screens. There are Lalique lighting fixtures, doors, and screens available to collectors today and some were even installed in Park Avenue, New York, apartments.

Lalique glass relates to both fashion and furnishing and for this reason it continued in popularity with the buying public. Many of the pieces have the graceful affectations of Art Nouveau but with an order and simplicity of Art Deco. But Lalique glass has held little interest for collectors and there are those who term Lalique as glorified pressed glass. Indeed Lalique glass has been neglected by the antique collector for almost twenty years. However, now within the last few years the number of collectors of Lalique glass has increased enormously and with the present interest in Art Deco and the art and decoration of the 1920s and 1930s, especially that of France, Lalique glass has again come into its own. In addition to scores of private collectors Lalique is now collected by many museums including the Chrysler Museum at Norfolk, Virginia, The Toledo Museum of Art, The Smithsonian Institution and others both in America and abroad.

Iron-mounted glass lamp. Hemispherical shade in grey glass deep molded with pattern of crescents. Shade engraved on rim in script. "R. Lalique." c.1925.

Light cover, body vertically ribbed and fan-shaped crystal engraved with prunus. Height, 16¼ inches. Lalique. c.1925. (Christie's. Photo, A.C. Cooper.)

Lamp, two figurines holding wreath set on bronze stand. c.1926. (Collection of Charles and Mary Magriel.)

Chandelier or lustre, Bucarest design. R. Lalique. (Breves Gallery catalogue, 1928.)